A History of Greece

Chap 4 & 5

PALGRAVE ESSENTIAL HISTORIES
General Editor: Jeremy Black

This series of compact, readable and informative national histories is designed to appeal to anyone wishing to gain a broad understanding of a country's history.

Published

A History of the Low Countries   *Paul Arblaster*
A History of Italy   *Claudia Baldoli*
A History of Russia   *Roger Bartlett*
A History of Spain (2nd edn)   *Simon Barton*
A History of the British Isles (2nd edn)   *Jeremy Black*
A History of Israel   *Ahron Bregman*
A History of Ireland   *Mike Cronin*
A History of Greece   *Nicholas Doumanis*
A History of the Pacific Islands   *Steven Roger Fischer*
A History of the United States (3rd edn)   *Philip Jenkins*
A History of Denmark   *Knud J. V. Jespersen*
A History of Poland   *Anita J. Prazmowska*
A History of India   *Peter Robb*
A History of China (2nd edn)   *J. A. G. Roberts*
A History of Germany   *Peter Wende*

Series Standing Order
ISBN 1–4039–3811–3 hardback
ISBN 1–4039–3812–1 paperback

If you would like to receive future titles in this series as they are published, you can make use of the standing order facility. To place a standing order please contact your bookseller or, in case of difficulty, write to us at the address below with your name and address, the name of the series and one of the ISBNs above. Please state with which title you wish to begin your standing order. (If you live outside the United Kingdom we may not have the rights for your area, in which case we will forward your order to the publisher concerned.)

Customer Services Department, Macmillan Distribution Ltd
Houndmills, Basingstoke, Hampshire RG21 6XS, England

A History of Greece

Nicholas Doumanis

First published 2010 by
PALGRAVE MACMILLAN

Palgrave Macmillan in the UK is an imprint of Macmillan Publishers Limited, registered in England, company number 785998, of Houndmills, Basingstoke, Hampshire RG21 6XS.

Palgrave Macmillan in the US is a division of St Martin's Press LLC, 175 Fifth Avenue, New York, NY 10010.

Palgrave Macmillan is the global academic imprint of the above companies and has companies and representatives throughout the world.

Palgrave® and Macmillan® are registered trademarks in the United States, the United Kingdom, Europe and other countries.

ISBN 978-1-4039-8613-9   hardback
ISBN 978-1-4039-8614-6   paperback

This book is printed on paper suitable for recycling and made from fully managed and sustained forest sources. Logging, pulping and manufacturing processes are expected to conform to the environmental regulations of the country of origin.

A catalogue record for this book is available from the British Library.

A catalog record for this book is available from the Library of Congress.

10   9   8   7   6   5   4   3   2   1
19   18   17   16   15   14   13   12   11   10

Printed in the UK by CPI William Clowes Beccles, NR34 7TL

Contents

List of Maps and Illustrations

MAPS

ILLUSTRATIONS

Preface

A *History of Greece* traces the story of Greek communities since the Bronze Age (*c*.3300–1200 BC), from the time when the Greek language was first spoken in the Aegean area. The book has been written for those who have often wondered what it is that Homer, Alexander the Great, the Byzantine emperors, and Zorba and Aristotle Onassis might have in common. What made each of them 'Greek'? Why has Greek culture survived in one of the world's most historically contested regions? Why is Greek among the world's oldest living languages?

For too long, these questions have been approached in the wrong way. Modern commentators have often worked with a fixed notion of Hellenism: that Greek culture is a specific entity that was set in stone during the Classical Era. Since the eighteenth century, modern Greeks have tried to force that Classical connection by having a contrived version of Classical Greek (*katharevousa*) as the national language, and by replacing current placenames with their original classical versions. Westerners, on the other hand, have often complained there is no resemblance between ancient and modern Greeks, and have therefore concluded there is no connection.

Astonishingly, the question of Greek continuity has seldom been approached with the understanding that cultures and ethnic groups evolve, often into something quite unrecognizable. This book follows the history of the Greeks as it unfolds, although an important feature of that process of unfolding has been the tendency to reconstitute Greekness in accordance with the Classical paradigm: in Roman, Byzantine and modern times, identities were refashioned through conscious imitation of the classical Greek tradition. The book also works on the assumption that no culture can develop within a vacuum. Greek culture was shaped and re-shaped through its relations with other cultures. Classical Greece was a unique little world, but it had been indelibly influenced by Egypt and the more established societies of the eastern Mediterranean. The transnational context is vital to our understanding of every stage in this long history. Greece might not exist today but for the West and its rise of global dominance, and for the fact that Westerners had a special interest in the Greek heritage.

A History of Greece is not about a nation, although the Greek nation is very much part of its bifurcating story. It wastes no time with such matters as bloodlines, even if such ideas have common currency among many Greeks today. Rather, *A History of Greece* will follow the fortunes of a cultural group that made sense of itself as an ethnic unit, or as a much broader cultural system or *oikoumene*, a term often used to designate 'the Greek world'. For most of the time frame covered here, this Greek *oikoumene* included populations that were often dispersed, but which were bound by Greek language, or education or religion. From the time of Herodotus to about the Age of Constantine, they described themselves as 'Hellenes' (*Ellines*), as they have also done since the nineteenth century, but for the entire period in-between they used the term 'Romans' (*Romanoi, Rhomoi*), in the sense that they identified with the *Hellenized* part of the Roman Empire and its legacy.

The book is primarily written for the general reader. The need for brevity has meant that many important topics have been sacrificed, hence there is very little on the Greek Orthodox Church and modern intellectual trends, and no discussion of the Christological debates of Late Antiquity, or Cavafy and Kazantzakis. A great deal of recent scholarship has been synthesized for this undertaking, but as far as possible I have tried to provide a seamless narrative.

* * *

I must begin by thanking Chrissie Verevis, who read the entire manuscript and provided a great deal of useful commentary. Another 'Cazzie', Nick Pappas, also read it and offered encouraging commentary, as did Milan Voykovic. In the course of writing this book I shamelessly exploited friends who work on aspects of Greek History. For the ancient eras, Ben Brown, Geoff Nathan and Shawn Ross suffered relentless questioning. Over a much longer period, I learned much from discussions with the following modern historians, anthropologists and polymaths: Petro Alexiou, Philip Carabott, David Close, Richard Clogg, Vicky Doulaveras, Effi Gazi, George Hatzikosmidis, Antonis Liakos, Margaret Poulos, Neni Panourgia, David Sutton, Yanis Varoukafis and Alfred Vincent. I'd also like to thank the many scholars whose works have given me an education in Greek history, but who I have not had the privilege to meet. They are listed in the bibliography. Crucial to the completion of this book have been the following providers of the *machiatto ristretto*: 'Black' Jimmy, Anthony, Albert, and the coffee cart lads outside my building. I thank the Faculty of Arts and Social Sciences at the University of New South Wales for various funding grants and sabbatical leave in 2004 and 2008. Thanks also to Terka Acton, Jenni Burrell, Kate Haines and Keith Povey for editorial input. Finally, there is my family. To my wonderful parents, Jack and Connie, my loving wife Helen, and our impossibly gorgeous daughter. This book, as indeed everything else, is for Daphne.

NOTE ON TRANSLITERATION

I have subscribed somewhat inconsistently to a convention followed by many ancient historians nowadays and have used transliterations that are more faithful to the original Greek: thus '*Kos*' instead of '*Cos*', and '*Palaiologos*' instead of '*Palaeologus*'. However, well-known Greek names and place-names, such as Corinth or Constantine Karamanlis, have not been altered (e.g. 'Korinth' and 'Konstantinos' Karamanlis).

NICHOLAS DOUMANIS

Acknowledgements

The author and publishers wish to thank the following for permission to reproduce copyright material:

The Nicholson Museum, University of Sydney, for the black figure vase depicting a battle scene between Greek and Amazon warriors (late sixth century BC).

Art Resource, New York, for the following images: Bronze figure, Zeus or Poseidon, from Artemesium, c.460 BC; Laocöon and Sons, c.200 BC; Zoe Panel, depicting Christ between Emperor Constantine IX Monomachus and Empress Zoe, 1028–1055; and propaganda poster, 'The patriotism of the Greeks: Greek resistance world war II, 1940–1941'.

The Benaki Museum, Athens, for the following: The Oath-taking in the Church of Aghia Lavra by Theodoros Vryzakis; painting depicting the Bazaar at Athens, by Edward Dodwell (c.1805); and The Orpheus Cinema, Athens, 1947, photograph by Dimitris A. Harissiadis.

Dr Kathryn Welch, University of Sydney, a photograph of the Temple of the Olympian Zeus, Athens.

Every effort has been made to contact all the copyright-holders, but if any have been inadvertently omitted the publishers will be pleased to make the necessary arrangement at the earliest opportunity.

I

Prehistory to 500 BC: Beginnings

Historic Athens lies at the heart of a triangular-shaped plain that widens as it slopes gently towards the Saronic Gulf. The plain barely contains the modern capital's burgeoning urban sprawl, while the four mountains (Parnes 1413 m, Pentelikon 1106 m, Hymettos 1037 m, Aegaleos 470 m) that form the landward perimeter rise so sharply that air pollution gets trapped and generates a lingering haze – Athenians have dubbed it *to nefos* (the Cloud). Around the centre of the plain lie a series of hills that include the cone-shaped Likavitos, which rises to 227 m above sea level and is crowned by a small, whitewashed church. The ancient city was founded a short distance away, at the foot of a 70-metre-high plateau large enough to fit a small settlement. In antiquity it served as a citadel (acropolis), but to this day the world knows it simply as *the* Acropolis. First-time visitors come essentially to see the Parthenon that now sits in splendid isolation on the plateau, but it is the plateau, this striking physical protrusion, where Athena and Poseidon did battle for the city, that enhances the temple's majesty and allows it to dominate the cityscape.

Indeed the entire Aegean basin, with its wild scattering of islands and craggy coastlines, gives the impression that it was created by a great celestial disturbance: the story told by geologists today might have resonated with the Greeks in Homer's day. Roughly 70 million years ago, the African plate began its movement towards the Eurasian plate, producing a depression that became the Mediterranean, along with a series of peninsulas (e.g. Italy, the Balkans and Anatolia), and mountain ranges (from the Pyrenees to the Alps) which continue along a south-eastern axis across the Balkans through to Turkey and Iran. The Pindus range, along with the Peloponnese, the Ionians, the southern Cyclades,

Crete, Karpathos and Rhodes, form part of the same mountain belt. A younger parallel range developed further west, consisting of Mt Olympus, eastern Thessaly, Eubeoa, eastern Attica and the northern Cycladic Islands. Greece, Anatolia and southern Italy straddle the unstable tectonic juncture that is marked by a line of volcanos (e.g. Nisyros, Santorini (Thira), Melos, Etna, Vesuvius). On rare occasions, one can see new terrain forming with the naked eye.

Geography is fundamental to our understanding of Greek history. For example, the mountain chains that cover most of the mainland and that hindered overland communications were ideal for banditry and for villages and towns wishing to live beyond the reach of the state, the so-called *agrafa* (unregistered). With only a small proportion of Greece amenable to intensive agriculture, local communities have been particularly dependent on seaborne trade for staple foods and on other maritime activities for income. A low population threshold has also meant that Greeks have had a tradition of emigration that can be traced back to the earliest times.

Greece was never equipped in an ecological sense to be a major population hub. It set a contrast to the much richer and heavily populated civilizations that emerged in Mesopotamia and Egypt, where intensive agriculture enjoyed a dependable source of irrigation from the Euphrates, Tigris and Nile rivers. The average Greek farmer was forced to contend with capricious rainfall that could vary annually in terms of volume and distribution. The rains arrive with airstreams from northern Europe, but they are unpredictable because the Balkan mountain ranges form a barrier. During the winter months, when roughly 80 per cent of annual rainfall is received, the rain precipitates with little consistency even over short distances, while it is not unusual to experience double or half the annual average rainfall in a given year. Farmers since before Homer's time have adapted to such challenges by favouring crops that require relatively little hydration, especially olives, vines and cereals, and by anticipating one crop failure every four to five years. In *Works and Days*, Hesiod, Homer's near contemporary, harangues his lazy brother about the need to work hard and be resourceful: 'O noble Perseus, keep my words in mind, and work till hunger is your enemy'.[1] Since Hesiod's day, farmers have minimized risk through mixed cropping (growing different crops on the same plot) and by using dispersed parcels of land, which have helped to distribute the risk of crop failure. Reliance on communal support networks also explains the persistent preference for clustering in village settlements.

FROM EARLY HOMINIDS TO THE FIRST FARMERS

Europe's earliest hominids arrived via Anatolia as early as 800,000 years ago, although the only Greek site that has yielded much information is a cave at Petrálona, 35 km south of Thessaloniki, which contains hominid remains dating back to 300,000 or even 400,000 years ago. The archaeological record improves marginally for the period between 55,000 to 30,000 years ago, with clear signs of the presence of Neanderthals in Thessaly, Epirus and the northern Peloponnese, and some evidence of the first anatomically modern humans. (The majority of scholars agree that *Homo sapiens* emerged in Africa about 250,000 years ago, from where they migrated to other continents and superseded all other hominid species.) We attain a slightly clearer picture of human activity in Greece from the time of the Last Glacial Maximum (*c*.20,000 years ago), when ice sheets covered northern Europe and the southern half of the continent was a cold, windswept, steppe land. About 18,000 years ago, the sea level was about 120 m lower than it is today, which meant many Aegean islands were joined to the mainland. The central Cyclades Islands, from Andros down to Ios, formed a single island that was home to such things as pygmy elephants and other dwarf megafauna.

What set *Homo sapiens* apart from other hominids was their exceptional capacity to acquire, store and accumulate knowledge, and it appears that the changing climatic conditions following the Last Glacial Maximum created new challenges that fostered greater human virtuosity and cognitive development. Our best information on late Palaeolithic Greece comes from the Franchthi Cave near the modern town of Nafplion. Prehistorians have discerned sequential alterations in diet and technologies that corresponded with changes in environment. At the beginning of the Last Glacial Maximum, the cave served as a shelter for hunters of wild horses and cattle that grazed the nearby plains. By 14,000 years ago, the evidence points to a warming climate and forestation, which provided excellent cover for smaller game such as deer. By that stage, the Franchthi Cave dwellers had improved their foraging skills and lived on a diverse range of fruits, vegetables, cereals, nuts, fish and shellfish. By 12,000 or 11,000 years ago, the occupants of the cave had clearly become skilled seafarers since they could travel as far as Melos to extract obsidian, a natural form of glass from which was made very sharp and highly prized tools. Beyond Franchthi and several other sites, however, there is precious little evidence of human activity, which may mean Greece did not attract, or could not support, large numbers of foragers.

The first great transformation in human history took place from about 11,000 or 10,000 years ago with the Neolithic Revolution, when direct intervention in plant reproductive processes created a more stable source of staple foods. Agriculture required sedentary living, which led to population increases and, eventually, more complex societies. Immigrants from Anatolia and the Near East (Syria/Palestine/Mesopotamia/Egypt) introduced farming skills and knowledge to Greece as early as 9000 years ago, or 7000 BC. These newcomers also grazed goats, pigs and cattle, and among their material possessions were fire-clay figurines, pottery and tools used specifically for farming chores. From 7000–5500 BC, most farming communities were concentrated in the wide and well-irrigated plain of Thessaly, but during the subsequent phase (5500–4000 BC) we find settlements appearing throughout the mainland and islands. Towards the end of the Neolithic Era (4500/3200 BC) there were many more farming villages across the Balkans. The typical house was made of mudbrick and timber, and it contained household necessities (ovens, kitchenware, etc.) and storage room for tools and food. Each house was packed tightly with several other residences, and each locality was part of a regional exchange network. Occasionally, archaeologists unearth luxury goods that had clearly travelled from the Near East and perhaps beyond.

Eventually, this lively but unexceptional world of dispersed villages was to form the basis of more complex societies. More than 4000 years after the arrival of the earliest farmers, we begin to see very early signs of urbanization, wealth accumulation, the emergence of social elites and increasingly sophisticated economic networks. The end of the fourth millennium BC marks the onset of the Aegean Bronze Age, so-called because bronze had come into common use.

THE EARLY AND MIDDLE BRONZE AGE (*c.*3300–1500 BC)

Complex societies emerged where farming communities were able to produce enough surplus wealth to support specialist occupations not directly related to food production, such as craftsmen, priests, scribes and warriors. Throughout the Early Bronze Age (3300–2000 BC), agriculture in southern Mesopotamia sustained a dense patchwork of urban centres, while Egypt, the world's first territorial state, developed the technical and managerial expertise to build structures as massive as the Great Pyramids at Giza. It was during this period that we also find early signs of societal complexity in the Aegean area. Sometime during the

Map 1 The Aegean during the Bronze and early Iron Age

period 2700–2200 BC, large buildings were erected at Lerna and Tiryns in the north-western Peloponnese, as well as at Troy (specifically Troy II) and Poliochni on Limnos. In each case, construction required a range of craft specializations. The so-called 'House of Tiles' at Lerna, for example, was 25 × 12 m in size, with an elaborately designed structure that included corridors and a variety of rooms. The building also featured fired clay roof tiles, wood-sheathed doorjambs and stucco-plastered walls. Archaeologists ascribe great significance to such sites because they presuppose the existence of craft specializations, social hierarchies and regional exchange networks that can only exist with complex societies.

5

There is nothing about these Early Bronze Age cultures that can be meaningfully described as 'Greek', although scholars have speculated that the Greek language was introduced to the region sometime during this era. Along with Persian, north Indian and most European tongues, Greek belongs to the Indo-European family of languages, and it appears that an early form of Greek or proto-Greek was imported sometime between 2700 and 2000 BC. Experts nowadays tend to believe that Greek took on its basic form when it fused with indigenous Aegean and western Anatolian languages, and where it took on such un-Indo-European characteristics as the suffix 'inth' (as in Kor*inth*os/Cor*inth*). Scholars continue to use sophisticated linguistic, archaeological and even DNA analysis to speculate about an earlier date for the 'coming of the Greeks', although the only conclusive evidence comes from the very end of the Bronze Age, with the advent of written Greek. With good reason, therefore, scholars prefer to talk of an 'Aegean' rather than a 'Greek' Bronze Age.

The Cyclades Islands provided the setting for the most distinctive cultures during the Early Bronze Age. Seaborne trade flourished, as the islands formed a physical chain between the Greek mainland on the one hand, and Crete and the Near East on the other, and because some islands were good sources of minerals. Centres such as Kastri and Chalandriani on Syros also developed distinctive craft specializations that were in high demand and which were imitated throughout the Aegean basin and indeed beyond. Cycladic art is best known for the highly abstract and schematic marble figurines that depict (mostly) women standing upright with folded arms. Only noses, breasts and limbs are defined, and sometimes ears and the pubic area. These minimalist figurines have drawn a great deal of interest from modern abstract artists and sculptors, although recent scientific studies have confirmed that the smooth surfaces were once illustrated with detailed facial features, tattoos and jewellery.

By 2200 BC, the Aegean basin, as indeed the entire eastern Mediterranean world, experienced an economic downturn and depopulation. A significant exception was Crete, a relatively fertile island that could support a much larger population than all the Cycladic Islands combined, and where archaeologists have discerned a gradual improvement in material wealth. By 1900 BC, Cretans had played a leading role in the revival of eastern Mediterranean trade, and by 1600 BC they had built cities and palaces that could be compared to anything in the Near East in terms of sophistication and scale.

'Minoan Civilization', as it was later named, was distinguished by a series of independent but closely engaged cities. The largest, Knossos, at its height had as many as 15,000 inhabitants. Other cities like Kato Zakro, Phaistos, Malia and Gournia ranged between 5000 and 10,000 inhabitants, and also featured street drainage, sewerage and other planned amenities. Each city was the centre of a regionally administered polity that operated with a bureaucracy and a writing system: the Cretan script, Linear A. This, however, cannot be deciphered, but it was undoubtedly used for accounting purposes. Government administration was located in a monumental and multifunctional building or 'palace' that also served as the centre of trade, worship and entertainment. In essence, most, if not all, significant public activity was centred in the palace. The labyrinthine structure unearthed at Knossos consisted of 1300 rooms that provided a variety of civic functions.

As with the earlier Bronze Age cultures, the Minoans were not necessarily 'Greek', but they did have an enormous impact on the earliest Greek-speaking societies on the mainland. Their most important legacy was as purveyors of culture and ideas from the Near East, particularly Egypt. Crete itself was very much a part of the Near Eastern orbit: its administration, economic organization and architecture were strongly influenced by eastern models. The Minoans also left their own particular imprint on the wider Aegean world, and the clearest measure of that influence was the popularity of Minoan art. Some of the most striking examples of Minoan society can be seen at Akrotiri on the island of Santorini, where frescos depict typically Minoan subject matter, such as exotic fauna and women engaged in various day-to-day and ceremonial activities. On the mainland, artists made a habit of copying the uniquely Minoan motif of boys engaged in bull leaping, while women are usually depicted in Cretan dress, along with Cretan hairstyles, jewellery and make-up. At some point after 1400 BC, for reasons for which we can only guess, Minoan civilization went into decline and power shifted to the mainland, where new palace-centred states had also adapted Minoan forms of bureaucracy and architecture.

THE MYCENAEANS (c.1500–1200 BC)

There was also much that separated the Minoans and the mainlanders. Artwork uncovered by archaeologists at Mycenae, the site after which this civilization was named, appears to celebrate martial qualities by depicting warriors, warfare and other such subject matter. At great expense, Mycenaeans built large *tholoi* (tombs) for elite warriors and

7

their military paraphernalia. Whereas the Minoans had no need for defensive walls, the 'Mycenaeans' invested much of their wealth in fortifications and citadels. Initially, the archaeologists who uncovered Mycenae and other Late Bronze Age centres believed that they had found the cities and palaces of the warrior kings described in Homer's epics, but it soon transpired that the resemblances were superficial. Mycenaean society was structurally sophisticated and had more in common with the Egypt of Ramesses II (1279–1212 BC) and the Assyrian kingdom of Shalmaneser I (1263–1234 BC) than with the tiny warrior chiefdom of Odysseus' Ithaca.

More so than the Minoans, the Mycenaeans formed part of an interconnected set of eastern Mediterranean states and cultures. Much like Egypt, Assyria and the Hittite kingdom, the Mycenaeans had centralized states that were ruled by kings, who lived in fortified palaces and were surrounded by scribes that operated complex bureaucracies. Mycenaean rulers also formed part of a trans-Mediterranean elite that was connected through diplomacy and the exchanging of gifts, and which appeared to conform with a common aristocratic lifestyle. Archaeologists have also noted the growth and intensity of inter-Mediterranean trade in this Late Bronze Age period. Most of our information comes from palace documentation, but a great deal of insight is now provided by shipwrecks that have been examined by marine archaeologists. A Phoenician shipwreck discovered off Ulu Burun in southern Turkey, and dated to 1325 BC, was found to contain 12 tonnes of cargo bound for the Greek mainland. Much of it included raw and manufactured goods from Syria, Canaan and Egypt, such as musical instruments, ivory tusks, hippopotamus teeth, fishing equipment and a gold scarab belonging to Queen Nefertiti of Egypt.

What makes the Mycenaeans especially important in terms of Greek history, however, is language. Among the ruins at Mycenae, Pylos, Tiryns and Thebes were also found numerous clay tablets that featured a linear script. Dubbed 'Linear B', the script revealed patterned combinations that formed syllables, which in turn rendered words that resembled the earliest known forms of Greek. For example, the Linear B words *kunaja* and *pamako* corresponded to the Greek words *gune* (woman) and *pharmako* (medicine). Among the words deciphered are terms that are easily identified in Modern Greek: *antropos* (man), *ipos* (horse) and *tranion* (desk).

The decipherment of Linear B in the 1950s confirmed Greek as one of the world's oldest living languages, while also permitting a more intimate understanding of Mycenaean society. At Pylos, for example, the fabled city of King Nestor, the records do indeed refer to kings (*wanax* – singular), a secondary figure that might have been a war leader (*lawagetus*), a court (*hequetai*), district administrators (*korete*) and deputies (*prokorete*), and what appears to be a council of elders (*gerosija*). All these terms survive in classical Greek (*laos-agein, heretai, prokoitos, gerousia*), except for *wanax* – the 'w' sound was to disappear altogether from Greek. Land tenure arrangements suggest a highly stratified society that included a large population of free subjects described as *damon*. For the most part, the Linear B tablets consist of bureaucratic accounts, but we also learn something about religion, including the names of later Greek gods. Thus 'Diwonusojo' becomes 'Dionysus', 'Era' becomes 'Hera' and 'Posedaone' becomes 'Poseidon'. Zeus, Athena, Hermes and Apollo are also evident in the Mycenaean pantheon.

The records give no insight, however, as to why Mycenaean civilization collapsed. The material record shows that there was a breakdown around 1200 BC, followed by a short recovery, and then a final collapse by 1125 BC. Palaces were abandoned and communities migrated to the islands and overseas: thus migrants from Arcadia in the central Peloponnese settled on Cyprus. Aegean communities became smaller, more dispersed and self-sufficient. Literacy disappeared and links with the wider world were limited. Many scholars refer to the onset of a 'dark age'.

THE EARLY IRON AGE (*c.*1200–800 BC)

The destruction of Mycenae was part of a much wider calamity that affected every part of the eastern Mediterranean. Near Eastern records indicate waves of disruptive mass migration movements, the breakdown of regional trading networks and the destruction of cities all along the Syrian coastline. The identity of the invaders, however, remains a mystery, and it is quite likely that there were other, perhaps more telling, reasons for the general breakdown, including climate change. As it happened, some state systems recovered more quickly than others, but the impact on Mycenaean civilization was irreparable. Sometime between 1130 and 1125 BC, the palace economies ceased to function. An explanation might be that the international framework of political, cultural and gift exchange that had sustained elite groups across the eastern Mediterranean had not recovered, and that the Mycenaean order, which seemed particularly dependent on those links, could not be

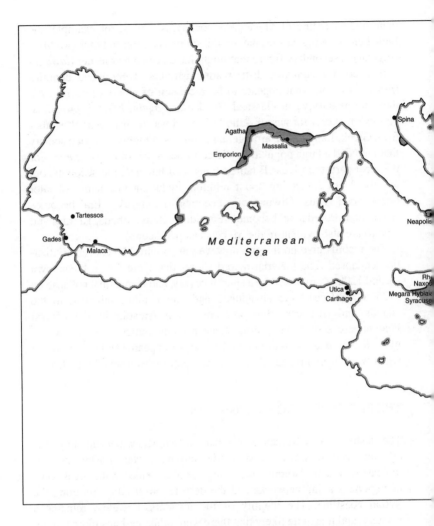

Map 2 Greek settlement expansion during the Archaic period

reconstituted. Without the eastern Mediterranean network, elites lost an essential source of wealth, and the palaces, bureaucrats and craftsmen became redundant.

The ensuing period was a 'dark age' in the sense that we have no written record. What we know about it is inferred from archaeological research, and the material record shows that between 1200 and 1000 BC, the Aegean world had fewer and smaller settlements, and hardly any monumental structures (e.g. palaces, citadels and tombs) that might suggest societal complexity. Rather, we find this world had reverted to much simpler patterns of organization, and yet there were also early signs of a new kind of world in the making.

Regional trading networks can be traced by the distribution of simple geometric pottery styles and regional dialects. Certain communities, particularly on the island of Euboea, continued to engage with Near Eastern centres. For that reason, the Euboean centre of Lefkandi, the most illuminating archaeological site of that period, appears to have retained the rudiments of a complex society. It features a villa roughly 10 × 45 m, with internal and external colonnades. Construction would have required specialized craftsmen and somewhere between 500 and 2000 working days to build. The period is also distinguished by close connections with iron-producing communities on Cyprus, which introduced iron to the Aegean world.

The 'dark age' is best viewed as a transitional period, when a Near Eastern model of societal organization disappeared, and when a rather different society begins to emerge. The key development is the formation of a new Aegean elite. The most powerful figures in this period were chiefs or regional strongmen who liked to be buried with their weapons and armour in elaborate graves. The rediscovery of such graves has yielded a consistent pattern of practices that apply throughout the Greek mainland and the islands, thus suggesting a social order that was distinguishable by a common lifestyle and set of values. Compared to the Mycenaean warrior tombs, these graves reveal an elite of modest means, and not unlike the kings depicted in the Homeric epics that, despite their great status, were not necessarily wealthy. It was sometime during this dark age that the epics attributed to Homer were composed.

One can glean other developments from the material record, including the patterning of regional Greek dialects, although the way these dialects were transmitted is hard to explain. Certainly, the conventional view that attributed this process to the Dorian, Ionian and Aeolian invasions has been firmly discredited. Overall, we know that by 800 BC a very distinct society was in the making. There were significant continuities dating back to the Late Bronze Age, such as the gods, language and such concepts as *damon*, which appears also to refer to an administrative unit. Otherwise the new Aegean world was significantly different to that created by the Mycenaeans, as much as it was to anything found in the Near East.

THE BIRTH OF GREECE (*c*.800–600 BC)

By the eighth century, Aegean communities had proliferated and become more prosperous. Gravesites reveal an increasingly rich repository of materials that indicate the growth of manufacturing and increased contact with the Near East. Another sign of material prosperity is the construction of temples or religious sanctuaries, along with the material offerings ('votives') deposited by worshippers.

The most concrete manifestation of growth, however, is land reclamation and urbanization. In fact, the period is marked by the *synoikismos* (urban coalescence) of smaller village communities into larger and hence stronger communal units known as *poleis* (sing. *polis*). The advantages of *synoikismos* were many. As a larger unit, the *polis* was better placed to compete militarily and economically in an increasingly competitive interregional environment. The historian Thucydides noted that under the leadership of Theseus, Athens became a *polis* when the scattered settlements of Attica agreed to abandon their local institutions and accepted a common political authority. From an economic perspective, urban centres served as the focus of local exchange and production, while, in terms of security, the *polis* could mobilize more warriors and finance expensive fortifications. In time, the *polis* became the focus of political life, law-making, economic activity and cult practices. What emerged was the 'city-state'.

It is important to bear in mind that large parts of the Greek-speaking world retained older forms of political organization or developed different systems, and that these polities came to play an important part in Greek history. Thus, in many parts of Greece, such as Aetolia and Arcadia, scattered communities chose to form federations based on ethnic or tribal affiliations. In Macedonia and Epiros, on the other hand, Homeric-styled kings continued to wield power. It was the *polis*, however, that was responsible for creating a distinctively 'Greek' civilization. The *polis* became the focus of identity and political sovereignty, subsuming all other loyalties, including ethnic, tribal and kinship ties. It came to symbolize all its members, and not just its elites, and provided an environment in which cultural creativity and rethinking paradigms were possible.

As *poleis* were being formed in Greece, new ones were also being established outside the Aegean region. The first overseas farming settlement was established by communities from Euboea at Kyme (Cumae) in the Bay of Naples. Other settler colonies were soon created along the Bay and eastern Sicily, including Naples (Neapoli) and Syracuse, which was founded by the Corinthians. The Greek cities of southern Italy became so numerous that the entire region was later known as 'Greater Greece' (*Megali Ellas, Magna Graecia* in Latin). Other regions that featured a significant number of Greek settlements included the entire Black Sea littoral, coastal Libya and Provence. Among the numerous cities founded were Massalia (Marseille) and Byzantion (Constantinople/ Istanbul). Significantly, these settlements were not colonies, insofar as they were independent entities that nevertheless retained familial bonds with the founding *poleis* in old Greece.

Relations between natives and settlers also varied. A most intriguing feature of Greek 'colonization' is the extent to which indigenous peoples might have influenced the overseas *poleis*, especially as we cannot assume that 'natives' were more backward or less refined than the Greeks. It does appear, however, that along these frontier zones Greek settlers retained a more acute sense of their own homeland identity, and it may be that these overseas settlers were pioneers in formulating Greek identity. Their determination to retain ancestral links was reflected in the unusually large temples that were built in places like Agrigento, and in the large number of dedications deposited at religious centres back in 'Old Greece', particularly Delphi. And yet it is also clear that the overseas Greeks were strongly influenced by indigenous peoples and their ways. Cultural mixing was reflected in artwork and perpetuated through intermarriage. Herodotus of Halikarnassos, for example, the celebrated father of history and among the first to write about the Greeks as a distinct *ethnos* (people), was of mixed Greek and Karian stock.

The most important extraneous influence on Greek culture in these formative years was the Near East. Historians speak of an 'orientalizing' period (around the eighth and seventh centuries), when Greek artists invented a highly original approach to art by adapting and refashioning eastern traditions and techniques. Early Greek interest in sculpting human figures, for example, was directly inspired by long-standing

Egyptian traditions. Greek social elites also looked to their much richer counterparts in Egypt, Persia and Phoenicia to learn about how to act and behave as aristocrats. They adopted lifestyles of conspicuous consumption and such seemingly trivial traits as reclining on couches and giving dinner parties. They also relearned the fundamental skill of literacy. The many variations of the Greek alphabet were based directly on an existing Phoenician script, but, as with everything else, such borrowings were adapted in creative and wholly innovative ways. Thus, the Greeks added vowels to the alphabet, and by the time of Herodotus they had invented prose literature.

THE QUESTION OF AUTHORITY

Trends from 900 BC onwards reveal a commonplace pattern of an emerging complex society: population growth, urbanization, craft industries, fine art and literacy. What sets the Greeks apart, however, was the absence of monarchies. In most ancient civilizations, control over surplus wealth, symbols of power and military resources were concentrated in the hands of an exclusive social elite. Supreme authority was symbolically embodied in the person of the reigning monarch, who ruled with the assistance of bureaucrats and court officials drawn from the ranks of the elite. State propaganda affirmed the monarchy's divinity or divinely sanctioned authority. Within nearly every premodern society, monarchy proved the most stable and enduring state form, and in each case the principle of monarchical power was rarely questioned.

The key to understanding the Greeks, and what indeed made them unique, is not so much that they rejected the principle of monarchy, which they did emphatically, but the fact that sovereign authority remained a matter of constant deliberation, which in turn led to novel political experimentation.

Any discussion of the re-emergence of states in the Aegean must begin with the *basileis* (sing. *basileus*; social elites). It was this element that inevitably commandeered efforts to create state institutions, if anything to safeguard and further develop their particular interests. The archaeological record clearly attests to an expanding elite. For much of the eighth century, inventories from gravesites reveal that the warrior class enjoyed increasing material wealth, and most items recovered from temple sites also appear to symbolize the power and status of the *basileis*, especially horse figurines. (Since only prosperous individuals

Image 1 Hellenism and Gender: late sixth-century vase depicting a battle between Greeks and 'barbarous' Amazons (*courtesy of the Nicholson Museum Sydney (NM 98.25)*).

could afford the luxury of a high-maintenance domesticated animal that had limited use in agriculture, the horse was an item of luxury that symbolized elite exclusivity.)

Early Greek poetry gives us much insight into the mental universe of this rising elite. Most extant poems celebrate the divine calling of aristocrats and their warrior ethos. When it came to drafting law codes and inventing political systems, these *kaloi* (beautiful) people believed it was vital that power be shared amongst fellow *kaloi*, but that they should also rule on behalf of commoners or the *kakoi* (bad). The inferences regarding leadership and political responsibility are clear. In Homer's epics, which are our fundamental source for aristocratic values in this period, the *basileis* claim privileged status by promoting their god-like nature, and commoners are expected to treat them with reverence and honour them with gifts.

The *basileis* are a separate caste that could be distinguished by their lifestyle. For example, the typical Greek aristocrat met his peers at a gymnasium (*gymnasion*), where he exercised and competed nude in a range of sports (e.g. boxing, wrestling, running). Only the wealthy had the leisure to commit time and energy to training and participating in organized games, such as the Olympics. The number and scale of these contests increased over time, and they attracted aristocratic participation from far and wide. Another peculiarly Greek practice was the symposium. These were drinking parties that were held in an *andron* (men's room) and which involved a series of practices that included alcohol consumption, entertainment, sex and intelligent conversation. Knowing the correct 'form' in a symposium, advised the sixth century poet Theognis, was the mark of a well-bred aristocrat:

> Drink with these men, and eat and sit with them, and court them, for their power is great. From them you will learn goodness. Men of little worth will spoil the natural quality of your birth.[2]

Typically, the 'good' and 'beautiful' identified much more with social peers from rival *poleis* than with their own commoners. Powerful bonds were established through intermarriage and a generous form of hospitality known as *xeneia*, which produced enduring interregional bonds that were meant to be as powerful as any blood relationship. Thus at one point in *The Iliad*, the *basileis* Diomedes and Glaucus meet on the battlefield but cannot fight because their fathers were tied by *xeneia*. The two affirm that bond by exchanging armour (6.119f.). Breaking the rules of *xeneia* might incur divine retribution. Paris violated the hospitality of Menelaus by running off with his wife, an indiscretion that precipitated the Trojan War.

Perhaps the key question in any examination of the early Greek aristocracy is why it failed to acquire the level of authority and power enjoyed by its Near Eastern counterparts. And why did the Greek *poleis* fail to develop into monarchies? First, Greek aristocrats were much poorer by comparison. The average *basileus* estate was tiny when compared to that of an Egyptian provincial governor or a Persian nobleman. No single Greek aristocrat had the means to build a grand palace or have a temple built in his name. And no aristocrat was meant to dominate his peers. Rather, the 'beautiful' were forced to share power, as is made apparent in *The Iliad*. For ten years, the 'kings' are encamped outside the walls of Troy, and they must function as a community in which all decisions require deliberation. Hierarchy certainly exists among the *basileis*. Agamemnon is the most 'kingly' of kings (*basileutatos*), and Achilles holds a rank too low to be worthy of his daughter's hand. But when Agamemnon's leadership is found wanting, Achilles can appeal to the authority of his peers.

Another factor that set Greek elites apart from their much richer eastern contemporaries was the fact that the notion of hereditary authority had little purchase in Greek thinking. An aristocrat's worth was measured by his achievements, not his birth. Hence most elite practices featured an *agon* (contest). Accomplishments on the battlefield were the ultimate source of kudos, but there were other sources, including sporting competitions. The fame of the greatest athletes, such as Milo of Kroton, an Olympic champion on six occasions, endured into Roman times. Poets, too, won esteem through competitions, as later would playwrights. Esteem had to be earned; a *basileus* was engaged in a lifelong *agon* to affirm his standing.

This competitive mode had profound implications for Greek state formation. From the outset, that process featured compromises among aristocrats that produced oligarchic systems of government. The political history of Archaic Greece (800–480 BC) is characterized by the determination of aristocratic clans to uphold their authority through constitutional means, while trying to contain the aspirations of the commoners. The patrician families of Corinth, for example, who were known collectively as the Bacchiads, jealously guarded all positions of state responsibility. At Athens, power was monopolized by the 'Eupatrids' or 'the well-born'. When Athens was threatened by public disorder in the 590s, an aristocrat named Solon was asked to draw up a constitution that appeased the discontented commoners while guaranteeing the power of his social peers. Lauded by some as the father of democracy, Solon instituted a 'timocracy' (*time* meaning honour) in which political rights were based on strict property qualifications.

POLIS AND COMMUNITY

Since power was always contested, the Greeks had to invent politics. Aristocrats seeking communal respect and authority were required to compete for state offices, to use speech in order to persuade others of their entitlement and to undertake their state responsibilities under intense peer scrutiny. At the same time, however, competing aristocrats faced pressure from the broader community, which also sought a stake in the political order. In essence, the political history of the early Greek city-states was the search for institutional resolutions to competing elite and non-elite interests.

Why were the aristocrats susceptible to pressure 'from below'? And how did political struggles sometimes lead to the creation of such curious state systems as democracy? One well-subscribed argument has it that changes in warfare had the effect of extending power to lower social levels. During the Archaic period, Greek warfare was transformed gradually from a rather primitive contest between chariot-riding warriors and their personal retinues to carefully structured clashes between heavy infantries that required numbers and great discipline. The propertied *mesoi* (middling sort), namely non-aristocrats who could nevertheless supply their own armour and weaponry, were arranged in a very tight and highly disciplined formation known as the phalanx. Each phalanx required every hoplite ('armed one') to cover the flank of the hoplite to his right, and thus form a wall of shields. The formation consisted of several rows that hurled their full weight in unison against an opposing phalanx. In this form of warfare, which remained the most elementary feature of Greek and Roman battles, collective discipline was fundamental. One would expect, therefore, that the *mesoi* who formed this new hoplite class might seek a greater role in state decision-making or be drawn into the conflicts *between* aristocratic factions.

Either way, military changes generated greater social involvement in political life. Another reason for social inclusion was the sacrosanct value ascribed to the concept of *koinos* (community). If there was one point on which Greeks of all social classes had come to agree upon, it was that community was a source of legitimacy, and that those in authority must serve the common interest. In Homer, *hoi polloi* (commoners) are not meant to speak when the *basileis* hold council, but they are present. For Hesiod, the *basileis* were entitled to positions of authority so long as they served the community competently and honourably. The ideology of community was also reflected in the nature of hoplite warfare, which required of each hoplite to function in unison with fellow members of the *koinos*.

Legal developments are most illuminating on this score. As Archaic communities expanded and became more complex, the workings of justice became less arbitrary and less susceptible to the whims of personality. By the sixth century, the law became more transparent. The *basileis* generated law as an impersonal standard that was applicable to the entire community. Thus, law codes were inscribed on walls for public knowledge and hence to make the law common property. Some of the earliest law inscriptions come from late seventh-century Tiryns, and these give details about magistracies and the mechanisms for checking the power of those holding office. The laws of Drakon of Athens (621 BC) were said to be so harsh that they were written in blood. Among the most famous lawmakers of the age was Lykourgos of Sparta, whose 'Great Rhetra' described the workings of the Spartan constitution. Another was Solon of Athens, who opened up the Athenian political system to the lower social orders. Each of these aristocratic lawgivers were caught in the tension between upholding the authority of elites while ensuring that institutions and laws ultimately served the interests of the *koinos*.

The ascendancy of the *koinos* over aristocratic exclusivity can be discerned from the physical environment of each *polis*. Here, too, the Greeks invented something quite unique. The dominant feature of most cities in the ancient world was the king's palace, along with other monumental structures and shrines that symbolized his authority. All the great monuments of Egypt and Mesopotamia, such as the great temples, the ziggurats, pyramids and tomb complexes, performed that role to some degree. No Greek community could muster the resources needed to construct monuments of comparable scale. Rather, each *polis* erected much smaller structures that reflected the interests of the community, including the archetypically Greek temple. The first stone temples were constructed in Corinth in a style known as 'Doric', with fluted columns, elaborate metopes and terracotta tiling. 'Doric' was quickly copied by Corinth's neighbours in the Peloponnese and by the city-states of Ionia, the central Aegean coastal region of Asia Minor. Here, the Ionians soon developed their own style ('Ionic'), which was distinguished principally by the folding or rolled volute at the apex of each column. During the course of the Archaic period, aristocrats stopped arranging elaborate private tombs and found greater meaning through making endowments or contributions towards temple construction. Significantly, temples were never associated with particular benefactors.

Indeed everything about the *polis* and its physical environment symbolized 'community'. The *agora*, for example, was much more than just a marketplace. It was a specifically designated public space that served as the focus of community governance, communications and festive activity. All institutions and public meetings were located there. The new cities of southern Italy, such as Megara Hyblaia, were planned around an *agora*, while older cities like Athens had to clear space within the city precincts and place boundary markers to demarcate its limits. The planning of newer cities reflected the public interest in other important ways, such as in the equitable allotments of housing and the allocation of space for public buildings such as temples, law courts and the *bouleuterion* (assembly house). Other public features included water supply and waste disposal. Older cities, such as Smyrna in Asia Minor, orchestrated an urban overhaul by clearing the unplanned clusters of housing and creating a rational urban order.

Intense civic involvement and collaboration was required in the life of every *polis*. In warfare, we see a synergy of communal and aristocratic interests. The semi-mythical Lelantine War (*c.*733 or 720 or 648 BC) may have been the last of the old style military encounters. The geographer Strabo notes that the Eritreans boasted 600 cavalrymen and 60 charioteers,[3] while Plutarch claims the Chalcidians won when an ally, a Thessalian *basileus* named Kleomachos, routed the enemy cavalry by leading his own cavalry charge.[4] When hoplite warfare became the norm, battles were seen as a contest between communities. Whereas the old warfare was individualistic and frenzied, the phalanx could only function properly if movements were synchronized and if each individual hoplite maintained self-discipline. The phalanx therefore served as an analogue for communal harmony. To retain their leadership of *polis* life, the aristocrats had no choice but to find their place *within* the community. In hoplite warfare, they claimed the front ranks of the phalanx, as the legendary King Leonidas was to do at Thermopylae in 479 BC.

EARLY GREEK THOUGHT

Early political thought was conditioned by the conflicting values of community order and aristocratic competition, or, how to balance the spirit of *agon* and the desire for social harmony. Early Greek philosophy placed a premium on self-control and moderation, or as one Delphic aphorism put it: 'Nothing in excess'. An aristocrat had to accommodate the imperatives of personal honour with communal values by maintaining a sense of proportion (*sophrosyne*). While being trained from a very young age to become elite warriors, Spartan youth were expected to carry themselves with a measured decorum, to control their passions and instincts. Aristocrats also believed *agon* could be tempered through adherence to procedures. All city-state political systems invented an elaborate and strictly observed range of voting, decision-making and vetting practices.

In fact, process and method, in lieu of divine intervention, underpinned all aspects of Greek thought. The Greeks developed frameworks that gave thinkers free reign to ask questions about all phenomena, such as the structure of the universe and the rules by which it operates. If authority was a subject that was open to discussion, then so too was everything else. If nature was deemed distinct from the supernatural, then nature itself had to be explained. What was its composition? How did it work? What were its origins?

Some answers proposed by the earliest thinkers might seem bizarre. Thus, the sixth-century thinker Thales believed the earth floated on water, and that earthquakes were a refraction of much wilder liquid tempests underneath. And yet what is significant about Thales' theory is that there is no reference to supernatural intervention. Secular theorization became the hallmark of an enduring culture of intellectual exchange in Thales' home town, Miletos, and the results would set the stage for an intellectual revolution in the fifth and fourth centuries. The mid-sixth-century thinker Anaximander, another Milesian, wrote the first natural history of life, as well as the first map that distinguished oceans and landmasses. His work on astronomy, in which he ventured a theory about the universe orbiting the earth, was also the first known book of prose. Yet another Milesian, Anaximenes (writing in the 520s), continued the discussion on the composition of substances and how they transformed into new ones: in other words, how and what causes change. Of even greater moment in the early history of science was the work of Pythagoras of Samos. Pythagoras used mathematics to understand celestial arrangements and to show that the universe was a system governed by mathematically substantiated laws. His famous theorem, which determines the length of the hypotenuse of a triangle, helped him establish an analytical framework for the *kosmos* or 'ordered whole'.

Greek investigations into *physis* (nature) did not imply any principled subscription to rationalism or secularism. The divine realm was implied in Greek scientific thinking, even if it was kept firmly to one side. Thales reasoned that the gods were an expression of an ultimate god, while Pythagoras assumed the mechanics of the universe were a reflection of the divine. Xenophanes of Kolophon went so far as to apply his understanding of nature to the metaphysical realm, and reasoned that there was only one god. Rational inquiry was in no sense considered blasphemous, and it was to remain a standard feature of Greek education throughout antiquity and well into the Byzantine era.

Why so much intellectual achievement in one region? Why Ionia? The short answer is that Ionian *poleis* were more tightly connected with broader Mediterranean networks, and therefore more exposed to the transmission of ideas and culture. The Ionian *poleis* of Asia Minor also bordered on Lydia, a sophisticated non-Greek kingdom through which Ionian thinkers absorbed a good deal of Near Eastern thinking on mathematics and astronomy. It was via the Ionians that the rest of the Greek world came to adopt the Lydian invention of coinage. The eastern Greeks were also responsible for inventing hoplite warfare and the trireme, the archetypal Greek naval vessel.

The Ionian spirit of invention extended to the arts, particularly poetry. Ionia produced Homer, whose epics remained the primary reference for values and moral education, and Sappho of Lesbos, perhaps the greatest female poet of antiquity. Overall, the Ionians set the pace when it came to intellectual and cultural matters. When it came to politics, however, the most creative experiments were taking place in Greece proper.

TYRANNY AND ITS ALTERNATIVES (*c*.650–500 BC)

By the latter half of the seventh century, the Greek city-state faced its first significant challenge. Wealth disparities had widened significantly and indebtedness among the poor was becoming a major source of communal discord. In these troubled times the *polis* become susceptible to a new kind of 'strong man'.

The first case of one-man rule or 'tyranny' arose in the wealthy city of Corinth. Positioned near the isthmus that joined the Peloponnese with the mainland, the Corinthians had privileged access to the Ionian and Aegean seas and spawned some of the largest settlements in Italy. The ruling patrician families of Corinth, the Bacchiads, grew rich by 'exploiting harbour trade without limit',[5] but ruled their fellow Corinthians as if they were kings. In 657, a Bacchiad 'black sheep' named Kypselos seized power and was said to have enjoyed popular

23

support. Indeed, so popular was Kypselos that he ruled for three decades and was known for not requiring bodyguards. In 625 he was succeeded by his son, Periander, who ruled for an even longer period (to 585), but his arbitrary style of rule made him progressively unpopular. The dynasty ended a mere three years after Periander's death, when his nephew Psammetichos was overthrown in a popular uprising, following which oligarchic rule was restored.

Other tyrants of note included Polykrates of Samos, who was responsible for Pythagoras' flight to southern Italy; Pheidon of Argos, who is described as a king as well as a tyrant, possibly because he needed the support of hoplites; and Orthagoras of Sikyon, who was succeeded by his son Myron, but who was then overthrown by another tyrant named Kleisthenes (c.600). Tyrants sought to entrench their personal authority by securing popular assent. Thus, Periander earned praise for his building activity and for patronizing festivals, as did the tyrants who ruled Athens for much of the second half of the sixth century. It could be said that tyranny was a form of early kingship, but, as it happened, no tyrant managed to launch a durable dynasty. Crucially, the tyrants failed to secure aristocratic support or suppress all opposition. In turn, aristocrats found tyranny to be a humiliating experience and thereafter deemed any form of arbitrary authority anathema. In fact, the mere threat of tyranny led some *poleis* to create quite novel political systems. The most renowned cases were those of Sparta and Athens.

Of all the Greeks, the Romans admired the Spartans most. For Sparta achieved social equilibrium at home and yet managed to be Greece's greatest military power. The Romans could relate to Sparta's ostensible balance of monarchical, aristocratic and popular interests in its constitutional arrangements. By securing the homefront, the Spartans were free to exercise military domination over their neighbours. In its classic form, the Spartan political system featured two kings or *basileis* drawn from two separate dynasties (the Agiads and Eurypontids). The *basileis* led their fellow *Spartiates* on campaign and managed judicial and religious functions at home. Kings were expected to rule with the *gerousia*, literally a council of 'elders' (members were over 60), who were the arbiters of the law. The conduct of kings and the *gerousia* was monitored by five annually elected *ephors* (overseers), while government decisions made by the *gerousia* required the approval of an assembly, which consisted of all Spartan men over the age of 30. Stringent checks and balances were meant to minimize change. The Spartan assembly, for example, the supposedly democratic feature of the constitution, was not allowed to deliberate or amend the *gerousia*'s proposals.

By securing stability at home the Spartans sought to dominate the Greek world. To this end, they created a professional standing army. All Spartan boys were taken from their families at a young age, raised in barracks and drilled in the arts of warfare. The supremely disciplined Spartan phalanx became unbeatable. With it, they were also able to force neighbours to join a military league dominated by Sparta. To support its professional army, however, Spartan society committed itself to a rather callous social experiment. Sometime in the ninth century they forced the *periokoi* (surrounding inhabitants) to perform most of the other roles required of a properly functioning society (e.g. merchants, craftsmen, builders), while sometime during the latter half of the eighth century the population of the neighbouring region of Messenia was reduced to slavery. Spartan society came to depend completely on a vast *helot* (serf) population for its primary production, while at the same time becoming paranoid about the prospect of a serf revolt. Ironically, keeping the *helots* in check became the essential purpose of the professional army. That paranoia worsened over time, as the *helot* population expanded and Spartan numbers contracted.

The Athenian search for a stable political order followed a different path. Since the seventh century, this search had been driven by the need to end aristocratic feuding and growing social disparities. Social violence was avoided in 594, when Solon was entrusted to draw up a new constitution. Solon's motives were to provide equal justice to the 'bad' (*kakoi*) and the 'good' (*agathoi*), and therefore he enacted changes that guaranteed every male landholder a share in political power: 'I gave to the people as much privilege as is sufficient for them, not detracting from their honour or reaching out to take it.'[6]

Solon's reforms failed to secure civic stability, for in 546 BC another aristocrat named Peisistratus became tyrant after two failed attempts. He and his sons ruled Athens for the next 36 years, during which time they tried to entrench their authority by promoting festivals and inventing new civic traditions. In 510, however, the tyranny collapsed and Athens was again consumed in aristocratic feuding. In the summer of 508, Kleisthenes, a seasoned political figure, proposed that power be shared between all Athenians, regardless of class or property qualifications. His motives were probably driven by political self-interest rather than principle, but the effect of his reforms was to institute a form of 'people power' or *demokratia* (democracy). To put into effect the kinds of reforms and institutional frameworks required, Kleisthenes reorganized Attica into a series of equal-sized constituencies known as a 'demes'. The aim was to break the influence of kinship or tribal loyalties and have people identify instead with their local *deme*. The state also required citizen involvement in the deliberations and execution of state power.

Therefore, in Sparta and in Athens, the questions 'who has power?' and 'who governs?' led to wildly different solutions. Governance was effectively handed over to the community itself, although membership of that community, or 'citizenship', was restricted to adult males. Such constitutional experimentation had the effect of reinforcing the notion of the community as a sovereign entity, and *polis*-dwelling Greeks came to recognize that notion as being uniquely Greek.

HELLAS

But what did it mean to be Greek? When did Greeks begin to see themselves as 'Greeks' (Hellenes)? When did they become a self-conscious group? Thus far we have described the making of a coherent culture based in Greece but which also transcended much of the Mediterranean world. It is impossible to tell, however, when members of that culture became a self-conscious entity. We can trace 'Greek' culture deep into the Bronze Age, but the mere existence of these traits does not presuppose Greek ethnic consciousness.

The consensus among scholars nowadays is that 'Greekness' or 'Hellenism' was constituted historically. The fifth-century historian Thucydides understood this perfectly well. In the first chapter of his famous *History*, he noted the near absence of the word 'Hellas' in Homer's epics, which led him to conclude that Greek consciousness was developed sometime after. In contrast to modern-day nationalists, who see ethnicity as a timeless essence, he reasoned that collective identity was generated through ongoing contact between the Greek communities (1.3.1–3).

It is certainly true that later Greeks developed myths in order to explain their own origins, but these myths were inventions and are of very little value as historical sources. Tracing the etymology of the term Hellas (Greece) does not get us very far. In *The Iliad* it is designated as a specific part of Thessaly, and in *The Odyssey* it is also applied to the mainland. For the late-seventh-century poet Alkman, the term does appear to cover all the Greeks: he refers to the kidnapping of Helen by Paris as having slighted Hellas. Overall, the scarcity of 'Hellas' and

26

'Hellenes' in the archaic literature suggests there was little interest in, or need for, a collective ethnic term; but the mere existence of the term does suggest some interest in the concept.

Tracing the objective conditions that made Greek ethnogenesis possible is relatively easy. We have already mentioned the likelihood that elites across the Greek world subscribed to a common culture during the 'dark age', and that for the Archaic Era we have detailed knowledge of a transregional aristocratic lifestyle, which included participation in 'Panhellenic' (all-Greek) festivals such as the Olympic Games. It is certainly true that participants had to be 'Greek', subject to a strict ethnic lineage test, and yet while the traditional launch of the Olympics is 776 BC, we only know about the application of the test in Classical times. None of these developments could determine the making of an ethnic identity, but we do see the accumulation throughout the Archaic period of a common set of cultural traits that were shared among the Mediterranean's Greek-speakers, particularly among the *poleis*. The *polis* as an urban form, and the 'way of life' associated with being a member of a *polis*, later came to dominate thinking about who was, or who was not, a Hellene.

And yet, determining when and why Hellas eventually became important in Greek thinking is difficult. A standard argument has it that Hellenism was promoted through Delphi, the most important pilgrimage centre in the Greek world, while a recent argument ascribes that role to Olympia and the increasing popularity of its games. Ethnic consciousness often arises when a given culture is under challenge. It may be that 'Greekness' was articulated first among the overseas colonies of Italy or the Black Sea, where settlers engaged more directly with hostile indigenous peoples, such as the Sicels of Sicily. Here, the compulsion to define 'self' was greater than in Old Greece, where the existence of small groups of indigenous non-Greeks, like the Pelasgians and Dryopes, was of little account. Elsewhere, Greek settlers were probably always in the minority, and it was in the overseas settlements like Megara Hyblaia where greater effort was expended in creating cities that were quintessentially Greek in appearance.

As is often the case, ethnicity is constituted most effectively in times of war. In the Greek world, Hellenism achieved a newfound resonance during a desperate struggle against Persia, a foreign power that threatened to overtake the Greek world. It was at the beginning of the fifth century, during which time an alliance of Greek *poleis* staged a heroic war of resistance against Persia, that Hellenism was probably born.

2

Classical Greece (500–359 BC): The Golden Age of the *Polis*

In 480 BC, the Great King Xerxes (519–465 BC) marched his massive multi-ethnic army into Greece. Herodotus claims that the Persian expedition was the greatest the Greek world had ever seen: 'For what nation of Asia did Xerxes not lead to Hellas? What body of water did his forces not drink dry except for the greatest of rivers?' (7.20–21).[1] With an estimated land force of some 100,000 men, perhaps many more, Xerxes proceeded slowly through Macedonia and Thessaly, deliberately so because he expected many *poleis* to capitulate without a fight, and many indeed did. However, 31 refused to yield. Led by the Spartans, these *poleis* engaged the enemy first at Thermopylae (literally, the 'gates of fire'), the narrow passage to southern Greece and where Persian numbers might not be an advantage. After two days of heavy fighting, however, the Greeks abandoned the pass once the enemy had found a way to circumvent their position. A small force of 300 Spartans led by King Leonidas, along with a number of Thespians and Thebans, fought on to face inevitable death. Herodotus says of Leonidas that he 'perceived that it would be ignoble for him to leave the pass, and that if he were to remain, he would secure lasting glory and assure that the posterity of Sparta would not be obliterated' (7.220.2).[2] After Thermopylae, the Greeks mustered more formidable numbers and managed to defeat the Persians and drive them out of Europe.

That Leonidas and his 300 should choose a suicide mission rather than live to fight another day might seem irrational, but it gives some idea as to what made the Greeks unique. Whereas the Persian army was fighting for its king and the prospect of material reward, the Greeks were sacrificing their lives for ideals.

By convention, historians see the Persian Wars as marking the point where the Archaic Era is succeeded by the Classical: when a world in the

28

making had finally come of age. The ensuing decades witnessed the explosion of creativity that set the foundations of Western culture. The age produced the great playwrights Aeschylus, Sophocles, Euripides and Aristophanes; the historians Herodotus and Thucydides; the Parthenon, the quintessential expression of Greek architecture and sculpture; the radical democracy of the mid-fifth century; and the Athenian thinker Socrates, who, together with Plato and Aristotle, created Western philosophy. It was this Greek revolution, the archetypal 'classic' era, which inspired the other great cultural and intellectual revolutions: that of Augustan Rome, the Renaissance, the Enlightenment and what we refer to as 'the Modern'. As the classicist Simon Goldhill has put it: 'To speak of culture in the modern West is to speak Greek'.[3]

What made the Classical Era 'Greek'? One can think of at least two basic reasons. First, all forms of innovative endeavour, in learning and strictly artistic fields, from areas as distinct as political reform and urban planning, were underscored by a peculiarly Greek approach to knowledge. To 'speak Greek' is to invite critical thinking. Second, the Persian Wars provided the moment when Greekness became meaningful to every *polis* and its citizenry. Greekness became an important measure of moral worth. For Athens, the acknowledged hub of Greek cultural activity, a powerful motivation was the desire to *lead* that Greek world.

The significance of the Classical period in the long run of Greek history was to provide the superlative paradigm of 'Greekness' or 'Hellenism'. Classical Greece was held up in succeeding eras as a reference point for 'authentic' Hellenism, while the language of classical literature, specifically the Attic dialect, was to remain the unquestioned standard for *real* Greek. The tendency of all later Greek-speaking societies to reconstitute cultural authenticity by paying homage to that legacy, serves as the principal explanation for why Greek has survived as a living language.

THE PERSIAN WARS (490–479 BC)

The rise of the Achaemenid Persian Empire was sudden. Its founder, Cyrus (557–530 BC), came to power in the southern Iranian kingdom of Parsa (modern Fars) and went on to conquer the entire Near East. By the end of the century, his successors had built an empire that stretched from Asia Minor to the Indus Valley, including Egypt and parts of Central Asia. It was the first 'world' empire, but the question that exercises historians more nowadays is not how world empires were built but how they were maintained. How did premodern societies manage to control empires of such scale? The Persians led the way by creating a template of imperial governance that was copied by later empires. This template featured a sophisticated provincial system that included powerful governors (satraps), an elaborate road system that ensured swift communications and a massive imperial army that drew on the military expertise of many peoples. Critically, the Persians learned to absorb conquered elites into the imperial order and subscribed to an ideology of cultural toleration. Cyrus and his successors saw the realm as one that embraced humanity in all its diversity.

In 547, Cyrus seized Lydia and its capital, Sardis, and brought the many Greek city-states of Asia Minor under his control. The main burden of subjugation was tribute, and Greek tyrants and oligarchs were now forced to curry favour with the local Persian governor based in Sardis. Otherwise, the eastern *poleis* functioned much as before. From the outset, the Persian presence in Asia Minor cast a shadow across the Aegean. In 506, for example, Athens nominally submitted to imperial authority in exchange for assistance against Kleomenes of Sparta. Later, the *polis* of Aegina tried to lobby Persian support against its rival Athens.

Direct intervention did come, however, after Athens and the city of Eritrea intrigued against the Great King. In 499, a number of *poleis* in Asia Minor revolted against Persian authority, with Athens and Eritrea providing military support. After the revolt failed (494), the Persians sent two naval expeditions across the Aegean. The first was wrecked off the coast of Mt Athos in 492, but the second (490) sacked Eritrea following a six-day siege and moved on to deal directly with Athens. The Persians beached their ships in a cove on the northern coast of Attica and marched into the plain of Marathon, where they engaged a force of Athenian and Plataean hoplites. Herodotus reports that a numerically inferior hoplite army forced the enemy back to their ships and inflicted heavy casualties. A race to Athens ensued, but the hoplites arrived first, forcing the Persians to call off the expedition and to sail back across the Aegean. The Athenians and much of the Greek world were thereafter preoccupied with the prospect of inevitable Persian retaliation.

In 481, Persian heralds arrived in mainland Greece, demanding submission to the Great King. The Spartans and the Athenians made their positions clear by killing the messengers. Along with the other unyielding Greeks, the Spartans convened a council at the Isthmus of

Corinth and formed the Hellenic League. As the acknowledged masters of hoplite warfare, the Spartans took command of the alliance, and although the League suffered defeat in the first land battle at Thermopylae, the heroic stand by Leonidas and his 300 Spartans inspired the other Greeks to keep fighting.

The Persians marched onto Athens and discovered that the inhabitants had abandoned the city for the neighbouring island of Salamis. Since the victory at Marathon in 490, the Athenians, led by the politician Themistocles, had planned such an evacuation in the event of another Persian invasion, while channelling most of their energies into building a large navy, believing that Persian power could be counteracted more effectively at sea. As it happened, an Athenian-led naval force struck a major blow when the Persian fleet was lured into the narrow straits between the island of Salamis and the mainland, where it became crowded and immobilized. With much of his fleet destroyed, Xerxes, in a fit of rage, had his Phoenician captains executed and then personally abandoned the campaign, leaving his general Mardonius to finish the conquest of Greece. The Persians wintered in Thessaly, as the Spartans and their Peloponnesian allies busily fortified the Isthmus of Corinth. The following spring, the League raised a formidable force of 40,000 hoplites and 70,000 light armed troops and marched north of the Isthmus to Plataea, where it faced a still larger Persian army. After days of manoeuvring, the combatants eventually engaged in open battle, where the Greek hoplites won a decisive victory and Mardonius was killed.

Greek unity had defeated the Great King, but the Greeks also seemed to think that the resources of the Persian Empire were boundless. The threat of a Persian retaliation remained, and the Greeks continued to live under a cloud until well into the fourth century.

BECOMING GREEK

The consensus among ancient historians is that the Persian Wars gave 'Greekness' its special purchase. 'Hellenes' began to see themselves as a people linked by blood, and who regarded Hellenism as a way of life that was superior to anything else. It is Herodotus who provides the first unequivocal evidence of Greek self-consciousness. At one point during hostilities, the Athenians refused a Persian offer to switch sides. The main reason was Persian spoliation of religious sanctuaries, but it also had to do with *to hellenikon* (the fact of being Greek):

> First and greatest of all is religion . . . Then there is the fact of being Greeks
> – we are one and the same blood, and use one and the same tongue, we
> have in common the establishments of the gods and the sacrifices we
> perform in their honour, and we share the same customary ways. For the
> Athenians to be traitors to all that would not be well. (8.144.2)[4]

As with the Trojan War, the recent struggle saw a combination of
Greeks fighting heroically, only this time the aim was to retain political
independence. Leonidas and his 300 appeared intent on self-sacrifice to
create a legend, so that like Troy the new war would have lasting meaning.
The mere fact that we remember the 300 suggests that Leonidas' suicide
mission had achieved its aim. Thereafter, we find Greek-speaking polities
wishing to be seen as members of a Greek *ethnos*, with closer attention
now being paid to genealogical traditions that could prove ethnic ties. By
the same token, the *poleis* that failed to support the war against Persia
were forced to somehow live down or disguise the shame.

The significance now ascribed to Hellenism can also be gleaned from
the Greek preoccupation with 'barbarians' or non-Greeks. The barbarian
became a commonplace figure in tragedy. When the playwright
Aeschylus entered *The Persians* at the Great Dionysia festival in 472,
memories of the war were still fresh. The play focuses on the woes of
Xerxes after the destruction of his fleet at the Battle of Salamis, and it
relates the tragic consequences of the Great King's *hubris* (overweening
pride) and Persian *habrosyne* (luxury-loving), whilst the Greeks extolled
sophrosyne (comportment, moderation) and *timi* (honour). *The Persians*
can also be read as a subtle meditation on human mortality, but it is clear
that his audience found it useful to explore values through the prism of
Greekness. In drama as in other art forms, the Greeks revealed a proclivity for defining subject matter by juxtaposing opposites (male/female,
Greeks/Persians), and the intense interest in barbarians after the Persian
Wars was essentially about defining the Hellenic self.

In subsequent literature we find much cruder depictions of the
Greek/non-Greek, or Greek/barbarian, polarity. The barbarian is
accorded such base qualities as *deilia* (cowardice) and *amathia* (stupid-
ity, ignorance) once ascribed to commoners, whereas Greekness
conjures aristocratic virtues such as *andreia* (courage). Hellenism relates
to positive governance, intelligence and physical robustness, whilst the
barbaric corresponds to despotism, servility and flabbiness. In a medical
tract attributed to Hippocrates of Kos, the father of Western medicine, it
is written that:

> The small variations of climate to which the Asians are subject . . . account for their mental flabbiness and cowardice . . . they are not subject to those physical changes and the mental stimulation which sharpen tempers and induce recklessness and hot-headedness . . . Such things appear to me to cause the feebleness of the Asiatic race, but the contributing cause lies in their customs; for the greater part live under monarchical rule.[5]

The body was thought to symbolize Greeks in the most telling way. By the fifth century, possessing a moderately muscular, finely toned, male body not only reflected a personal sense of proportion and beauty, but it also captured the essence of Hellenism.

Many modern commentators have likened the clash between the Greeks and Persia as a clash between Western and 'oriental' civilizations, between the values of democracy and liberty on the one hand, and authoritarianism and conformity on the other. While such views find some support from ancient sources, it ought to be noted that the Greeks were capable of seeing the virtues and attractions of barbarians. Neither Aeschylus nor Herodotus demonize the Persians. Aeschylus' Xerxes, as with every figure in Greek tragedy, is not a caricature villain but a complex human figure whose deeds and experiences were meant to elicit moral reflection.

THE GROWTH OF INTERSTATE DISORDER (c.478–445 BC)

Although only 31 of the thousand or so Greek *poleis* fought against Persia, it was still seen as a 'Greek' victory: the list of 31 now enjoyed as much prestige as the celebrated list that fought against Troy. Collective memory of the Persian Wars became a reference for values associated with Hellas, and yet it did little to promote ongoing unity.

Indeed, the fifth and fourth centuries were consumed by wars *amongst* the Greeks, initially between the protagonists Sparta and Athens, then by a series of contests that included Sparta, Athens, Thebes and Macedonia. The issue always was leadership (*hegemonia*). Leadership of Hellas carried great prestige, and a mantle that the hypercompetitive Greeks were always likely to contest. Sparta enjoyed immense esteem as *hegemon* during the Persian Wars, while Athens, having earned kudos from the Battle of Salamis, was keen to pursue its own claims. The Persians had also shown that with empire came power, wealth and influence. No sooner had the Persian threat subsided than an intense competition for *hegemonia* began in earnest.

Map 3 Classical Greece

Initially, however, there was little sign of dissension within the Hellenic League. Immediately after the Battle of Plataea, the most pressing concern was the renewal of Persian aggression. King Leotychidas headed a force to punish the Thessalians for collaborating with the Persians, while the other Spartan king, Pausanias, led an allied naval expedition to expel the Persians from Cyprus. He then followed up by liberating the city of Byzantion. However, his Spartan compatriots back home were deeply ambivalent about their new role as *hegemon*. Foreign adventures were seen as a distraction from pressing local concerns, particularly the permanent threat posed by the helots. When Pausanias was recalled following accusations that he had treated his allies with contempt, and for lining his own pockets with vast sums of money, Spartan society was forced to confront the issue of *hegemonia*. With some hesitation, the leadership of the League was handed over to the eager Athenians. Besides, the struggle against Persia required more naval power.

The Athenians had good reason to want to continue the struggle, for it was the coastal *poleis* that were most vulnerable to Persian reprisals – Phoenician naval power remained a force to be reckoned with. Thus in 477, a new league of mainly seaborne city-states was formed, including most of the Aegean Islands. Among the few exceptions was Melos, a prosperous island that retained close links with Sparta. The so-called Delian League supported a permanent fleet, with the larger cities like Athens providing the ships and crews, and the smaller members paying annual dues to a treasury on the island of Delos, site of a major religious sanctuary.

It did not take long before the Athenians came to see the league as a means of shoring up their particular interests, especially as the treasury at Delos provided an enormous annual bounty. The League's most impressive feat was the destruction of a Persian naval force off the southern coast of Anatolia in 467, the Battle of Eurymedon, otherwise most of its activities were directed at prohibiting League members from pulling out. Not two years after the League's formation, the Athenian general Kimon captured the Persian stronghold at Eion, on the northern Aegean coast, and converted this lucrative trading post into an Athenian settlement. When Naxos threatened to withdraw from the League, it was besieged and compelled to remain. In 465, another League member, Thasos, rebelled because its own trading and mining interests on the mainland had been usurped by the Athenians.

By Greek standards, Athens had become a superpower. It was certainly the supreme naval power. Other possible rivals were Sparta, still the dominant land power, and Syracuse, the dominant force in Sicily. Syracuse was too remote to impact directly on Athenian interests, but Sparta watched the growth of Athenian power with a mixture of envy and anxiety. Since 478, Sparta and Athens had maintained the pretense of being allies, but relations effectively broke down in 462 over a curious incident during a major helot revolt that raged between 465 and 455. An Athenian contingent led by Kimon, who had strong personal links in Sparta, came to the aid of its erstwhile ally, but after the failed seige of a rebel stronghold the Athenians were sent home. This snub unleashed a political storm in Athens, and the alliance was severed. The pro-Spartan Kimon was discredited, and Athens, now led by his rival Pericles, pursued a policy of isolating Sparta through an alliance with Sparta's key Peloponnesian rival, Argos, and with Megara, traditional rival of Corinth, Sparta's strongest Peloponnesian ally. The clearest indication of Athenian anticipation of hostilities with Sparta came with the construction of the long walls between the city and its main port, Piraeus. In the event of a land invasion, the Athenians could hold out as long as the city enjoyed access to its principal port.

However, the Athenians now ran the risk of fighting wars on many fronts. The struggle against Persia continued. Seeking to exploit an Egyptian rebellion against Persian rule, the League became involved in a drawn-out conflict that drained resources and sapped morale. The venture ended in abject disaster in 454, with the destruction of an entire naval squadron, although the Athenians used the defeat as an excuse to transfer the League's treasury from Delos to Athens, thus removing any lingering pretence of a 'league'. Meanwhile, another military adventure in central Greece brought the Athenian 'empire' to its knees. Since 457 the Athenians had been trying to extend their domination over Boeotia in Central Greece, but by 447 the Boeotians had the Athenians on the run. This humiliation coincided with revolts in Euboea and by Megara's decision to rejoin the Peloponnesian League. When a Spartan-led army descended on Attica, the Athenians had no choice but to sue for peace. In 446/5, the Spartans and Athenians agreed to a Thirty Year Peace. The terms stipulated that each alliance must desist from interfering in the affairs of the other party; members of each alliance could not switch allegiance; and disputes had to be submitted to arbitration. A troubled and short-lived peace ensued, but the Athenians found time to focus their inestimable energies in more creative directions.

PERICLEAN ATHENS: POLITICS AND THEATRE

From an Athenian perspective at least, the struggle with Sparta was also a contest between competing visions of Hellenism. Spartans took pride in their austere lifestyle and their laconic or economical use of words. Their preoccupation with military preparedness came at the expense of cultural achievement. Ostensibly, the Spartans were a society of 'equals', but their constitutional arrangements were deeply conservative. They looked suspiciously upon the radical system being developed by the Athenians, and were opposed to Athenian attempts to promote democracy further afield. The Athenians, in turn, came to see themselves as the embodiment of Hellenism. In his famous 'Funeral Oration' of 430, found in Thucydides' *History*, Pericles exhorts the Athenians as 'the school to the rest of Greece' (2.41).

That Athens had grown rich and powerful was proof of the citizenry's extraordinary attributes. Commentators pointed to Athenian *polygragmosyne*, meaning their 'exceptionally enterprising nature', that set a contrast to the unimaginative and convention-bound Spartans. By the mid-fifth century, most Athenians believed success was a function of radical democracy, for it allowed full expression of the citzenry's wisdom and dynamic qualities. The story of Athens dominates the fifth century, for it was the force driving change in the Aegean world and because the great bulk of our sources were from Athens. Moreover, it was the Athenians who did most to fashion the ideological and aesthetic nature of Hellenism in its 'classic' form. The 'Classical Greek Heritage', as it is understood today, was largely an Athenian invention.

Since the reforms enacted under Kleisthenes, the Athenian political system had developed into a full democracy. From 487, candidates for the archonship, the state's leading office, were chosen by lot. Theoretically, the position was open to landless citizens, including the oarsmen who powered the city's warships, and who had thus obtained a measure of political importance. Complete democratization was realized in 461, when all positions of public responsibility, save for that of *strategos* (general), were also chosen by lot. The *Areopagos*, which functioned like a council of elders, had its powers severely curtailed. All issues of political and legal importance were thereafter subjected to open deliberation and required popular assent.

Since the Athenian citizenry was sovereign, each citizen was expected to speak out, to contribute to open debate and to vote. Pericles denounced the apolitical, the indifferent and those who remained mute at public meetings as not deserving of citizenship. The success of the political order depended on passionate commitment. Military leadership required special talent, but according to the dominant ideology of the mid-fifth century, all other matters of public interest were best resolved by the collective wisdom of the Athenian citizenry. Through the meeting of many minds that had been schooled in life's experiences, the citizenry could be expected to produce the best resolutions to a given problem. In Aeschylus' *Eumenides*, which was first performed in 458, a vicious cycle of intergenerational killings within an *oikos* (single house) was resolved when Orestes, who was responsible for killing his own mother, and was tormented thereafter by the Erinyes (spirits of vengeance), had his case resolved by an Athenian court. Opposing counsel argued his case, the jury deliberated, and a vote was taken. The moral of the story was that a tragic cycle of recriminations left to fester by the gods was resolved satisfactorily by common wisdom.

Theatre was conceived as a tool of civic education, for if the citizenry was to be entrusted with power, it was important that every citizen exercise his mind. He was expected to think for himself, and no art form could elicit intellectual and moral reflection more compellingly than a dramatic performance. Greek drama was an invention of the sixth century, but it was after the Persian Wars when the 'classic' plays were written and performed, first by Aeschylus (*c*.525–456) in the second quarter of the fifth century, and then by Sophocles (*c*.495–406) and Euripides (*c*.480–406) in the latter half of the century. No other art form could command as much emotional impact. Plays such as *Oedipus the King*, *The Supplicants* and *Trojan Women* probed the most difficult issues, forcing audiences to think about justice, moral obligation, piety, community and family.

Drama was financed and organized by the Athenian public, and performances were held during the Great Dionysia festival, held over several days between the end of February and the beginning of March. Before each daily performance, audiences were entreated to elaborate state rituals that celebrated Athenian society, its generals, the empire and war dead. What appeared to be exercises in state legitimation were then followed by plays that often *questioned* all forms of authority and mercilessly lampooned men in power. In the plays of Aristophanes, our only surviving comedies from the fifth century, generals are attacked, politicians are mocked and wars are questioned, even current conflicts. *Lysistrata*, performed in 411, when Athens was fully embroiled in its struggle against Sparta, had the women of Athens, Sparta and Thebes forcing a termination to hostilities by agreeing to deny sex to their husbands. No society since, let alone one at war, permitted its moral and institutional foundations to be tested so searchingly. Democratic Athens deliberately gave its playwrights carte blanche so that the citizenry could think about all issues.

The democratic *polis* secured for citizens an open society, but one should always keep in mind that the majority of people living in Athens were not citizens. Very little of what was offered by the *polis* was meant for women, who were designated no space in the public sphere. Aristotle gave scientific reasoning for the exclusion: women are the product of insufficiently developed foetuses owing to a lack of vital heat. Thus, the female body is an insufficiently developed male, which explains the lack of self-control and other inadequacies. As with the first democratic experiments of the modern era, male political freedom gave free reign to male gender biases.

TEMPLES AND BODIES

By Greek standards, Athens was a megacity. It had a population of 100,000 or so Athenians, and perhaps an additional 200,000 people consisting of foreign residents and slaves. It was during the mid-fifth century that Athens pilfered the Delian League's funds and commissioned a series of grandiose public works, including a new temple complex on the Acropolis. The centrepiece was the Parthenon. The architects Iktinos and Kallikrates set to work on a Doric structure using Parian marble, on a 69.5 × 30.8 metre plan, and featuring 46 outer columns. When it was finished in 438, it had a running series of elaborate sculptures along the inner and outer entablatures, along with a 12-metre-high statue of the goddess Athena, made of gold and ivory, housed within the temple's inner sanctum. By all accounts, the precisely proportioned Parthenon is the finest Greek temple there is. At the time it was the largest and most ornate building in the Greek world, having surpassed the slightly older Temple of Zeus at Olympia.

The construction of the Parthenon and the rest of the Acropolis complex confirmed Athens as the cultural hub of the Greek world. As intended, visitors found the cityscapes awe-inspiring. The poet Pindar was fined by his native Thebes for praising Athens as the 'divine city; shining, violet-wreathed, song-inspiring pillar of Greece'. The Athenians rewarded him with money and made him an honoured guest.

The Athenian desire to be the 'education of Hellas' must be borne in mind when reading such works as the Parthenon's frieze. It featured a procession of mortals, heroes and immortals, measuring 150 metres in length, and took several years to complete (442–438). Viewers were meant to look up and follow the frieze while walking astride the long colonnade, although *what* they were meant to read has been the subject of endless debate. There is a narrative, but no easy clues are provided, and deliberately so, it seems. Does the Parthenon Frieze simply depict the Panathenaia procession? Or does it say something about war, or what it meant to be an Athenian? Since the procession appears to evoke social harmony, was the frieze designed as an antidote to civic disharmony? Nowadays, half the frieze can be found in the British Museum, and the other half in the New Acropolis Museum, thus making it impossible for modern viewers to read the entire procession in its intended sequence. Yet even if reassembled, in all likelihood the frieze will not impart an unequivocal message. As with Greek drama, the intention of Greek art was to stimulate the mind and open discussion.

The frieze also draws our attention to the Greek preoccupation with aesthetics, namely the nature and meaning of beauty. The sculptures on the frieze served as a prototype for how to depict the human body, and it was renowned sculptors like Pheidias and (later) Polykleitos who defined beauty in accordance with the physical body. A resonant tradition was launched that was sustained under Roman dominion, revived during the Renaissance by the Italian masters, and continues to inform modern aesthetics regarding bodies as objects of beauty. The more contemporary resonance of classical sculpture is the body cult as displayed in nearly every media form, from cinema to the beauty industry. After all, it was Greek society that made a fetish of the ideal human physique: moderately toned and well proportioned. Dietics and gymnasiums were important matters for the *polis* citizenry, for the *polis* needed men fit for battle; but there was also an ideological imperative at work. Individuals subscribed to values that were evoked by the finely crafted body, such as balance, symmetry and moderation. Priapus, the heinous fertility god wielding a massive phallus, was repellent precisely because he lacked bodily proportion. Inevitably, this obsession with physical beauty also had the effect of underscoring social prejudices. Thus, the physically handicapped fared much worse in Greek society than the mentally impaired. Thersites, *The Iliad*'s best known and most impudent commoner, has a suitably deformed body.

Overall, the student of Classical Greece finds the sublime was not far removed from the abhorrent. Indeed we find that civil conflict and theatre, imperialism and the Parthenon, philosophy and misogyny, and slavery and democracy were linked, sometimes intimately so. Athens transferred full sovereignty to its citizenry, but as a consequence it became a much more belligerent, if not reckless, state. The mere fact that Athenians were 'enslaving' other Greeks was troubling to some citizens, and there was always a significant element of the citizenry that *did not* believe that full democracy equated with good governance. Thucydides' study of the Peloponnesian War demonstrated this point repeatedly, such as when the Athenian citizenry ordered the massacre of the entire male population of Melos in 416. Among the defenders of radical democracy were the itinerant thinkers/educators known as the 'Sophists', such as Protagoras (*c*.481–411), who argued that 'man was the measure of all things'. Some claimed that if laws, morals and traditions were created by man, then they could just as easily be *unmade*. To their critics, the Sophists were clearly proffering moral relativism.

Opponents of radical democracy began their own search to reconstitute a moral foundation for the *polis*, and they were led by a bizarre looking figure who was the butt of Aristophanes' *The Clouds* (419). Ugly, flabby and stout, Socrates (469–399) was not the physical embodiment of Greek ideals, nor did he play a significant role in politics. Yet it is difficult to think of another fifth-century Greek who had such an impact on posterity. The main difference between Socrates and his Sophist contemporaries was that he did not believe *aretê* (virtue) could be taught. Rather, he believed each individual had to struggle throughout life to achieve *aretê*, which he equated with knowledge. Each man had to recognize his own ignorance, so that 'to know thyself' one had to test all assumptions with analytical rigour and to engage in discussions about morals and other salient matters. Socrates made ethics the central concern of philosophical inquiry. No single individual did more to extol the Greek imperative to educate by bringing before the public (*en meson*) all matters of personal and civic importance. What theatre did through performance, Socrates did through conversation and relentless inquiry.

STRUGGLE FOR MASTERY I: 431–404 BC

The reasons for the outbreak of war between Athens and Sparta in 431 BC have been the subject of endless debate; suffice it to say that

Spartan–Athenian antagonism had remained unchanged since the end of the Persian Wars. The catalyst for war was a complex series of Athenian interventions in the affairs of three *poleis* that had close ties to Corinth: Kerkyra (Corfu), Potidaea and Megara. Corinth and other Peloponnesian League members found Athenian meddling provocative enough to warrant a declaration of war, and Sparta was more or less forced to act.

Spartan hesitation may partly be gleaned from the speech Thucydides (1.80.3) puts in the mouth of King Archidamus:

> But a struggle with a people who live in a distant land, who have also extraordinary familiarity with the sea, and who are in the highest level of preparation in every department: with wealth private and public, with ships, horses, and hoplites, a population size such as no other Hellenic place can equal, and lastly a large number of tributary allies – what can justify us in rashly beginning such a struggle?[6]

Athens was indeed a very rich *polis*, but its hoplite force totalled only 13,000, a figure perhaps three times smaller than what the Peloponnesians could muster. Its basic strategy was to avoid land battles and use its sea power to maximum effect. Athens therefore expected to win the war by attrition. As Pericles reminded the Athenian Assembly, 'the Peloponnesians are without experience in long wars across sea, from the strict limit which poverty imposes on their attacks upon each other' (1.141.3).[7]

Predictably, the Spartans led a force of 30,000 into Attica in the spring of 431, besieging the city and spending much of their time destroying olive trees and other crops. The pattern was repeated almost annually until 425. With equal regularity, the Athenians retaliated by attacking Peloponnesian coastal towns, where they were sometimes able to install their own garrisons (e.g. at Pylos and Methana). Athens enjoyed a series of successes. In 425, the Athenian general Kleon trapped 120 Spartans and 170 of their allies on an islet (Sphakteria) off Pylos. For reasons that are not altogether clear, the Spartans offered peace terms that the Athenians cockily refused. The Spartans then changed strategy by attacking Athenian food and revenue sources in Thrace. An expeditionary force marched overland and attacked Athenian interests on the northern Aegean coastline, including Amphipolis (422), a vital source of gold and silver. After the Athenians failed to retake Amphipolis, both Athens and Sparta were exhausted and ready to arrange a truce.

The Peace of Nikias (421), brokered between King Pleistonax and the Athenian politician Nikias, was meant to last for 50 years, but was

Image 2 Body beautiful: this bronze figure of Zeus or Poseidon perfectly illustrates the Greek ideals of balance and proportion (National Archaeological Museum, Athens) (*photo credit:Vanni/Art Resource, New York*).

broken after six. The peace had been opposed by powerful elements within Sparta and Athens, and the Corinthians refused to be signatories. War resumed in 415, when an ambitious young aristocrat named Alcibiades convinced the Assembly to support the Sicilian city of Egesta against a neighbouring *polis* (Selinus), which in effect meant war against Syracuse, the largest Sicilian *polis* and ally of Sparta. Thucydides argues that the real purpose of Athenian policy was to see if Sicily and its vast resources could be brought under Athenian control. Sixty ships set sail in the spring of 415, but Alcibiades was then recalled to answer accusations of impiety, and he decided instead to flee to Sparta. The expedition itself ended in disaster. With Spartan help, and with the advice of Alcibiades, Syracuse inflicted the first significant military defeat on the Athenians. Worse still, King Agis of Sparta, again on the advice of Alcibiades, invaded Attica and established a fortress in the north-eastern hills (Dekelea), within close proximity to farmland.

Ironically, it was Athens that lost the war by attrition, although it managed to fight on for another ten years, despite many defections by its allies to the Spartan camp, and despite a series of regime changes, including an oligarchic coup of 411. With Persian financial assistance, the Peloponnesians were eventually able to build a navy that could match that of Athens, and under the able generalship of Lysander, the Spartans won a major battle off Lesbos in 406, and a more decisive victory off Aegospotami the following year. Having destroyed the Athenian navy, the Spartans blockaded Athens, which they starved into submission by early 404. Lysander installed the so-called 'Thirty Tyrants', a regime composed of Athenians who were hostile to radical democracy, and which launched a wave of violent recriminations against their political opponents. As many as 1500 were executed in the ensuing terror, but the regime's democratic opponents rallied outside the city walls. By 403, when Athens seemed on the verge of civil war, the parties were forced to conciliate under Spartan supervision.

CONSEQUENCES OF WAR: ART, PHILOSOPHY AND THE *POLIS*

The Peloponnesian conflict changed Greek society in a number of far-reaching ways. Traditionally, war had been a heavily ritualized, convention-bound activity that functioned more like a contest for symbols. The stakes were limited, and only a handful of *poleis* had ever been destroyed as a result of war. All that changed during the course of the late fifth century. When Athens surrendered in 404, the Thebans argued that the city should be obliterated. The Spartans resisted the temptation, even though the Athenians had put the entire male population of Melos, which had originally been a Spartan settlement, to the sword. We have already noted that the unprecedented brutalities committed during the Peloponnesian War had led the Athenians to produce less sanguine assessments of human nature. The year after the massacres at Melos, Euripides staged his relentlessly bleak *Trojan Women*, a play focusing on the plight of widows and orphans in the wake of Troy's brutal demise. For Thucydides, the blame lay with *demos*, the ostensible source of common wisdom. Easy success against tiny Melos, he argued, whetted the Athenian people's appetite for further aggression, thinking they could then bully more formidable adversaries like Syracuse: '*hoi polloi* were ignorant of the great size of the island (Sicily), of the large size of its Greek and barbarian population' (6.1.1).[8] Although an admirer of Pericles, Thucydides clearly believed that his less scrupulous political successors had accumulated power by pandering to the feckless *hoi polloi*. Athens was a democracy in name, but in practice it allowed 'the rule of the foremost men' (2.65.9).[9]

The greatest malaise in the Greek world, however, was the growth of *stasis* (civil conflict). During the course of the Peloponnesian War, *stasis* had become endemic and threatened the moral foundations of the *polis*. Thucydides commented on the 'general deterioration of character', for since *stasis* was not governed by the normal conventions of open conflict, it produced acts of bloodcurdling savagery. Regarding a civil war that broke out in Kerkyra in 427, Thucydides reports that: 'There were fathers who killed their sons; men were dragged from temples and butchered on the very altars; some were actually walled up in the temple of Dionysus and died there' (3.81).[10] Significantly, *stasis* and interstate politics were intimately linked. Time and again, faction leaders were willing to sacrifice the sovereignty of their own *polis* if it meant they could bludgeon their rivals and secure their favoured form of government. Sparta and Athens were lobbied regularly to intervene by factions against their fellow countrymen. It had been a war of ideology as much as it was about the mastery over Hellas.

Stasis was seen as a revelation of all that was wrong with the *polis*, but the Athenian philosopher Plato (*c*.428–347) wryly contended that each *polis* was in fact two contending *poleis*, hence the question of how power should be managed was bound to remain an open one. In the fourth century, people continued to discuss issues that had taxed Greek minds before the Persian Wars: what *is* the best form of government? Which best served the community? Plato's disenchantment with democracy and the relativist views of Sophists like Protagoras led him to write a series of long and highly theoretical treaties, and in doing so he invented political philosophy. He produced a series of works (e.g. *The Laws, The Republic*) through which he explicated a theory of knowledge on which he based his theories of governance. One of the hallmarks of Platonic thinking is that the *polis* requires the expertise of specialists, and in his ideal *polis*, Kallipolis ('Good City'), authority is invested in a philosopher king.

By the beginning of the fourth century, in the wake of the greatest and bloodiest war in Greek history, there was a prevailing sense among the Greeks that their crisis-ridden world was in decline. Athens, once touted by its citizens as 'the education of Greece', was shattered by the defeat, but even more so by internal bloodletting. The *stasis* experienced by Plato and his contemporaries under the Thirty Tyrants was so traumatic that in 403, when the vicious oligarchic dictatorship was brought to an end, the Athenians had no choice but to subscribe to an amnesty, that is, to pledge willfully to forget enmities so that the community might survive.

Decadence, however real or imagined, can nevertheless be a stimulus to cultural creativity and intellectual ferment. In post-war Athens it fostered the greatest intellectual revolution of premodern times, particularly in the field of philosophy, and especially because of Plato and Aristotle. Many philosophers in the Modern Era have subscribed to the view that all subsequent Western philosophy is basically 'a series of footnotes to Plato', while Aristotle (384–322) created an alternative school of thought whose scale and impact was similarly immeasurable. Plato founded 'The Academy' in 387, a school that attracted students from throughout the Greek world, while Aristotle, a non-Athenian from Stagira, taught at the Lyceum on the other side of town. Whereas Plato's approach was heavily abstract and influenced by his love of mathematics, Aristotle was far more interested in determining the laws of nature empirically, by observing and classifying natural phenomena. If Plato placed faith in his Republic to mould the perfect citizen, Aristotle first asked his students to collect information on existing *poleis* and their histories, and then build a theory of politics that accounted for 'natural' inequalities (such as class, gender or master/slave). In his *Politics*, Aristotle came to the conclusion that the best *polis* was one governed by a democratic aristocracy.

Broader cultural developments reveal a Greek world somewhat more self-critical and less encumbered by conventions. It also appears that *poleis* other than Athens now had the financial capacity to refurbish public spaces with impressive monuments. The period is known for its somewhat baroque-looking sculptures and architecture, and is symbolized by the Corinthian column, with its ornate capital adorned with acanthus leaves. In sculpture, one finds a predilection for more flowing drapery, of statues in more challenging poses, including the S-curve made famous by Praxiteles, the greatest sculptor of his age. The works of Praxiteles also reflect much greater interest in the female body. The fourth century produced the greatest female masterpieces of Classical Greece, including the famous 'Aphrodite of Knidos' that was commissioned by the people of Kos. The Koans rejected it after finding the sculpture too erotic, so it was taken to nearby Knidos, where Aphrodite became a tourist attraction.

Fourth-century art also revealed greater interest in portraying humanity in less idealistic ways. Among the most discussed temples in Greek art history is the Temple of Apollo at Bassae, an odd structure found in the open countryside of Arcadia. The frieze was produced sometime after 400, and it entreats the viewer to mythical scenes of mortals fighting centaurs and amazons. In contrast to the Parthenon frieze, Bassae presents the observer with unsettling violent scenes, featuring distressed faces and contorted bodies. The Bassae frieze is extremely provocative and elicits an emotional response.

The fourth century also witnessed a more determined effort to revamp the physical environment of the *polis* along orthogonal 'Hippodamian' lines. We find much more attention given to the rational configuration of public spaces and public buildings. There is also greater adherence to a unified architectural style for all public buildings, and to the beautification of public spaces with monuments and statues. The search for greater precision is well illustrated by such cities as Priene in Asia Minor, a city that was forced to relocate to a new site in 352, and which was rebuilt along a perfect grid pattern. The civic identity of the Priene was encapsulated by the positioning of the *agora* and the main public buildings, each of which was physically linked by sheltered colonnades. Even the non-polis peoples of the north had begun to adopt Hippodamian rules. King Archelaus IV of Macedonia (413–399) founded a new capital at Pella, where the city was arranged in the orthogonal manner, and where the royal palace was located within the civic centre. Elsewhere, the *polis* reflected egalitarian ideals. In this period we find less interest in temple construction and more in public utilities, such as gymnasia, theatres and strictly administrative buildings such as *bouleteria* (civic assembly houses).

STRUGGLE FOR MASTERY II: 404–359 BC

The defeat of Athens did not bring an end to interstate discord, nor did it mollify factional rivalries within city-states. In fact, the new era of Spartan domination appeared to exacerbate political tensions at each level. Among the former tributaries of the Athenian Empire, Lysander replaced democracies with handpicked oligarchies. Tribute was still extracted from these 'liberated' *poleis*, with a good portion pocketed by Lysander himself, making him phenomenally rich by Greek standards. Initially, the new era of Spartan *hegemonia* featured a campaign to liberate Greek *poleis* under Persian rule. Lysander and then King Agesilaos II (400–360) led the Spartans to a series of stunning victories against the Persians, including one outside the provincial capital Sardis in 395. However, Spartan success had the effect of unnerving even such stout old allies as Corinth. With Persian support, Corinth, Argos, Athens and the Boeotians formed an anti-Spartan alliance, but the ensuing Corinthian War (394–387) was inconclusive, and after 389, despite a series of setbacks, the Spartans prevailed with Persian financial support – the Ionian Greek *poleis* that had been liberated only a few years before were ignominiously handed back in return for Persian gold. In 387, the Spartans imposed an advantageous settlement (the King's Peace) that prohibited major cities from forming leagues that might challenge their *hegemonia*. Thus, Thebes could no longer dominate Boeotia, Athens again was forced to relinquish its tributaries, and Corinth was compelled to rejoin the Peloponnesian League.

The King's Peace was an attempt to forge a stable interstate order under Spartan domination, but Sparta's chief protagonists were not easily restrained. In fact, the Greeks were incapable of creating an interstate system that might balance the interests of the greatest powers and limit the recourse to war. During the course of the 370s, Spartan *hegemonia* began to unravel. Athens rebuilt its fleet and was able to capitalize on anti-Spartan sentiment by organizing a new maritime alliance that included many *poleis* in Asia Minor. The incident that triggered the next major interstate war occurred in 379, when an anti-Spartan faction in Thebes, with Athenian connivance, assassinated the city's pro-Spartan oligarchy and expelled the Spartan garrison. In the ensuing conflict, the new Athenian alliance destroyed the Spartan navy in two major naval encounters (376 and 375), while Thebes, after having reconstituted the Boeotian confederation, defeated the Spartans at Tegyra in 375. Thebes then dealt a decisive blow in 371 at the Battle of Leuktra. Led by the

49

tactical genius Epaminondas, the Thebans employed deeper rows of hoplites to the left side of their phalanx, thus adding enough extra weight to smash the more finely balanced right side of the opposing phalanx.

Leuktra proved to be a turning point in Greek history, for it exposed a fatal weakness in the Spartan social structure. For by 371, the total number of Spartan citizens had shrunk to about 1300, a mere fraction of the citizenry that fought Persia a little over a century earlier. In more recent times, the Spartans had been making up the numbers by hiring mercenaries, but nothing had been done to expand their citizen base. Of the 700 hoplites who fought at Leuktra, 400 had been killed, and Sparta suddenly found itself vulnerable to complete annihilation. So desperate were matters that King Agesilaos ignored the Spartan prohibition of retreat and allowed the 400 survivors to return home. It took a single battle to expose Sparta's vulnerability, and worse was to come. For the Thebans then took the unprecedented step of invading the Spartan homeland with 40,000 hoplites, who ravaged the countryside. Only flooding stopped a direct attack on the city. The real harm was rendered when the Thebans liberated the helots, thus denying the Spartan military system its economic foundation. The Thebans reorganized the helots of Messenia into a new anti-Spartan state, and prompted the equally anti-Spartan Arcadians of the central Peloponnese to form a confederacy. Within a very short space of time, Sparta had been reduced to a marginal entity.

The Theban quest for *hegemonia* merely confirmed that no Greek *polis* was capable of enforcing a stable interstate order. After Leuktra, the Thebans busily attempted to assert their authority over the Peloponnese, Thessaly and the Aegean, where some attempt was made to compete against Athenian naval power. It soon transpired, however, that Theban success was attributable to battlefield tactics and the exceptional talents of two generals, Pelopidas and Epaminondas. Otherwise, the Thebans lacked the financial capacity to sustain their geopolitical ambitions. Tellingly, Theban domination began to unravel not long after the deaths of its two military geniuses.

THE CONSEQUENCES OF ENDEMIC WAR

During the fourth century, Greek warfare had been transformed in important ways. Traditionally, battles had been contests between rival phalanx formations, and the protagonists abided by rules and rituals. At the end of the Peloponnesian War, however, many conventions had disappeared. Contemporary observers noted that fighting now took place in every season, during night and day. Warfare had also become more sophisticated. Generals were forced to think more strategically when it came to logistics and battlefield tactics. Indicative of the new importance of tactics were specific books that dealt with warfare, such as Xenephon's *Horsemanship* and *Cavalry Commander*. Auxiliaries now played a more telling role in battles, while Philip II of Macedonia, who entered the scene in the 350s, introduced ambushes and other 'surprise' tactics. Fourth-century *strategoi* accorded much greater importance to cavalry, skirmishes, archers, slingers and light infantry. Particularly prominent were peltasts, whose main role was to hurl heavy javelins to unsettle the opposing phalanx. The richer *poleis* began to employ mercenaries – the growing pool of soldiers for hire was an inevitable outcome of endemic warfare. In other words, the Greeks began to flout conventions as warfare became more expensive and the stakes increased.

In what ways did these developments impact upon the *polis*? Historians of state formation find that change is often driven by the exigencies of warfare. States must maintain parity with rivals or risk annihilation. To raise the taxes needed to finance larger armies, bigger fortresses and more warships, states refine their fiscal systems and bureaucracies. In less sophisticated polities such as the feudal monarchies of medieval Europe, the crown extended its control over social elites, which in turn were meant to supply it with military retinues. The *polis* did not lend itself to either approach. Politics remained a strictly amateur affair, and most *poleis* were too small to support bureaucracies. Nor did the Greek city-state have the capacity to grow into a larger state. The *polis* was an exclusive entity that was not open to absorbing outsiders. In Athens, citizenship was restricted to males with two Athenian parents, and there was no scope for including such distinguished foreigners as Pindar, Herodotus and Aristotle. As one scholar of state formation has noted, the Greek city-state was a 'dead end'.[11]

Rather, to meet their security needs, many fourth-century *poleis* pooled their resources by forming leagues and confederacies. The Boeotian League might have been the first such league, but culturally coherent groups such as the Achaeans, Aetolians and Arcadians, which were bound by common tradition, origin myths and institutions, and which covered vast territories by Greek standards, came to play significant roles in interstate politics during the fourth and third centuries.

The future, however, belonged to centralized kingdoms that could, with much greater efficiency, muster the financial and manpower reserves of vast territories, and on a scale that was well beyond the ambit of even the largest confederation. The beginning of the end of the independent Greek city-state can be traced to 359, when Philip II of Macedonia brought his traditionally factious kingdom under his firm control. He then extended his authority across the southern Balkans and into Thessaly, and by 338 he had forced most Greek states into an alliance. Philip's success can be attributed to a number of factors, but his arch critic, the Athenian orator Demosthenes, raised the essential point that:

> his personal control of all activities, open or secret, his combined position in command of an army, state and exchequer, his invariable presence with his forces, give him a real superiority in military speed and efficiency.[12]

Until the advent of Philip II, the Greek world had existed in splendid isolation, being somewhat beyond the reach of Persia and therefore free to engage in petty wars and civil conflicts. Philip's Macedonia had the power to impose peace at both levels, and drew the Greek world into an international mainstream that was dominated by great monarchies. Thereafter, the individual *polis* played a relatively insignificant role on the international stage. Some *poleis* such as Rhodes were able to pursue an independent 'foreign policy', but they could do so only by playing off the greater powers against each other.

By that stage, however, the Greek *polis* had already established a powerful cultural legacy. Even at the beginning of the fourth century, there was already a sense that the pinnacle of human achievement had been reached: that the tragedies of Aeschylus, Sophocles and Euripides could not be bettered. It was this 'classical' culture that the Macedonian kings were to disseminate beyond the Near East, as far as Samarkand in Central Asia and the Indus Valley in India, and which the Romans would later bring to Britain and the rest of western Europe. In other words, it was from the mid-fourth century that the culture of the *polis* began its transformation into a 'world' culture.

3

....

The Hellenistic Era (359–327 BC): From Philip II to Augustus

One of the greatest monuments of antiquity, listed among the Seven Wonders of the Ancient World, was the great Mausoleum that dominated Halikarnassos (modern Bodrum), a major *polis* on the southwest shoreline of Asia Minor. As with many overseas colonies, the inhabitants of Halikarnassos were a blend of Greek and indigenous peoples: here, the local rulers actively promoted Greek and Karian culture. The Mausoleum itself was also a synthesis of different cultural influences. While it featured 36 Ionic columns and an elaborate series of sculptures to rival the Parthenon frieze, this massive structure, 45 m high with a 38.4 × 32 m base, was the tomb of Mausolus, the local satrap and effective ruler of a large region that included nearby islands and Crete. When Mausolus made Halikarnassos his capital in 370, he also had built a magnificent palace. The city also had an *agora*, a gymnasium, a theatre and other quintessential features of the *polis*; and its urban plan followed the Hippodamian grid pattern. But it was the Mausoleum that gave the city its distinction; and, although it looked Greek, it served a decidedly un-Greek function. That Mausolos could build something so ostentatious and grand was clear testimony of his enormous personal power. He was sufficiently 'Hellenized', as many Karians were by this stage, but Halikarnassos was as much *his* city as it was the community's. The day-to-day running of the city remained in the hands of the citizenry, but they were no longer sovereign.

The fourth century augured a radically different world to that which had been familiar to the Greeks of the mid-fifth century. Philip II, a much more powerful and enterprising despot than Mausolos, was able to impose his authority over most of the Greek city-states, as did his successor Alexander. The ensuing 'Hellenistic' period was an age of kings, but the historians who first coined the term in the nineteenth century were cognizant of the fact that the rise of territorial states like Macedonia did not augur the end of the *polis*. On the contrary, the *polis* became the administrative and cultural bedrock of a succession of empires, including the Roman Empire. Indeed, under the Hellenistic kings and the Romans, the world between the Atlantic and India found unity through a network of Greek or quasi-Greek cities. From the late fourth century, we find Hellenism becoming a 'world' culture.

MACEDONIA UNDER PHILIP II

In 338, Macedonia defeated an alliance of *poleis* at the Battle of Chaeronea. The following year, Philip chaired a congress at Corinth at which he proposed a solution to Greek division and instability. He impressed upon the Greeks the need to channel their energies against Persia, recalling the fact that the Great King Xerxes had angered the gods by despoiling sacred sites, and there was still the need to liberate the Greeks in Persian-controlled Asia Minor. Philip could count on the moral support of many leading Greeks who saw the Persians as the most pressing problem, including the Athenian politician Isokrates, who had long been calling upon the Greeks to unite and confront the real enemy. The League of Corinth was formed, and its signatories were committed to bringing an end to *stasis* and interstate war. All disputes between states had to be submitted to arbitration, and, as a safeguard against civil instability, members were not permitted to make constitutional changes – Philip had already ensured that pro-Macedonian elites were already at the helm in most city-states.

The League of Corinth was conceived as a Panhellenic ('all-Greek') organization, and, for the first time, most of the *poleis* of Greece proper were politically united. Only Sparta, the western Greeks and other distant *poleis* were not included. The League was formally established to protect the freedom and autonomy of the Greeks. The interests of its members were represented in a *synedrion* (council), a formal body of which Philip was the presiding member. In reality, the *synedrion* was a tool with which Philip could control the Greeks and wage his imperial ambitions in the east. His ultimate ambition was to challenge the might of Persia, and for that immense task he needed Greek manpower and resources, or at the very least he would need to secure his base while campaigning in Asia. Philip's propaganda did indeed appear to generate enthusiasm among many Greeks, and there was also the promise of loot. At the same time, four strategically placed Macedonian garrisons were left behind to keep the Greeks in check. With carrot and stick, Philip channelled the combined power of the Greeks against the world's greatest empire. In 336 the League voted to wage a Panhellenic crusade against Persia, and Philip was formally granted the right to requisition manpower and other resources from each of the member states.

That Philip managed to unite Macedonia, let alone the rest of the Greek world, astounded many at the time. How did a kingdom composed of 'resourceless vagabonds', of shepherds dressed in skins, as Philip's own son was meant to have said, become masters of Greece? Macedonia had been a backwater that seemed unchanged since the days of Homer. The kingdom's population was primarily composed of highland pastoralists and peasant communities strewn across the lowlands. Macedonian monarchs were forced to contend with a powerful nobility, while having only nominal authority over the lords who dominated the kingdom's highlands. Macedonia's aristocrats likened themselves to the *basileis* of the Homeric epics, particularly those selected to be the king's *hetairoi* (companions), who formed his court and elite cavalry corps. The king and his *hetairoi* caroused in raucous drinking parties, where tempers often flared and where the exchange of insults could lead to bloodshed. Monarchical succession was a particularly fraught affair. Archelaus I (*c.*413–399) started his reign by slaying an uncle, cousin and half-brother. The incumbent also had to secure the loyalty of the more powerful *hetairoi*, who might throw their weight behind a rival family claimant. Certainly, Philip and his son, Alexander, remained wary of the *hetairoi* and their traditional entitlements, particularly the right to 'elect' the king.

The Greekness of the Macedonians was as much a controversial matter in Classical times as it has been recently, but what is indisputable is the profound importance of Macedonia *in* Greek history. When serious interest in defining Hellenism was first entertained in the wake of the Persian Wars, it was the *polis*-Greeks who set its terms. Herodotus claims Hellenism can be defined through blood ties, religion, language and way of life, and it was clear that the Macedonians could not meet all these criteria. King Alexander I (*c.*498–454) was initially refused the right to compete at the Olympic Games until it was determined that his ancestry could be traced to impeccably Greek Argos. On a more objective level, Macedonian religion was recognizably Greek, regional peculiarities notwithstanding, and social elites received a Greek education: for obvious reasons Macedonians were especially drawn to Homer. It is much harder to identify the culture of the general population, but recent epigraphy studies at Pella suggest that the Macedonian language was a form of Greek related to a northwest dialect of the Mount Olympus region. Where the Macedonians failed the test of 'Hellenicity' was the 'way of life' criterion, which essentially meant the 'way of life of the *polis*', and in the years leading to the Battle of Chaeronia, when Philip was seeking to impose his hegemony over southern Greece, the non-Greekness of the Macedonians became an article of faith among Philip's opponents. Be that as it may, Macedonia's elites had always insisted that they were part of the Greek world, and Philip intended to lead that world in a 'Panhellenic' venture against a common enemy.

The prestige of the Macedonian monarchy had been enhanced during the course of the fifth century, when Alexander I, Perdikkas II and Archelaus I expanded the kingdom and came to dominate Macedonia's neighbours to the north (Illyria) and east (Thrace). They also promoted the Hellenization of the Macedonian nobility by patronizing Greek artists and promoting the local Olympia festivals to Panhellenic status. The early fourth century featured a series of troubled reigns, and when Philip II assumed power in 359, he moved quickly to eliminate rival claimants. Domestically, he acquired unassailable authority once he established Macedonia's domination of the Balkans. Through deft diplomacy, marriage alliances and above all sheer military force, Philip brought Illyria, Thrace, Epiros and southern Greece under his personal authority. By the time he was ready to move against the southern Greek states, he had at his disposal immense financial resources, including mines rich in silver and gold, and vast fiscal revenues from his newly conquered territories. Like the Great King of Persia, Philip could finance a standing army that was well drilled and properly armed. And unlike his Greek opponents, he had enough manpower reserves to overcome many setbacks. Moreover, as a ruler who had attained absolute power, Philip could mobilize his resources quickly, thus giving him a decisive advantage against any combination of Greek states.

The most important factor explaining Philip's ascendancy was his extraordinary political and military talent. Within a short space of time, he managed to unite his kingdom under his personal authority and was later able to divide and dominate the hopelessly divided Greeks. As a younger man he spent several years as a hostage at Thebes, where he studied the arts of war under the tutelage of Epaminondas and Pelopidas. On becoming king, Philip remodelled the Macedonian army and created a phalanx that could break any infantry formation of its day. Each infantryman was armed with a *sarissa* (pike) so long, up to 4.5 m, that it had to be held with both hands. Together, these infantrymen formed an impenetrable wall of spikes, though they were drilled in such a way as to make the phalanx flexible and highly mobile. Philip also learned how to coordinate the various elements of his army (cavalry, archers, slingers and skirmishers) during battle. Within a short space of time, he made traditional Greek approaches to warfare redundant.

In 336, Philip was ready to take on the might of Persia. An advance guard led by Parmenio ventured into Asia Minor in 336, but it was forced to return on hearing of Philip's assassination. During a typically boisterous Macedonian festival, the king was murdered. At that point, the kingdom was expected to fall into disarray. His son, Alexander, was still in his late teens, and it was inevitable that formidable generals like Parmenio would make a bid for the throne. Buoyed by Philip's assassination, the Greeks took the opportunity to renounce the League and proclaim their independence. However, Alexander rose to the occasion quickly and decisively. Within a few weeks; he had nullified his potential rivals at home and reasserted Macedonian authority over southern Greece. Parmenio proved useful in restoring control over Illyria and Thrace. When Thebes revolted a second time in 335, Alexander set an example by destroying the city and selling the survivors into slavery. The young king managed to restore his dynastic authority to the point where he could pursue his father's dream of conquering Asia.

His reign would be short, yet it proved to be a watershed in Greek history. Alexander the Great conquered much of the known world and made it his personal domain. States not yet conquered sent embassies to win his favour, and many peoples within his empire worshipped him as a living god. This self-proclaimed son of Zeus, undoubtedly the most powerful figure in Greek antiquity, began his reign as the champion of Panhellenism.

ALEXANDER THE GREAT

Alexander claimed the Persian Empire following a series of major battles. After an opening encounter at Granicus (334) in Asia Minor, he won a second major victory at Issus (333) in northern Syria, and dealt the decisive blow at Gaugamela (331) in northern Mesopotamia. It was at Gaugamela that Alexander's reputation as a great conqueror was confirmed, and where the Persian king, Darius III, effectively conceded his realm. But Alexander wanted much more. Arrian, our best source, believed the young king was possessed by a *pothos* (passion) to continue conquering:

> he would not have been able to remain satisfied with his conquests so far, not even if he had added Europe to Asia and the British Isles to Europe. He would always have been seeking out some unknown land, attempting to rival himself not anybody else. (7.1.4)[1]

He drove his army relentlessly eastwards, through the Hindu Kush to the western extremities of the Himalayas and down into the Indus Valley. Only the threat of mutiny stopped the next move into the Ganges River basin. Forced back to Babylon in 325, Alexander began his reign as the legitimate successor of the Persian Empire, but it did not last long. In 323, at the young age of 33, Alexander died of fever.

Since then, an untold number of studies and biographies have been written about him, particularly about his generalship, political ambitions, legacy and personality. That he achieved so much within a short space of time has attracted endless commentary, but what is really astonishing is the fact that he lived as long as he did. For Alexander lived up to the Homeric warrior ethos quite literally. In fact, he sought to surpass his hero Achilles by engaging with the enemy in hand-to-hand combat, placing himself regularly in extreme danger and surviving several near-fatal wounds. His Macedonian followers remained loyal because of his extraordinary courage, but there was also the fact that he always led them to victory. He was a brilliant military tactician who regularly prevailed over vastly superior numbers. At Gaugamela, his 47,000 men defeated a Persian army that was at least twice as large and numbered perhaps as many as 250,000.

Alexander also knew how to consolidate his conquests. The Persian Empire was a seasoned polity, and he and his successors were wise to adopt its existing administrative apparatus. Moreover, local elites were absorbed into the new imperial power structure, and Alexander was sensitive to local traditions. In the east he adopted *proskynesis* (prostration), a submissive gesture of bowing, to which his Macedonian elites took deep offence. He was gleefully welcomed by Egyptian elites who made him pharaoh, and while he did not assume the Persian crown he nevertheless proclaimed himself ruler of 'Asia'. In Babylon, his imperial capital, he adopted some of the local royal regalia. He married three women for political purposes, including the Bactrian princess Roxane, and he ordered 3000 Macedonian soldiers to take Persian brides.

What was the purpose of this enormous empire? Was he driven merely by *pothos* or did he have a political vision for the world? And did he always intend it to be a 'Greek' world empire? Later biographers like Arrian liked to think he did. In his *Anabasis*, Arrian has Alexander tell Darius that

> your ancestors came to Macedonia and the rest of Greece and attacked us without provocation. I, as leader (hegemon) of the Greeks and wishing to take vengeance on the Persians, have crossed into Asia. (2.14)[2]

Alexander certainly maintained that his invasion of Persian territory was a Panhellenic venture. After the Battle of Granicus, his treatment of Greek prisoners of war was exceptionally harsh because they had 'fought against Greece for barbarians' (Arrian 3.23).[3] With each battle, Alexander took special care to draw links with the Persian Wars in order to reaffirm the historical and specifically Hellenic nature of the mission. The burning of Persepolis appears to have been a symbolic act of vengeance for the Persian Wars, while the dismissal of League contingents at Ekbatana in June 330 clearly signalled that the crusade was over. That he mistrusted his Greek allies and handled them ruthlessly when it suited does not mean he was disingenuous about his support for Panhellenism. It does appear, however, that the cause seemed less important to him after the Persian monarchy had been destroyed. Rather, for the rest of his reign he focused on the 'universal' nature of his monarchy, believing it was his destiny to forge the unity of humankind.

Overall, most experts agree that Panhellenism was not his primary motive, and even as a secondary motive it lost its currency once the Persian Empire was his. Ultimately, what mattered was his personal destiny and his place among the gods. As he led his army into what is now Afghanistan and Pakistan, his *hetairoi* grew increasingly uncomfortable with his autocratic style. After killing his cavalry commander Kleitos for questioning his achievements, Alexander sat in his tent and refused to eat or drink for three days, but he emerged when told that, as son of Zeus, justice was essentially 'whatever the king does, by whatever means' (Arrian 4.9).[4] As more and more of the world came into his possession, Alexander experienced a personal apotheosis.

A world empire might have been fitting for a living god, but the 'god' in question did not manage to live long enough to create a durable imperial structure. As it happened, the empire built by Philip and Alexander owed much more to charisma and exceptional talent than to any systems of governance. Quite predictably, the *hetairoi*, like highly competitive Homeric *basileis*, fought tenaciously to assume Alexander's mantle – but none could possibly fill his shoes. When the dust finally settled, there was not one powerful kingdom but several.

HELLENISTIC KINGDOMS (323–*c*.250 BC)

The fact that Alexander had heirs was of little account to his ruthlessly ambitious *hetairoi*, especially given that his half-brother, Philip Arrhidaeus, was mentally handicapped, and his son by Roxanne was not yet born. The most senior figure, Perdikkas, assumed the role of regent, but rival generals were also quick to see his regency as a ruse for his personal ambitions, and within a short space of time he was forced to fight against many other aspiring *diadochoi* (successors). In the heady contest that followed, most of the *diadochoi* were assassinated or fell in battle, including Perdikkas, who was murdered in 320 during a military campaign in Egypt. Back in Macedonia, Alexander's mother Olympias had been promoting the cause of her infant grandson and had her stepson murdered in 317. In 311, Kassander, ruler of Macedonia at the time, organized the disposal of the young Alexander IV and Roxane. By 307, the *diadochoi* had formally assumed the title 'king' (*basileus*).

Perhaps the canniest of his *diadochoi* was Ptolemy, later Ptolemy I Soter ('the Saviour', 323–282), the first to secure a territorial power-base. He chose Egypt, the richest and yet most strategically defensible province in the empire. The rest took an all-or-nothing approach, although only Perdikkas and two other *diadochoi* would ever come close to claiming the empire in its entirety. Following Perdikkas' assassination in Egypt, the strongest general was Antigonos Monophthalmos ('the One-Eyed'), an exact contemporary of Philip II. Despite his advanced age, Antigonos had seized much of Alexander's empire, but his rivals combined to bring an end to his bid at the Battle of Ipsos in 301. Antigonos died fighting, aged 81. Twenty years later, Seleukos Nikator (312–281) had succeeded in reconquering all of Alexander's Asian territories (Syria, Mesopotamia, Persia, Afghanistan and, temporarily, the Indus Valley), but he was assassinated during his campaign to claim Macedonia.

By that stage things had settled and a series of successor states known as the Hellenistic kingdoms took on their basic shape. The Ptolemies retained control of Egypt, and at times also held Cyprus and parts of Levant and the Aegean. The descendants of Seleukos Nikator (the Seleukids) retained the lion's share, namely the Near East, Persia and central Asia, although by 248 the Parthians had begun to reclaim central Iran. In 256, a breakaway Hellenistic state, complete with Greek-styled urban centres, was established in Bactria (roughly Afghanistan and southern Uzbekistan): it lasted for more than a century. Around 180, a further secessionist kingdom, dubbed by modern scholars as the Indo-Greek Kingdom, emerged in the Indus Valley and extended its control across the Ganges basin.

In the Mediterranean, a series of middle-sized kingdoms emerged. In 277, Antigonos Gonatos established the Antogonid dynasty in Macedonia, while in Anatolia (roughly modern-day Turkey) a series of formidable territorial states were formed, including Pergamon and Pontus. The central Mediterranean was contested by Carthage and Rome, and for a short period Syracuse could be ranked among the region's powers. In 304, Agathokles, the tyrant of Syracuse, had himself proclaimed the king of a united Sicily, but within 60 years his squabbling successors were forced to relinquish the Mediterranean's largest island to Rome.

The legend of Alexander shaped the ideology and purpose of the Hellenistic monarchies. These were warring entities, for each king made it his goal to claim Alexander's mantle by reunifying his empire. Thus each Hellenistic kingdom existed to promote its ruler's military glory and to fulfil his personal aspirations. Kings were constantly invading the domain of other kings, using large professional armies that fought not for the state but for its monarch. Massive fiscal revenues allowed some monarchies, particularly the Seleukids, to field armies that were more than double the size of the armies raised by Philip II. Incessant campaigning, however, had the effect of precipitating an 'arms race' that depleted even the largest treasuries.

Legitimacy was a key problem for all Hellenistic kings, particularly as none of Alexander's successors had royal pedigree. The new kings therefore had to invent new traditions and promote their special relationship with the gods. For Greek-speaking audiences, they created official titles that signified divinity, such as *soteros* (the saviour) and even *theos* (the god). They also tried to live up to non-Greek expectations of kingship. Before their Egyptian subjects, the Ptolemies looked and behaved like pharaohs, who were seen as living gods – Ptolemaic iconography gave every impression that the dynasty had gone completely native.

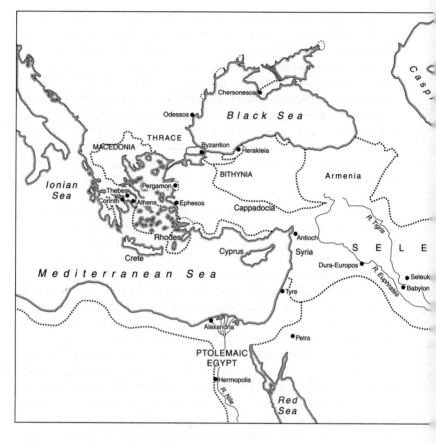

Map 4 The Hellenistic Kingdoms *c*. 270 BC

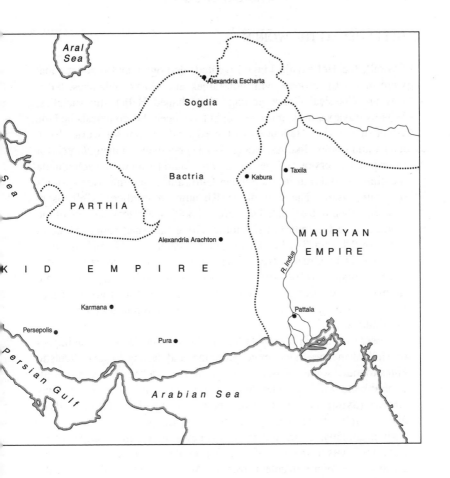

HELLENIZING THE WORLD

Overall, the Hellenistic kings invented ideologies and practices that were meant to resonate with non-Greek and Greek audiences, but it was the Classical Greek heritage that shaped Hellenistic societies. Whatever Alexander's motives might have been, his conquests had the effect of carrying Hellenism to the edge of the known world. Even later Indian rulers like Ashoka (269–232) persisted in using Greek for inscriptions. Versions of the Greek *polis* could be found in such remote locations as Bahrain in the Persian Gulf, and along the river systems of central Asia. The city of Aï Khanum in northern Afghanistan boasted a theatre that seated upwards of 6000 spectators and one of the world's largest gymnasiums. Another city established about 180 BC in northern Pakistan, Taxila, had a Hippodamian urban plan and Buddhist monuments in Greek design. The formation of the so-called Indo-Greek kingdom (*c.*180–10 BC), a vast state with a quasi-Hellenic ruling elite, featured the fusion of Greek and Buddhist artistic traditions that also appeared to influence Chinese sculptural depictions of the Buddha.

Closer to home, in Mesopotamia, the Levant and Anatolia, the impact of Hellenism was much more profound and lasting. The Hellenistic kings founded some 100 new cities that were modelled on the *polis*, with several being much grander than anything found in Greece itself. Thus Antioch (Syria) and Seleukia (Mesopotamia) might have had upwards of 500,000 inhabitants, while Alexandria in Egypt had as many as a million. Initially, the inhabitants of the new *poleis* were mostly soldiers and immigrants from Greece proper: Alexander's conquests hastened the greatest migration movement from the Aegean region, with merchants, scholars, artisans and labourers seeking their fortunes in the 'new world' of the Hellenistic East. Each new city was meant to function as a *polis*, with all the requisite civic institutions and rituals, and all the amenities and entertainments. Needless to say, the medium of all these *poleis* was Greek, as were the entertainments and the arts. The new *poleis* also had indigenous peoples that, over time, were Hellenized either completely or partially.

It was during this era that Greekness became a primary identity. The Greek immigrants that flocked to Asia and Egypt found a greater need to define their culture in relation to indigenous 'barbarians', the more so because Hellenism was the culture favoured by the kings. In fact, the Hellenistic monarchies were keen to be seen as 'Greek' monarchies, hence the efforts to found archetypically Greek cities. Thus, the rulers of Pergamon tried to conceal their questionable Greekness by fabricating a genealogical link with Alexander. The Attalids transformed Pergamon into one of the greatest Greek cities in the Mediterranean and made lavish donations to such established prestigious Panhellenic centres as Delphi. The Seleukids did not try to Hellenize Babylon, but they constructed a new city on the River Tigris called Seleukia, a major centre that continued to function as a *polis* long after it had passed under Parthian rule.

By all accounts, Alexandria was the greatest city of the Hellenistic era, especially as it showed what a Greek city might look like if money were no object. The geographer Strabo presents Alexandria as a masterpiece of urban design: 'The shape of the area of the city is like a clock; the long sides of it are those washed by the two seas ... The whole city is criss-crossed with streets suitable for the traffic of horses and carriages' (17.8). It also had great monuments such as the Pharos, the grand lighthouse and one of the Seven Wonders, and the Mouseion, an educational academy that rivalled the schools of Athens. The Great Library possessed the world's largest collection of books, perhaps as many as 700,000. Inevitably, the city became a magnet for scholars, making Alexandria the unrivalled centre of Greek learning, although there were challengers. Eumenes II (197–159 BC) did his best to promote Pergamon by building a library that held a respectable 200,000 books – the Pergamenes also invented parchment when the Ptolemies refused to export papyrus to them.

It was language that underscored the unity of the Hellenistic world. Attic Greek, the immensely prestigious language of the Classics, served as the basis for a new *koine dialektos* (common dialect) or 'Koine' that became the standard medium throughout the Hellenistic world. Although there is some evidence that other Greeks resented the domination of Attic, Koine became the language of government business and education, and all philosophical tracts, works of science, drama or poetry, and even religious works, were produced in the language that could secure the widest readership. In the new *poleis*, to which Greek immigrants would have imported many mutually incomprehensible dialects, Koine became a useful compromise medium. Another important development was the spread of Koine into Asia Minor and the rest of Anatolia, where it gradually supplanted indigenous languages.

Since Hellenism was the dominant culture of the Hellenistic states, it was inevitable that many non-Greeks would also adopt Greek culture and language. The Jews of Alexandria, for example, became a Greek-

speaking community that was to benefit greatly from a Greek transla-
tion of the Torah under the auspices of Ptolemy II Philadelphos
(282–246). Over time, as the flow of Greek immigrants from the
Aegean dried up, Hellenistic authorities found it necessary to promote
Hellenism among native elites. By the second century BC, the Ptolemaic
monarchy saw fit to make Greek identity a legal status that could be
bestowed on subjects. In other words, it was now possible to 'become'
Greek, the prerequisites being a Greek education and the acquisition of
Greek language and lifestyle. More on this matter will be said in later
chapters, suffice it to say here that Alexander's successors determined
that Hellenism need not be an exclusive ethnicity, even though 'ethnic'
Greeks continued to believe in the importance of genealogical criteria.
The making of Hellenism into an inclusive culture was the single most
important reason why it was to remain a world culture for more than a
millennium.

To be sure, the Hellenistic state did not impose Greek ways upon
subject peoples, if anything to avoid needless social disorder. The
Maccabean Revolt of 167, a significant moment of Jewish resistance
under Seleukid rule, began as a struggle in Jerusalem between traditionalist and Hellenizing Jews. Overall, tensions between Hellenized and
non-Hellenized groups had nothing to do with any attempts at forced
assimilation. Indeed, ethnic Greeks continued to see themselves in
exclusive terms, and retained a haughty 'colonialist' attitude to subject
peoples. With Hellenism upgraded as the culture of prestige, and given
that Alexander's empire had been won legitimately 'by the spear'
(conquest), the Greeks seemed initially at least to be uninterested in
other cultures. In fact, Greek visitors were known to dismiss Alexandria
and the Greek cities of Asia as superficially Greek and much too
'barbaric'. Reverse snobbery was also rife. One travel guide was known
to warn those intending to visit Athens and other 'historic' centres that
they might appear somewhat dilapidated and that amenities, such as
fountains, are either lacking or antiquated.

Conflict between Greek and non-Greek subjects, for the most part,
was associated with Greeks restricting access to *polis* citizenship and
civic institutions, particularly the gymnasium. In time, however, the
tendency was for confluence and syncretism. Greek writings from this
period show a marked tendency to blur the boundaries with 'the Other'.
There was much enthusiasm for constructing genealogies to demonstrate
blood ties between say Greek and Egyptian heroes, gods and peoples,
and to acknowledge say Phoenician accomplishments in the natural

sciences or the Jewish contribution to philosophical learning. Meanwhile, eastern religions came to exert a powerful influence on the Greeks. None went as far as the Indo-Greek kings in converting to an alternative religious systems – Menander I (*c.*155–130) might have been a convert to Buddhism, while Menander II (*c.*90–85) certainly was. Meanwhile, eastern cults were popular among Greeks, and some figured prominently at such traditional Hellenic religious centres as Delos. Cultural synthesis took many other forms as well. At Aï Khanum, archaeologists uncovered a Mesopotamian-styled temple containing what appears to be a massive statue of Zeus. Here, people worshipped a goddess that was read as Artemis by the Greeks and a familiar moon goddess by locals. At Philadelphia in Egypt, worshippers had temples dedicated to both Greek and Egyptian gods, especially deities like Isis and Sarapis, who appealed to both groups.

The world had changed after Alexander's conquests, but it is important not to exaggerate the impact of Hellenism on the indigenous societies of Asia and Egypt. Generally speaking, Hellenism was an urban phenomenon. The vast majority of the population, the peasantry, were largely untouched by its influence. There were also many important cities that were not Hellenized, such as Babylon, Jerusalem and Memphis. In Egypt, there was Alexandria and a handful of other 'oases' of Hellenism. Furthermore, it ought to be noted that throughout the Hellenistic East and beyond, Aramaic, the lingua franca of the Persian Empire, remained an 'international' language. Ashoka's inscriptions in the Punjab were written in both languages.

HELLENISM TRANSFORMED

In what ways did Greek culture change in the post-Alexandrian era? How were the *polis*, the values of community (*koinos*), and the function of art affected in this age of kings? Since the Peloponnesian War, endemic civic conflict and the excesses of radical democracy had made Greek society rather ambivalent about egalitarianism and the values of *koinos*. By the Hellenistic period, the *koinos* was still important, but the Greek world was now under the control of dynasts for whom the *koinos* was of secondary value at best. Rather, as Homeric-styled *basileis*, the Macedonians championed the values of elitism and private interests. In the meantime, individual Greeks had begun to amass fortunes that gave them enormous power and influence. And in contrast to earlier generations of aristocrats, the new *aristoi* (elites) had the private means to build huge public monuments and patronize artists.

These changes had an enormous impact on artistic production. The Hellenistic period was a great age of science, philosophy and literary production, and many of the great minds of this era, from Archimedes and Zeno to Polybios, had aristocratic pedigree. These were men who had the leisure to study, write, perform experiments and build expensive mechanical contraptions. With royal patronage, Greek schools were able to achieve new milestones in areas such as mechanics, engineering, astronomy, medical knowledge and geometry. Among the great luminaries of this era were Euclid (*c*.330–275), the father of geometry, the polymath Eratosthenes (*c*.276–194), who measured the circumference of the earth, and Hipparchos (*c*.190–120), who invented the astrolabe, discovered the precession of the equinoxes and showed how to predict solar eclipses.

More money also meant more art. The richest dynasties, the Seleukids, Attalids and Ptolemies, seemed to spare no expense as they lavished their capital cities with monuments made of marble. The Ptolemies, who maintained smaller armies and therefore had the most disposable wealth, were determined to make Alexandria the world's *megalopolis* (great city). The entire city was meant to be a spectacle, from its landmarks to its regular streetscapes. The Attalids sought to make Pergamon the new Athens. The city had its much vaunted sites, including the Sanctuary of Zeus, its famous gymnasia and a theatre that could seat 10,000 people. The city sprawled downwards along the side of a large hill, with the grand royal palace and the king's arsenal crowning the high ground. (Water was pumped upwards to this level by a sophisticated hydraulic system.)

Changes in Greek art reflected the new power structure as well as a deep-seated nostalgia for the Classical period. What made Hellenistic art distinctive was the manipulation of classical conventions to serve the new power elites and the vastly expanded market for art. Monarchs used the arts to project and legitimate their regal power. Much of what has survived is regal portraiture depicting the king in combat, hunting or with divine regalia. Lavish private patronage produced art that was often larger and more sumptuously detailed. Among the most emblematic Hellenistic sculptures is the Winged Victory (Nike) of Samothrace, a massive and lavishly draped female figure that now stands in the Louvre. It looks more 'baroque' than the typical classical statue, as do the figures that clutter the frieze of the Great Altar of Pergamon. In contrast to

Classical art, the new art conveys more explicit messages. Compared to the Parthenon frieze, the facial expressions and physical poses depicted in the Pergamene *gigantomachia* (celestial war) are expressive and confronting, leaving much less to the imagination.

Greek urban planning reached its zenith during the Hellenistic era. From Aï Khanum in central Asia to the Ephesos on Anatolia's Aegean coast, the new *poleis* exhibited the textbook symmetries of the Hippodamian system. What set the Hellenistic city apart, however, was the scale and impact of private benefaction. Inscriptions from this period show that individuals could treat their city as their own fiefdom. One particular notable from Samos by the name of Boulgaros was flattered with an inscription that listed his deeds for his community, including his profuse money-lending activities. It was 'resolved by the people to praise Boulgaros, son of Alexis, for his [excellence] and for his goodwill towards the citizens, and to crown him with a gold [crown] at the Dionysia'.[6] At the everyday level, however, the *polis* continued to function as it had in the past. In fact, civic institutions were even more assiduous about issuing inscriptions. It was the 'community' of Samos that issued the decree honouring Boulgaros. From a basic administrative perspective, Alexander and his successors recognized the value of retaining the *polis* and its institutions. Hellenistic kings treated the *poleis* as autonomous entities and generally observed the treaty arrangements that governed their relationships.

In the Hellenistic era, therefore, an accommodation was reached between monarchy and the *polis*. In many cases, kings portrayed themselves as liberators of cities, and in return the grateful cities granted divine honours and public monuments. The Ptolemies ruled native Egyptians as divine rulers with absolute powers, but the citizens of Alexandria, with their assemblies and magistrates, were treated differently. The later Ptolemies dispensed with these difficult citizen bodies, but they still looked to civic leaders to manage Alexandrian affairs.

GREECE AFTER ALEXANDER

Immediately after Alexander's death in 323, the Greek city-states made a bid to reclaim their independence. Alexander's regent in Macedonia, Antipater, defeated the insurgent Greeks at the Battle of Krannon (322), but neither he nor his successors were again able to control the lands to the south. Macedonia did indeed emerge as one of the major

Hellenistic kingdoms, but the old *poleis* had become much more adept at defending their interests. Indeed, the rivalries between the Hellenistic kingdoms made it easier for the Greeks to create space for manoeuvre. The Ptolemies were keen to counter Macedonian power in the Aegean, and they spent great sums supporting *poleis* and confederations. Indeed, the Macedonian dynasts were usually in the business of trying to win over the Greeks with promises of money and *eleutheria* (liberty).

Politically, the most powerful states in Greece were the confederations, particularly the Aetolian and Achaean leagues. The Aetolians, an ethnic group distributed among scattered settlements in western Greece, attracted little attention in Classical times but had since earned renown for their leading role in dealing with a Gallic invasion of 280. As a consequence, the Aetolian League became an important player in interstate politics and quickly brought most of central Greece under its control. The other major force was the Achaean League in the northern Peloponnese. Like the Aetolians, the Achaeans were united by dialect and blood, and during the third century they managed to drive the Macedonians out of southern Greece. Led by the enterprising Aratos of Sikyon (271–213), the League captured Corinth in 243, a Macedonian stronghold, and in 229 it expelled Macedonian garrisons from Argos and Athens.

An independent foreign policy was beyond the ambit of most individual *poleis*, the exception being Rhodes, Athens and Sparta. As a large island with five harbours, Rhodes was optimally placed along the main trunk route between Europe and the eastern Mediterranean. As a major maritime centre, it possessed the financial resources to build such monuments as the Colossus of Rhodes, another of the Ancient Wonders, and to maintain a formidable navy. Athens, on the other hand, ceased to figure as a maritime power, although it did manage to lead two (albeit unsuccessful) coalitions against Macedonia: the Lamian War in 323–322 and the Chremonidian War in 268–262. In 229, rich Athenians freed the city by bribing the Macedonian garrisons, but no thought was given thereafter to engaging in foreign adventures. Rather, Athens was content to trade on its historical importance and as one of the great centres of learning. Schools made famous by Plato and Aristotle would continue to operate well into Late Antiquity.

The Spartans, on the other hand, did seek to relive former glories. Sparta was a noticeable exclusion from Alexander's Panhellenic crusade, but its leaders continued to dream of restoring its hegemonic role in

Greek affairs. King Areus (309–265) rallied a Greek coalition against Macedonia in 280, challenged the Aetolians, and fought off an attack from King Pyrrhus of Epiros in 272. He was killed during an attack on a Macedonian fortress. By that stage, the citizen base of Sparta had sunk to as few as 700, and only a small proportion of that group owned most of the land. In 244, King Agis IV (244–241) sought to revive Sparta's military fortunes by resolving the land crisis. To rebuild the recruitment base, land had to be redistributed and debts cancelled, and the old Spartan education system had to be revived. Resistance from vested interests was strong, however, and when Agis lost face following a failed military venture he was tried and executed. Fifteen years later, King Kleomenes III (235–222) was able to implement land reforms after having won a succession of military campaigns in the northern Peloponnese between 229 and 227. Kleomenes also reorganized the Spartan political system, claiming to be restoring the traditional order when he was actually creating a Hellenistic-styled autocracy.

Kleomenes waged a formidable campaign to re-establish Spartan domination of the Peloponnese. Sparta's traditional Peloponnesian rivals naturally viewed its resurgence with great alarm, but what they found particularly disturbing was the fact that Kleomenes enjoyed the support of poorer citizens. Land concentration was a problem throughout southern Greece, and the discontented poor hoped Kleomenes would have their debts cancelled as well. In 225 he captured Argos and a year later besieged Corinth. The Achaean leader Aratos, who had done more than anyone to rid southern Greece of the Macedonians, now regarded Macedonia as the lesser evil. Led by Antigonos III, the Macedonians and the Achaeans defeated Kleomenes at Selassia in 222. Sparta was crushed, and his more radical social and political reforms were reversed.

How did the Hellenistic era affect the internal affairs of the *polis*? Did Macedonian domination bring an end to *stasis*? The short answer is no. Interstate conflict again became the normal state of affairs after the death of Alexander, only now the principal political divisions were between pro- and anti-Macedonian factions. At the same time, the new age of empires had broadened the horizons of most Greeks. The spirit of Panhellenism promoted by Philip and Alexander, and the fact that the Persian Empire was brought down by a Panhellenic crusade, had also left a deep impression on Greek minds. Indeed, they now ascribed much more importance to the ideal of Panhellenism. In diplomatic dealings, delegates usually invoked the Persian Wars and the battles of Thermopylae, Salamis and Plataea, which now served as historical

Image 3 The Laocoön Group: this Roman copy of a Hellenistic sculpture illustrates the move to a more expressive, if less subtle, mode in Greek art (Cortile del Belvedere, Museo Pio Clementino, Vatican Museums) (*photo credit: Vanni/Art Resource, New York*).

reference points for the Panhellenic ideal. In the Hellenistic era there was even greater interest in the Panhellenic festivals, while civic historians were busy writing local histories that proved the Hellenic credentials of their native *polis* – for the third century, the fragments of 800 such works of history have been noted by scholars. Greek identity, it seems, had become a primary identity.

ROMAN MILITARY EXPANSION (*c.*280–269 BC)

Heraklides Pontikos, a student of both Plato and Aristotle, and (possibly) the man responsible for the heliocentric (sun-centred) theory of the universe, is one of a mere handful of Classical Greek authors who mentions the Romans: he likens Rome to a Greek city, or assumes it is Greek. In fact, the Hellenistic world only really noticed the Romans from the 280s, after they had attacked the southern Italian *polis* of Taras. Its citizens requested military support from Pyrrhus, the itinerant ruler of Epiros, and the only Hellenistic monarch who seemed interested in roving westwards. Pyrrhus defeated the Romans in two battles, at Heraclea in 280 and at Asculum the following year, although the casualties suffered seemed excessive: hence the phrase 'Pyrrhic victory'.

The Romans did better at the battle at Beneventum in 275, after which Pyrrhus abandoned Italy for good. At least two reasons can be surmised here: the Senate, the executive body of the Roman state, would not accept a military defeat and had enormous manpower reserves at its disposal. Thus, it had the will and the means to put right any military setback. In contrast to all Greek city-states, the Roman city-state was open to absorbing other peoples, allowing it to expand and augment its power. By the third century, it already dominated central Italy by having its allies, client states and defeated enemies supply military levies rather than tribute. By numbers and gritted determination, the Romans survived the Second Punic War (220–201), a struggle during which they were pitted against Hannibal, one of antiquity's greatest generals. Despite crushing defeats at Trasimene (217) and Cannae (216), the Romans held out to win the war in 201. More than any other state in antiquity, Rome could win long wars through attrition.

What brought the Romans to Greece? Back in 215, Philip V of Macedonia (221–179) had forged an alliance with Hannibal, prompting Rome to align with Philip's enemies, Pergamon and Aetolia. However, the Romans were not ready to deal with Philip until they had defeated

Hannibal. On arrival, Rome was keen to rally as much Greek support as possible, and the fact that the leader of the expedition, Titus Quinctius Flamininus, was a Greek-speaking aristocrat and renowned 'philhellene' was probably no coincidence. Rome's greatest asset, however, was its military edge. The 'legion' was an infantry formation that was more flexible and adaptable than the Macedonian phalanx. At the Battle of Cynoscephalae in 197, Philip's phalanx was drawn onto uneven terrain, causing the hoplites to lose their footing and expose gaps between the long pikes. With their short swords, the Roman legionaries cut through their lines and slaughtered the Macedonians. The latter performed better at the Battle of Pydna in 168, but again strayed onto uneven ground, and the Romans inflicted yet another crushing defeat. The Macedonian phalanx was suddenly proven to be redundant.

In little over a decade, Rome was the undisputed *hegemon* of Greece, and by 146 Macedonia had been reduced to a Roman province. Meanwhile, one by one, the leading powers of Greece were humbled: first Sparta in 195, followed by the Aetolian League in 187, and finally the Achaean League in 146. The Romans also proved to be more than a match for the great Hellenistic empires further East. In 190, the Seleukid Antiochus III (223–187) was defeated decisively in Greece (Thermopylae) and again in Asia Minor (Magnesia). Quite suddenly, the Mediterranean in political terms had become a unipolar world. Such was the power of the Roman Senate that when Antiochus IV (175–164) tried to annex Egypt in 168, he was forced to abort his entire expedition after receiving a simple but pointed warning from a senatorial envoy.

Scholars remain deeply divided over what motivated the interventions in Greece: why did Rome seemed so determined to police the behaviour of the warring Greeks after Cynoscephalae, and to what extent did Rome's behaviour remain true to its stated intentions? Whether by design or accident, Roman domination of Greece was more or less complete by the middle of the second century BC. Why Roman ascendancy was not met with a 'Panhellenic' response, similar to that which defeated Xerxes back in 479, can be explained by the fact that Rome, at least initially, was drawn into Greek interstate politics to solve Greek interstate problems. Thus, Flamininus' legions effectively relieved the Greek world of Macedonian domination in 197. The following year at the Isthmian Games, he proclaimed the Greeks were 'free', stating that there would be no need for Roman garrisons or the payment of tribute (Polybios 18.46). Before Roman troops were withdrawn from Greece in

194, he spent much of his time settling disputes between the Greeks. It soon became clear, however, that the Roman conception of freedom (*libertas*) was conditional; it certainly did not allow any Greek state to conduct a foreign policy displeasing to the Roman Senate. Later interventions came when Greeks states violated treaties drawn up under Roman auspices, or when powers like Sparta or Aetolia threatened the independence of other Greeks.

As Polybios put it, Rome became woven into (*symploke*) the matrix of Greek politics. Roman domination of the East was gradual but irresistible. At the same time, Roman retribution was severe. In 149, the Achaean League took action against Sparta before a Roman senatorial commission could adjudicate the dispute in question. The Senate retaliated by ordering the removal of certain cities from the League, a course of action that precipitated a war. As the Corinthians were regarded as the most recalcitrant members of the league, and despite the fact that the city submitted to Roman forces without resistance, Corinth was sacked in 146 and the entire population was either put to the sword or sold into slavery. The following century, in 88 BC, the Greek *poleis* that supported Mithradates in his war against Rome were ransacked. Many of these cities took generations to recover.

The last part of Greece that was forced to yield to Roman authority was Crete, where in 69 BC, Caecilius Metellus, later named Creticus (the Cretan), seized the island after an arduous campaign. It was not until 27 BC, during the reign of Augustus Caesar, that Greece was made formally into a Roman province.

ROMAN HEGEMONY FROM REPUBLIC TO EMPIRE

The Achaean aristocrat, Polybios, who rivals Thucydides as the greatest historian of antiquity, was taken hostage for his part in the Third Macedonian War (171–168), though 'hostage' is hardly the appropriate term. His captivity was spent as the houseguest of fellow aristocrats in Rome, during which time he became familiar with the Scipiones, an extremely powerful patrician family that took a special interest in Greek culture and political affairs. Polybios came to admire Roman society and its systems of governance, and in his conceptually sophisticated or 'pragmatic' *History*, much of which has survived, he explains to his Greek readers why Rome came to dominate the Greek world. His *History* includes an analysis of Roman political and military institutions, showing how Rome managed to find a balance between the interests of its social groups.

Of Greek society, Polybios discerned some fundamental weaknesses:

> In our time, the whole of Greece has suffered a shortage of children and a general decrease of the population, and as a consequence some cities have become deserted and agricultural production has declined.(36.17)[7]

The Greeks had only themselves to blame, he adds, because 'men had fallen prey to inflated ambitions, love of money and indolence, with the result that they did not wish to marry'.

Polybios neglects to mention that the most obvious cause of Greek misery during the early years of Roman domination was imperial greed. If Rome was initially motivated by security, its ongoing incentive for interference in eastern affairs was financial. Plunder, indemnities and tribute greatly enriched the ruling class, and some of the wealth trickled down to the lower orders through various forms of patronage. Whilst the legions operated in the East, money flowed like a torrent to Rome. For example, after the defeat of Aetolia in 187, the Romans carried off nearly 40,000 kg of silver, 110 kg of gold, 785 bronze statues and 30 marble statues. For many ancient and modern historians, the hunger for booty is seen as the essential objective of Roman imperialism under the Republic.

Another problem were the devastations wrought by Rome's military campaigns in Greece, where competing generals commandeered vast quantities of local resources and left cities as large as Athens to starve. Such was the case during the war between Caesar and Pompey (49–45 BC), which was decided at Pharsalus in Thessaly. The Roman politician Cicero at the time wondered whether any part of Greece would be spared. The duration of the subsequent civil war between Mark Antony and Caesar's assassins made for a worse experience. Each camp looted Rhodes and the *poleis* of Anatolia, which, following the end of that conflict, also footed the bill for the decommissioning of 30 legions and a new war against the Parthians.

It was the massive pecuniary exactions and regular taxes that probably grated most with the Greek *poleis*. They were accustomed to regular taxation, but what made conditions particularly harsh was the fact that *publicani* (tax agents) were effectively given a licence to extort. The *publicani* became a highly influential pressure group in Roman politics by virtue of their financial strength; senators were known to hold shares in tax farming companies and generals often colluded with these contractors when on campaign. Territories formally defined as provinces could fare even worse if the governor was bent on self-enrichment. The most famous court case over provincial extortion was Cicero's prosecution of Gaius Verres (70 BC), who plundered Sicily so extensively that it could no longer serve as Rome's main source of grain. The historian Tacitus claimed that under the Republic the provinces were ransacked 'during the struggles of the powerful and [because of] the greed of the magistrates. The laws offered them no help because they were perverted by violence, favouritism and, most of all, by bribery' (*Annals*, 1.1–2).[8]

During the course of the first century BC, however, the Romans began to face up to the responsibilities of imperial governance. Corrupt governors and *publicani* were prosecuted more frequently, while conquerors like Pompey and Caesar also earned *auctoritas* (peer esteem) by establishing the frameworks of imperial administration. Thus in the 60s, Pompey, after destroying the Seleukid monarchy, performed important work in organizing the Near East, while Caesar, as dictator in the 40s, advanced the cause of imperial consolidation by introducing non-Romans into the Senate. It was Caesar's successors who, armed with autocratic powers, were able to organize provincial affairs in a more methodical fashion. By the first century AD, the provinces ceased to be regarded as cash cows that subsidized the excesses of the city of Rome. Emperors now ruled for the entire realm.

The *polis* and Hellenism found a new lease of life under the emperors. From the time of Augustus Caesar (31 BC–AD 14), the first of the emperors, the entire Mediterranean world came to enjoy the benefits of an enforced peace, the so-called 'Pax Romana'. With military campaigning now restricted to frontier zones, war became a dark and distant memory for the great majority of the emperor's subjects, including the Greeks, who were also required to desist from *stasis*. Civic elites were now expected to conduct their business in an orderly and competent fashion, and were monitored by governors that reported assiduously on provincial affairs to Rome. Ironically, therefore, the Greek *polis* had to be deprived of political freedom to realize its full potential as a civic order.

4

The Greek Roman Empire I (27 BC–AD 500): From the Pax Romana to Late Antiquity

Cornelius Sulla taught the Athenians a lesson they were never meant to forget. In 88 BC, Athens had thrown its support behind Mithradates of Pontus (120–63 BC), the last Hellenistic king to challenge the might of Rome, and perpetrator of a mass slaughter of Romans and Italians resident in Asia Minor. The 'city of Theseus' had got off lightly for previous breaches of Roman fealty, but this time it faced the wrath of the most ruthless Roman of his era, and one not particularly enamoured with things Greek. According to the biographer Plutarch (*c.*AD 50–120), Sulla besieged and starved the city of Athens and then he let loose his soldiers on its famine-stricken population: 'to this day their number [the dead] is estimated by the area of ground covered in blood . . . many people say it flowed out through the gates and washed out into the suburbs' (*Sulla,* 14).[1]

Within a few generations, however, the relationship between conqueror and subject would change. Residual bitterness persisted within elite Greek circles, but on balance the Athenians and most other peoples around the Mediterranean came to see the empire as a good thing. The orator Publius Aelius Aristides (AD 117–*c.*181), perhaps the most famous Greek of his age, provides the clearest enunciation of this sentiment in his famous 'Oration to Rome' of AD 143:

> You have measured and recorded the land of the entire civilized world; you have spanned the rivers with all kinds of bridges, and hewn highways through the mountains, and filled the barren stretches with posting-stations;

you have accustomed all areas to a settled and orderly way of life . . .
Though the citizens of Athens began the civilized life of today, this life in
its turn has been firmly established by you, who came later but who, men
say, are better. (102)[2]

These were the best of times, and he credits the Pax Romana with
providing the optimal conditions in which one could enjoy a civilized
'way of life'. Aristides was one of the leading luminaries of a renaissance of Greek scholarship known as the Second Sophistic (c.AD
60–230), during which time the bulk of the empire's significant literary
output was produced in Greek. As with most of his contemporaries,
Aristides could identify strongly with Rome while at the same time
being chauvinistically Greek.

The history of the Greeks under the Roman Empire is part of a longer
history of cultural accommodation. From its beginnings as an obscure
Latin city-state, through to its conquest of the entire Mediterranean
basin, Rome had been in constant contact with the Greek world, and it
was a relationship that was usually perceived as being symbiotic: of a
marriage of brains and brawn, culture and power. Recent scholarship has
rendered a more complicated picture, but there is no disputing the fact
that the Roman Empire, the most durable and culturally significant in the
history of Western civilization, would also be a 'Greek' Roman empire.

ORIGINS OF GRAECOMANIA

Why were the Romans so accommodating of Greek culture? Why did
they allow Hellenism to serve as the basis for cultural unity in the
Roman world? The Romans, as with the other peoples of Italy, had been
familiar with Greek culture since before the foundation of the Republic
in 507 BC. Archaeological research provides ample proof of the impact
of Greek art, religion and literacy. When it came to aristocratic lifestyles,
Italian elites took their cues from the Greeks of southern Italy. By the
Hellenistic Age, Roman elites had accepted Greek as the language of
paidea (education). Roman noblemen were expected to be proficient in
Greek and to be well versed in Greek Classical texts. In the 280s,
Pyrrhus of Epiros dealt with Roman envoys that spoke Greek; L.
Postumius Megellus' Greek was so bad that his offended audience pelted
him with excrement. By the very end of the third century, when Roman
legions first set foot on Greek soil, Roman writers had already composed

histories (*annales*) in Greek, and playwrights like Naevius had long been adapting Greek drama for Roman audiences. Titus Quinctius Flaminius, the general who defeated Philip V during the Second Macedonian War (200–197 BC), was proficient enough to conduct complex negotiations in Greek.

The most explicit testimony of Roman esteem for Hellenism was the determination to establish a genealogical connection with Greece through myth. The legend of Aeneas, the surviving prince of Troy who fled westwards to found a new settlement, was adapted to serve as Rome's foundation myth. From the late-third-century historian, Fabius Pictor, we learn that Aeneas encountered a Peloponnesian king named Evander, who was seeking to found a settlement and who was reputed to have introduced the alphabet to the peoples of the Latium Plain. The legend's classic and hence unalterable formulation was established in Virgil's epic poem, *The Aeneid*, written sometime in the late first century BC.

Roman society was certainly receptive to other cultural influences, particularly from the Etruscans and Carthaginians, but Greek culture had special purchase as a Mediterranean haute couture. With the growth of empire and more intimate contact with the Hellenistic world, Roman interest was transformed into something akin to graecomania: at least that is how it appeared to the leading politician and ardent traditionalist, Cato the Elder (234–149 BC). Throughout his long life, Cato berated his fellow *nobiles* (nobility) for neglecting too readily the more wholesome native traditions and moral codes. It was Rome's social elites who took to Greek ways, including nude bathing and sport. Cato's most virulent diatribe attacked everything Greek, claiming the Greeks were wicked by nature and that their literature was worth only a nodding acquaintance. It could be said that Cato invented Latin prose literature to counteract a Greek monopoly.

The fact was that the Roman *nobiles* were in awe of the Greek classical heritage. The imperial capital was inundated with Greek philosophers, doctors and educators, many being slaves and hostages, but each providing services in great demand. The city was also swamped by Greek art, much of it loot, but much of it also locally made reproductions. Greek artworks and artists inspired the Hellenization of Rome's physical environment, in architecture, sculpture and in the use of columns, particularly the Corinthian order.

As the *nobiles* became increasingly conscious of their role as the Mediterranean's ruling order, the need to master *and* compete with Hellenism became an imperative, especially if they were to retain control of the East. Moreover, to take on the appearance of a ruling power, the Romans had to adapt much of what they saw in the Hellenistic kingdoms. When he recast the political and cultural order, Augustus tried to elevate Latin and Latin literature to haute couture status, for which Greek and Greek classics provided the benchmarks. The poet Horace encouraged playwrights to find inspiration in the Greek Classics rather than earlier Latin dramatists like Plautus. The city of Rome, the capital of the world, had to compete with Alexandria or Antioch. Augustus might have been exaggerating when he claimed he 'found Rome a city of mud bricks, and left her clothed in marble', but the city did come to rival Alexandria in terms of grandeur.

Since the Romans first began to establish their dominion over the East, the relationship between Greece and Rome was often celebrated for its complementarity. It was usually typecast as a marriage between irresistible power and cultural sophistication. It was Horace who put it most pithily: 'Greece, the captive, took her savage victor captive, and brought the arts into rustic Latium' (*Epistles*, 2.1.156).[3] Needless to say, this notion of harmonized attributes belied a rather ambivalent relationship, as can be gleaned from reading between Horace's lines. Marriage, after all, is fraught with tensions. Greece, the female captive, through guile and trickery, snares the pristine conquering warrior. The Romans recognized the Greeks as the arbiters of high culture and learning, but they also scorned them as decadent and lacking in martial qualities. Horace elsewhere warned of the emasculating effects of becoming *too* Greek.

Such was the power of Hellenism that the Romans had to be mindful of cultural boundaries. Under the Republic (507–31 BC) and throughout the first century AD, Roman philhellenes were steadfast about the fact that they were *not* Greek. Graecomania was frowned upon. Cato, Cicero and Horace warned their countrymen not to forget those traditions and virtues that had given Rome the strength to rule the world. The Greeks, after all, were underlings: they were often described as *Graeculi* (Greeklings). Greek culture was revered, but it was also seen as a right of conquest, and as such it was meant to augment Roman culture, not supplant it. Cicero went so far as to argue that Romans had greater natural aptitude for learning and were better when they applied themselves to philosophy and oratory.

For the most part, however, Hellenism and being Roman were presented as complementary virtues. The greatest poet of the Augustan era, Virgil, encapsulated that interdependence in his classic reformulation of the saga of Aeneas:

Others will cast more tenderly in bronze
Their breathing figures, I can well believe,
And bring more lifelike portraits out of marble;
Argue eloquently, use the pointer
To trace the paths of heaven accurately
And accurately foretell the rising stars.
Roman remember by your strength to rule
Earth's people – for your arts are to be these:
To pacify, to impose the rule of law,
To spare the conquered, battle down the proud.[4]

IMPERIUM AND THE 'SWEETNESS OF PEACE'

The above passage also refers to an imperial mission. There had been some articulation of moral duty towards subject peoples and the bestowal of *humanitas* (civilization) before Virgil; but it was his patron Augustus who above all infused a sense of moral responsibility into provincial governance. For Virgil, *imperium* was the *artes* (means) 'to inculcate the habits of peacetime' (*Aeneid*, 6.852) so as to absorb subject peoples into what his contemporaries viewed as the *communis patria* (fatherland community). It was during the course of the Pax Romana that subjects became accustomed to imperial rule, and came to see the empire as a whole as a *communis patria*. The Greeks and other provincial peoples came to appreciate the merits of Roman *imperium* or simply showed passive acceptance. There were rare exceptions, such as the Jewish revolts of AD 66 and 132–135; otherwise the imperial state saw no reason to station garrisons within cities or provinces other than those that lined certain frontiers.

The Pax Romana had real meaning in the Greek East, where Rome's civil wars had brought great devastations. In the aftermath of these wars, Octavian Caesar, the last man standing, made it his purpose to seduce 'everyone with the sweetness of peace'. Protecting conquered subjects from the rapacious greed of private Roman interests was one of his objectives when reforming the provincial system. In 27 BC, Greece proper was made into a province labelled 'Achaea', while northern Greek *poleis* and regions were divided among the provinces of Epirus and Macedon. The *poleis* further east were distributed among a range of provinces that included Asia Minor and Bithynia. The provincial borders were to be redrawn many times, but approaches to provincial governance settled into an enduring pattern. Officials were now agents of the emperor, carrying precise instructions as to their roles and responsibilities, with limited scope for the pursuit of personal economic interests. A series of well-publicized prosecutions showed that Augustus and his successor Tiberius were serious about dealing with provincial malad-ministration. Petitions from the Greek *poleis* were also dealt with more conscientiously and efficiently. Tiberius was quite popular in the province of Asia Minor for authorizing a succession of trials against unscrupulous governors. The appreciative civic elders of the province then competed for the right to erect a temple in his honour.

Greece under the empire was still a world of city-states. Athens, Argos and Thebes functioned in much the same way as in the past. Traditional constitutional arrangements had been modified to assuage the Roman preference for oligarchy, but the basic Greek pattern of annual magistra-cies and assemblies were maintained. Athenian citizenship remained a jealously guarded right. Cities continued to issue their own laws, their own coins – 530 cities in the Greek East minted their own coins – and to use their own revenues for civic purposes. Diplomatic arrangements between city-states were maintained, while relations with Rome were defined by treaty arrangements. Many *poleis* remained nominally 'free' throughout the early empire: 'ambassadors' were despatched to Rome when necessary. In AD 239, for example, during a period of renewed civil war and dynastic turmoil, the emperor Gordian III responded to an embassy from Aphrodisias (Asia Minor) regarding the city's status:

> It was appropriate, Aphrodisians, to the antiquity of your city, to its good-will and friendship towards the Romans, for you to be disposed towards my kingship as you have shown in your decree addressed to me. In return . . . I maintain securely the enjoyment of all your existing rights which you have preserved up to the time of my kingship.[5]

The emperors found it very useful to maintain the facade of *polis* autonomy, for imperial governance depended on self-governing and self-financing cities. It was incumbent upon local elites to fund and manage the affairs of a city, and it therefore paid the emperor to indulge their interests and aspirations. The letters exchanged between Trajan and his conscientious governor of Bithynia, Pliny the Younger (AD 63–113), convey how attentive emperors could be to even the most mundane matters. For example:

> Pliny to Trajan: The public bath at Prusa, Sir, is old and dilapidated, and the people are anxious for it to be rebuilt. My own opinion is that you could suitably grant their petition . . .

Trajan to Pliny: If the building of a new bath at Prusa will not strain the city's finances, there is no reason why we should not grant their petition; provided no new tax is imposed and there is no further diversion of funds of theirs intended for essential services. (Pliny, *Letters*, x 23, 24)[6]

THE *POLEIS* UNDER THE EMPERORS

Pliny's letters are a vital source for the history of the Greek city under the early empire. But what kind of *istoria* (history) is it? Such pedantry would not have impressed Thucydides or Polybios, for whom history meant the study of politics and states. For the Greeks under the empire, however, *istoria* was something that was read about rather than experienced. It was the Romans who were now making *istoria*, thus the Greek historians in this period, men such as Arrian (AD *c*.86–146), Appian (AD *c*.95–165) and Cassius Dio (AD *c*.155–229), wrote either about the glorious Greek past, about the rise of Rome or about the emperors. The Greek celebrities of the Pax Romana were orators like Aelius Aristides, scientists like Galen (AD 129–*c*.200) or rich tycoons like Claudius Herodes Atticus of Athens (AD *c*.101–177), none of whom would have figured in a history written by Thucydides or Polybios.

The Pax Romana was not an eventful period in Greek history, which only serves to underscore the point made by Aristides in his 'Oration to Rome', that these were indeed the best of times. It was an age of civic and cultural vitality, particularly for Greek Asia Minor, where Aristides lived his entire life. Greece proper, where cities had been diminished both in number and size under the Republic, was also experiencing a period of renewal. New 'Greek' cities emerged under the Empire, including Patrae (Patras), Adrianople (Edirne) and Iconium (Konya), and many others were named in honour of emperors, such as Tiberias and Claudiopolis.

As the *Letters* of Pliny confirm, each *polis* was expected to function independently and responsibly. When asked whether the people of Amissos should be allowed to create a mutual-benefit society, Trajan told Pliny pointedly that:

If the citizens of Amissos, whose petition you send with your letter, are allowed by their own laws, granted them by formal treaty, to form a benefit society, there is no reason we should interfere: especially if the contributions are not used for riotous assemblies. (*Letters*, x 93)[7]

City patricians were also expected to foot the bill for the baths, aqueducts, festivals and much else. Some individual Greek aristocrats had the means to bankroll an entire *polis*, and some could even share their wealth with other *poleis*. The Athenian Claudius Herodes Atticus endowed buildings in Corinth, Troy and at Thermopylae. To the Athenians he left a stadium for the Panathenaic Games and the Herodion, a theatre on the south side of the Acropolis.

On a more mundane level, elites were required to carry out 'liturgies' or civic responsibilities. The empire demanded much of its civic leaders and imposed stiff penalties on those who shirked their responsibilities. For that reason, there were constant requests for dispensation; Aelius Aristides frequently cited ill health to absolve himself of his duties. After all, civic commitments could be quite onerous. The following extract from an inscription in the city of Kalindoia (Macedonia), dated AD 148, gives some indication:

> Since Apollonios, son of Apollonios of Kertimos, being a good man and deserving of every honour, having accepted spontaneously the priesthood of Zeus and Rome and Caesar of Augustus *divi filius*, has exhibited so much nobility, living up to the high reputation of his ancestors and his own virtue, as to omit no excess in expenditure on the gods and his native city, providing from his own resources throughout the year the sacrifices offered monthly by the city to Zeus and Caesar Augustus; and has also offered all manner of honours to the gods, and provided for its citizens feasting and lavish entertainment, similarly dining the whole populace, both en masse and by dining groups, and organizing the procession at festival so as to be varied and striking, and putting on contests in honour of Zeus and Caesar Augustus in elaborate and worthy style . . . Not only has he spared no expense, but he has made a statue of Caesar at his own cost, and has offered it as a permanent memorial of the beneficence of Augustus to all mankind.[8]

What did the likes of Apollonios get in return? In an earlier time, Cicero referred to people like Apollonios as *optimates* (the best of citizens), men who deserved the protection of the Roman state. Greek elites enjoyed legal privileges, such as immunity from corporal punishments, and were usually rewarded with Roman citizenship for their services. The Roman state also ensured that each *polis* was controlled by its *optimates*. Democratic constitutions were gradually phased out. Trajan's successor, Hadrian, strengthened the position of the propertied in Athens by awarding greater powers to the *Areopagus*, thus returning Athens to the kind of constitution that existed before democracy.

As the above inscription makes patently clear, what mattered most was how each city stood in relation to the emperor. Cities competed for his favour. As orator and philosopher Dio Chrysostom (AD 40/50–110) told his fellow Bithynians, being a *polis* left no room for complacency:

> Well you know that it is natural for a city's pride, its people's dignity, and its reputation with visitors and governors to be enhanced by its buildings, by its festivals, and by the fact that its citizens are immune from judicial scrutiny, and are not bunched together like some 'village'. (*Orations*, 40.10)[9]

To retain the honour of being a recognized *polis*, certain criteria had to be met. Population size and certain facilities, such as theatres and baths, were essential. Being a great cult centre or hosting prestigious festivals meant a great deal to the Greek city. Some could rest on their laurels, as did Athens, or enjoy prestige as a provincial capital. In essence, the *poleis* under the Roman Empire competed for symbolic capital, including such titles as 'first city' or 'metropolis'. In such cases, the emperor's favour meant everything. The *poleis* of Asia Minor, among the richest of the Greek world, appeared to work hardest at seeking the emperor's favour. Thus there were at least 34 emperor cults in Asia Minor by the end of the first century AD. Reckless out-bidding between political elites and rival cities often led to wild and irresponsible expenditure, occasionally prompting the emperor to enforce strict budgetary measures. For similar reasons, Hadrian's successor, Antoninus Pius (138–161), imposed limits on the number of professors that each city could appoint to its schools.

How 'Greek' were the *poleis* of the eastern Mediterranean world? Cities worthy of the name had the standard *polis* features, such as Hippodamian urban planning, an assembly, theatre, gymnasium, *agora* and *stoa*, but in no sense were they exclusively Greek. In the Levant and in Egypt especially, we find the *polis* featured a fusion of cultural influences. For example, in Bostrain in southern Syria, Greek games were held during an annual festival in honour of the local god Dusares. In nearby Palmyra, the most important religious site was the Temple of Bel, dedicated to a non-Greek god, although the temple featured strong Greek and Roman motifs. The Roman impact was also quite profound, particularly when it came to road and sewerage construction, aqueducts and the use of concrete. The Roman bathhouse, with its special heating systems and graduated heating spaces, was a prized feature of any Greek *polis*. It supplanted the much simpler pre-existing bathhouses, though in the Greek world it was often made to accommodate a Greek *palaestra* (exercise yard). The Greek East also took to gladiatorial contests, although they were normally staged in refurbished Greek theatres rather than Roman amphitheatres, of which very few were built in the East.

LIVING MUSEUMS: ATHENS, SPARTA AND THE AEGEAN WORLD

What of conditions in Greece proper? Well into the first century AD, Greeks continued to complain about *oliganthropia* (depopulation), a widely accepted measure of social malaise. To contemporaries, *oliganthropia* provided the clearest indication that Greece had been reduced to a backwater. Dio Chrysostom heard one landholder complain that 'over two-thirds of our land is a wilderness because of neglect and *oliganthropia*':

> I too own many acres, as I imagine some others do, not only in the mountains but also in the plains, and if anybody would till them, I should not only give him the chance for nothing but gladly pay money besides. (*Oration*, 7.34)[10]

Close study of recent archaeological data, however, reveals a more positive picture. Rural depopulation is confirmed, but the exodus appears to have been absorbed by new cities like Nicopolis (Epiros), founded by Augustus to celebrate his victory over Mark Antony at nearby Actium. Entire regions such as Boeotia had declined markedly, but the province of Achaea generally remained among the most highly urbanized parts of the empire. *Oliganthropia* might also be explained by the greater profitability of pastoralism, especially sheep and goat herding, and by the growth of large estates, a phenomenon that predated the Roman conquest. The provincial notables that owned the 'many acres' and complained about the ills of *oliganthropia*, including Dio Chrysostom himself, were probably the authors of the problem.

As with modern Greece, Roman Greece traded on its history. Athens and Sparta were especially well positioned to capitalize on Roman graecophilia and the interest of visitors from the Greek cities of the East. Sparta by this stage functioned much like any other Greek city, except that its inhabitants were expected to re-enact their history for the consumption of tourists. The Spartans had a series of historic monuments that commemorated its unrivalled military history, such as the Persian *stoa* that had been built with the spoils from the Battle of Plataea. There was so much to see that Pausanias, in his detailed description of Roman Sparta, was forced to restrict himself to highlights. Sparta was made into a living museum. During a visit in 21 BC, Augustus paid homage to Sparta's glorious past by eating in the common messes. By the late first century AD, tourists were treated to re-enactments of the Lykourgon education system, including its harsh regimes of training and sadistic punishments. There was even an attempt to revive the Doric dialect.

Athens was the greatest tourist magnet for obvious reasons. Young Roman and Greek aristocrats continued to come from far and wide to enrol in its prestigious schools, including the Academy and the Lyceum, while the more itinerant crowd could behold the city's famous landmarks. The centre of Roman Athens was cluttered with new buildings, with many classical sites now overshadowed by structures that were endowed by over-appreciative Hellenistic and Roman benefactors. Rome's esteem for Athens could be measured by the fact that it received the lion's share of Roman munificence. Augustus' son-in-law, Marcus Agrippa, was responsible for the Odeion, an auditorium that could hold up to a thousand spectators. Augustus himself oversaw the completion of the new *agora*, while the emperor Hadrian bestowed some of the cities greatest monuments, including the great Temple of Olympian Zeus and Hadrian's Library.

Inevitably, the Greeks were apt to exploit Roman philhellenism when necessity dictated. When applying for privileges, making claims against rival *poleis* or seeking mitigation against fines and other forms of punishment, city delegates always cited civic myths and histories in their defence, however irrelevant such stories might be to a given case. Emperors usually measured a city's worth by its historical and mythological significance, and by its past relations with Rome. Troy, for example, as the city of Aeneas, received tax-free status from the Emperor Claudius. A distinguished history was no guarantee of success, but it could help. Even the most obscure communities that rate a mention in Homer's epics and mythology, or those which fought during the Persian Wars, might expect favourable treatment. As such, the older *poleis* had an advantage over newer cities.

BEING GREEK IN THE SECOND CENTURY AD

Roman interest in Greek culture was always conditional, but it beca
less restrained under the empire. Under the first imperial dynasty, the
Julio-Claudians (31 BC–AD 68), the Romans continued to believe that
there was a time and place to speak Greek and to wear Greek attire.
Roman decorum placed strict demands on how one behaved in public
and private, and Greek language and Greek habits had no place in the
forum or during formal occasions that required traditional Roman attire
and protocols. Nero's ostentatious graecomania was thought to be symp-
tomatic of his degenerate character. A few decades later, however,
unqualified love of things Greek had become a virtue. It could be said of
the emperor Hadrian (AD 117–138) that he was possessed by graecomania. His villa at Tivoli was cluttered with an extraordinary collection of
Greek art replicas, and it was he who established the Greek tradition of
sporting a manicured beard.

Indeed by Hadrian's reign, Greek enjoyed a renewed ascendancy over
Latin. In terms of literary taste and production, Latin offered no compe-
tition. Romans actually preferred Greek myths, and they took to the
Greek approach of burying the dead in sculptured caskets (sarcophagi).
Such developments did not so much signify the Hellenization of the
empire as it did the formation of a more hybrid imperial culture in which
Hellenism played an indelible role. In Hadrian's empire, hybrid identities appeared to be the norm. The emperor himself was Spanish by birth,
Roman by necessity and Greek by choice. The great scholar Lucian (AD
c.120–180), whose mother tongue was Aramaic and who wrote and
delivered his works in Greek, also saw himself as a Roman: he tellingly
described Roman soldiers as *our* soldiers. Meanwhile, 'ethnic' Greeks
were playing important roles within the Roman imperial system.
Plutarch, for example, held significant imperial postings, while Herodes
Atticus was a Roman senator. The historian Cassius Dio was also a
senator, became a consul and held a series of governorships in Asia
Minor, Africa and the Balkans.

By the second century AD, therefore, imperial subjects were beginning
to identify with the empire, but it was an empire in which Greeks were
accorded a special place. In AD 131, Hadrian performed his most
poignant act as a philhellene when he oversaw the creation of the
Panhellenion, a league that included the better-known cities of Greece.
Its purpose appears to have been the promotion of Greek culture and
inter-Greek cultural exchanges, and while the evidence does not tell us

Map 5 The Roman Empire AD *c.*138

its precise purpose we do know that membership was restrictive. With some exceptions, only those cities and peoples that could trace their lineage to early Greek antiquity were eligible for admission.

Clearly, ethnicity or lineage still mattered to the Greeks in the second century, but it was equally apparent that one could also *become* Greek. Consider the case of Lucian, who could claim to be more 'Greek' than most, but who was born in Samosata in Aramaic-speaking Commagene (northern Syria), where social elites were educated in the Greek language and literature. Lucian was a renowned Greek orator and won fame and fortune touring through Italy and Gaul, although he was made to feel an outsider in Greece and Asia Minor, possibly because of his accent and the fact that he was Syrian. He went on to write some 80 works that included literary dialogues, satire, parodies and much else in Greek. He ranked among the most outstanding figures of a literary golden age.

For Lucian, 'Greekness' was fundamentally cultural, and under the Early Empire it was a prerequisite for elite status. Even in such places as Seleukia on the Euphrates, now a flourishing city under Parthian rule, being Greek meant having a Greek *paideia*. Lucian's advice makes clear that a Greek education was a rite of passage for any aspiring man of honour:

> You who are now a pauper, a son of a nobody . . . in a short while, you will inspire envy and jealousy in all, you will be honoured and raised, and held in good repute among the best people, and be regarded by those pre-eminent in birth and wealth . . . and be deemed worthy of office and promotion.[11]

What continued to set 'ethnic' Greeks apart, it seems, was a more pronounced cultural chauvinism and lingering resentment. The likes of Aelius Aristides continued to lament Greece's fall from grace and wished they had lived in more glorious times. The mid-second-century geographer Pausanias, whose detailed descriptions of significant Greek historical sites is a goldmine of information, gives scant regard for monuments endowed by Romans.

THE SECOND SOPHISTIC (AD *c*.60–230)

From the latter decades of the first century AD, educated Greeks found consolation in imitating the literary achievements of classical authors and by producing their works in 'pure' Greek, namely the Attic. Koine

Greek was seen as too base and unbecoming for the well educated. From the reign of Nero through to the mid-third century, a period remembered as 'the Second Sophistic' (AD c.60–250), we see an outpouring of high-brow Greek literature that dominated scholarship and learning through-out the Mediterranean world.

This search for a reconstituted Greek identity based on the distant past was the hallmark of this period, and its chief proponents were orators, who also happened to be the fashionable celebrities of the age. Oratory was an exceptionally useful talent. The law courts and civic assemblies required effective advocates. Among the competitive cities of Asia Minor, master rhetoricians were needed for settling disputes or for putting a particular city's case before the governor or the emperor himself. The discipline of oratory flourished among the empire's great schools, where it competed with philosophy as the most prestigious of disciplines. The best known orators, however, were not teachers but public performers like Dio Cocceianus of Prusa (AD c.40/50–110), who earned the name Dio Chrysostom ('golden mouth'); Favorinus (AD c.88–155), a native of Arlete (Provence) who toured Greece and earned the notice of Hadrian and Antoninus Pius, each of whom invited him into his inner circle; and Claudius Aelianus (AD 165/70–230/5), who became a noted speaker in his time, but who won lasting fame for writing on topics as varied as natural history and bucolic life.

Despite recurrent bouts of illness, Aelius Aristides managed to tour widely and perform before large crowds. The emperor Marcus Aurelius (161–180) was a fan and made a point of calling on Aristides during a visit to Smyrna. A typical performance by Aristides might feature a pane-gyric, of which 'Oration to Rome' is among his better known, or a *melete* (declamation), an exercise designed specifically to demonstrate an orator's wit, erudition and command of language. A *melete* was quite literally a rhetorical exercise, whereby speakers argued counterfactual positions on famous historical turning points, such as: should Nikias send a relief force to the Athenian soldiers trapped in Syracuse? Should the Athenians deliver Demosthenes to Philip? Audiences were enter-tained and moved by the orator's clever arguments, while aficionados were intrigued by rhetorical 'form': his mastery of Attic Greek, use of language and style of delivery.

The Second Sophistic's obsessions with the Classical era should not be construed as a rejection of Roman rule. For as Aristides' 'Oration to Rome' makes clear, Greek elites had reason to be grateful: if anything, only Rome was capable of fulfilling the promise of Greek civilization.

Image 4 Roman Hellenism: the colossal Temple of Olympian Zeus, completed under the auspices of the Emperor Hadrian, evokes a nostalgic 'Roman' vision of Greece (*photo courtesy of Dr Kathryn Welch, University of Sydney*).

Yet while memories of Classical Greece allowed Aristides and his fellow Greeks to feel rather special, it also gave cause for melancholy. Nostalgia for past glories reinforced the fact that they were yesterday's people, and that the present and the future belonged to Rome. Indeed, there was also something very 'Roman' about the Second Sophistic. To maintain good relations with the imperial centre, and to press their advantage over other imperial subjects, such as the Gauls and Egyptians, the Greeks had to appeal to what *Romans* liked about Greek history and letters. In that sense, the Second Sophistic pandered to Roman nostalgia for Hellas. The Greeks had to ingratiate themselves with such bearded graecomaniacs as Hadrian and Marcus Aurelius, who were enamoured with the Greek past rather than the present. Hadrian's building activities in Athens, where his great library and the temple to the Olympian Zeus overshadowed the surrounding buildings, constituted an imposition of his nostalgic vision of Athens. The Panhellenion was his way of forging Greek unity, putting into effect what the Greeks could never manage themselves, but according to his terms and under his supervision. In turn, the grateful Athenians erected an arch in his honour, which had an inscription stating that Athens was 'his' city.

THE EMPIRE AT BAY (AD *c*.170–400)

The end of the Pax Romana serves as the next watershed in our story. Imperial subjects, Greeks included, became more self-consciously 'Roman' as imperial security became a major and ongoing preoccupation. It was during the reign of Marcus Aurelius, particularly in the 170s, that Rome was struggling to defend its northern frontier. The combined impact of the Marcomanni, Quadi and Costoboci placed a severe strain on imperial resources – the Costoboci penetrated deep into the Balkans and as far as Greece. The fiscal and administrative apparatus of the Augustan system had worked well for the last 200 or so years, but Marcus and his successors were to face much more concerted 'barbarian' pressure than in the past. Such was the threat to Roman security that emperors of the succeeding Severan dynasty (AD 192–235) had to promote themselves explicitly as hardy military men. Marcus himself spent an inordinate length of his reign on the frontier, where we assume he penned (in Greek) many of his philosophical reflections (*Meditations*). Thereafter, emperors spent little, if any, time in the capital.

It was during the 50 or so years that followed the end of the Severan dynasty, however, that the empire faced the very real prospect of destruction. A new Persian dynasty, the Sassanids, particularly under Sharpur I (243–270), waged a series of aggressive wars in which Rome lost many legions and cities along the frontier. Not since Hannibal had Rome faced such a formidable adversary. Meanwhile, as Rome focused on its eastern borders, its northern defences were left exposed. In the early 250s and late 260s, Gothic raiders inundated the Aegean world and caused extensive destruction. We know very little about these terrible times, except that Corinth, Argos, Thessalonica and Sparta were sacked. Vast regions like Thessaly were laid waste. In 267/8, Athens too was looted, but we know of a spirited defence of the city led by an historian named P. Herrenius Dexippus, who was reported as having rallied the Athenians by invoking their glorious history. Many monuments in the Agora were destroyed and large parts of this historic area remained in ruins for more than a century.

This age of crisis had profound implications for the Greek city and its role within the imperial system. Under the Pax Romana, small government sufficed. Emperors were content to retain a rudimentary state apparatus that relied on civic elites to collect taxes and to perform most of the functions of government. That system could cope with the occasional frontier war, but it buckled under simultaneous Germanic and Persian pressure. There were also the inevitable side effects of endemic warfare, such as rampant inflation and soaring prices, which shattered civic finances and made it harder for cities to meet their municipal responsibilities. In the third century, therefore, the city ceased to be the fiscal bedrock of the imperial system. Military exigencies called for more direct central supervision of fiscal resources, though these were extremely difficult times for emperors to enforce the necessary structural adjustments. For the third century was also distinguished by a rapid succession of emperors, some of whom reigned for a few weeks. Sections of the army were quick to support rival usurpers, and the result was endemic civil war and rapid imperial succession. Emperors like Aurelian (270–275), who did manage to implement far-reaching reforms, lived a precarious existence. For all his considerable military and political achievements, Aurelian succumbed to a plot from within his own household.

From this era of unprecedented political turmoil and endemic violence there emerged a new system of imperial governance that consigned the

Greek city to a much more passive role. The new Roman Empire was a centrally managed bureaucratic state that was, out of sheer necessity, much more efficient at mobilizing imperial resources. By the reign of the great Diocletion (283–305), the empire could field an army of 258,000 men: 186,000 more than had been possible during the second century. Diocletion, who was most responsible for consolidating the new centralized system, recast the province as a smaller and much more effective unit of governance (diocese). The provincial capital, which now earned the label of *metropolis* (mother city), not only dominated every other provincial centre but also absorbed most of the educated talent. Greek cities such as Thessalonica, Antioch, Smyrna and Nicomedia figured among the early *metropoleis*. In such circumstances, the average Greek city lost much of its civic vitality. City elites lived in reduced circumstances and were less able to fund festivals and utilities. The schools that once groomed young men for civic responsibilities were now likely to provide essential training for provincial and imperial service in the *metropoleis*.

Yet historians of Late Antiquity and archaeologists warn against pronouncing the death of the *polis*. Archaeological research on the period has confirmed that cities might have been diminished by the experiences of the third century, but most continued to thrive, as they did in Greece. Archaeologists have shown that after the Gothic invasions, Greece enjoyed a gradual population revival. The number of *poleis* in Boeotia, which had plummeted from 70 in the Classical/Early Hellenistic Era to just 33 during the Pax Romana, had recovered to around 45 by Late Antiquity. On the island of Chios, the trend was similar: Classical 56, Pax Romana 10 and Late Antiquity 28. More impressive still was the resettlement of vast territories which were being progressively reclaimed for agriculture. Nor had emperors necessarily given up on the idea of the *polis* as the basic unit of governance. Indeed throughout the fourth century there were loud calls for restoring the prestige of civic elites and their traditional roles. The emperor Julian (361–363), perhaps the last of the graecomanics, envisaged a restored classical empire based on the Greek city.

Yet it remained a fact that civic elites were no longer capable of playing the role of administrators and benefactors. Only in North Africa, a region unscathed by the third-century crisis, were cities capable of functioning as in the past. In most ways, the *polis* as an independently operated entity was a thing of the past.

CULTURAL DIVERGENCE (AD c.230–400)

Diocletian recognized that the challenges of imperial governance were too great for a single imperial authority. He appointed a co-emperor and then organized another two junior emperors. About a century later, when the empire was divided into two states (in 395) for roughly similar reasons, the political border accorded closely with the linguistic fault line. For by that stage the western and eastern halves of the empire were much more discrete cultural units: a Greek empire in the East and a Latin one in the West. How might one explain this cultural divergence?

It seems that the Graeco-Roman synthesis began to unravel sometime during the crisis-ridden third century and with the rise of Christianity. The emperors of that era were drawn from military ranks and generally lacked an aristocrat's education. Diocletian had chosen the Greek city of Nicomedia as his administrative capital, but he needed Greek inter- preters. Tellingly, he required that Latin be used in government commu- nications. For Diocletian and for most of his fourth century successors, conformity to a single imperial language concurred with the centralizing tendencies of the late Roman state. During his reign and for much of the fourth century, therefore, Latin enjoyed pre-eminence over Greek. In the meantime, a cultural shift had been taking place within the Latin-speak- ing half of the empire. Whereas proficiency in Greek had been expected of any Roman aristocrat worthy of that rank, now the focus was in attain- ing excellent Latin. Even Constantine (306–337), a native Latin-speaker who was presumably educated in his native Illyria, was not at home with Greek. Although this extremely energetic emperor had chosen the Greek city of Byzantion as his new imperial capital, and engaged closely with Greek-speaking elites and bishops, Constantine was also known to need interpreters.

Meanwhile, although Greek continued to feature in West Roman education, qualified teachers were in rare supply and most cities could ill afford their services. The decline of Greek also had much to do with the renewal of Latin literature. Western education now revolved around Latin grammar and the mastery of classics such as Cicero's letters, Virgil's poetry and Tacitus' *Histories*. Certainly, Homer and the Attic playwrights were still being read in the West, but most readers had no Greek or inadequate Greek, and they much preferred Latin translations. The late-fourth-century monk Jerome performed an immense service to West Roman readers when he translated Greek theological texts into Latin.

It was Christianity, in fact, that played a key role in the making of two distinct Roman empires. It is certainly the case that Koine Greek was the original language of the Gospels and the Early Church, and the new faith spread initially through the Greek-speaking Jewish Diaspora. The greatest of the early missionaries, Paul, had a Greek education and preached throughout Anatolia and the Aegean world in Greek. The preaching circuit he followed was one often traversed by orators, and all his letters were to Greek cities. The books that form the New Testament were written in Koine, the language expected to find the largest possible audience. But Christianity also made headway among non-Greek speaking communities, in places such as rural Egypt, Syria, Armenia and Arabia, where it was vital that the message of the Gospels was diffused in vernacular tongues. The effect was to consolidate other vernaculars as written languages. By the fourth century, Syriac, Armenian and Coptic, the common vernacular in Egypt, were not just languages of prayer and liturgy, but of formal church administration and theology. Armenian script was invented in the fourth century to service the needs of an independent state as well as an independent 'national' Church.

Of special significance were Latin-speaking parishes in the western half of the Roman Empire. There, Latin became the language of church liturgy or 'mass', and Bibles could be found in a number of Latin translations. Another factor that contributed to the making of a distinct Latin Church was the influence that western bishops were to enjoy in civic affairs. Once Constantine had legalized Christianity and gave it a privileged position among the empire's religions, it was only a matter of time before the leaders of Christian communities began to test their role within society at large. This development had a most telling impact in the Latin West, where cities and communities were more regionally focused and less amenable to central imperial authority. Thus, western cities began to produce rather powerful figures such as Ossius of Cordoba (c.257–359) and Ambrose of Milan (339–397). The fearless Ambrose was the first Church leader to openly challenge imperial authority when he demanded that the emperor Theodosius I do penance for the massacre of 7000 unruly civilians in Thessalonica in 390.

Ambrose's indomitable stance set a precedent in Latin Church thinking in regard to the clergy's relationship with the state, particularly the Bishop of Rome, who enjoyed a position of symbolic primacy within the Church. The fact that Rome was the traditional capital of the Empire, and that it possessed the bones of St Peter and St Paul, gave its bishop a convincing claim to primacy. Perhaps the most important factor in the making of a distinctly 'Latin' Church, at least in these early stages, was the role played by the north African bishop, Augustine of Hippo (354–430), whose voluminous writings, particularly his *City of God* (426), did most to establish a coherent Latin theological tradition. Matters of Christian belief and practice had been hitherto defined in Greek by learned bishops in the East. Augustine made much of this arcane and (often) incomprehensible philosophical material more accessible to his Latin readership. He also created a series of uniquely Latin theological precepts, such as grace and predestination, thus setting the stage for the making of distinct Latin and Greek churches.

HELLENISM AS PAGANISM

Christianity is important in our story for another significant reason. Sometime during the course of the tumultuous third century, the term 'Hellenic' ceased to be an ethnic ascription. In fact, most of the empire's subjects, whatever their spoken vernacular might have been, came to identify themselves as *Romanoi* (Romans). To use modern terms, Rome had become a 'nation' or a commonwealth, with a firmly integrated society that was united in its concern for the empire's survival. In the meantime, with the spread of Christianity and its growing popularity at all social levels, the term 'Hellene' came to refer specifically to those who persisted with traditional religious thinking and practices. By the fourth century, 'Hellene' was an insult that Christians hurled at pagans.

From the reign of Constantine, therefore, the empire was marked by a new kind of social division. The Roman state became progressively Christianized, but it was forced to accommodate both pagan and Christian communities. Each group had their separate centres of learning. The Hellenes still had the highly prestigious schools of Athens, Alexandria and Pergamon, and it was at Athens that the emperor Julian, known to Christians as 'the Apostate', received his education and secretly renounced his Christian upbringing on becoming a 'Hellene'. Julian's great lament was that a civilization inspired by Classical Greece and built by pagan Rome was being usurped by Christianity. During his brief reign, Julian sought a Hellenic/pagan restoration, and many of his measures were designed to roll back the gains achieved by Christians. Thus, he withdrew financial subsidies awarded to churches and the monopoly on official sinecures enjoyed by Christians.

Christian and pagan thinkers had different visions of society and the cosmos, but they were each preoccupied by the notion of a supreme source of existence, which in turn provided common ground for intellectual engagement and debate. Thus, philosophers and theologians alike were inspired by the ideas of Neoplatonism, the dominant intellectual tradition of Late Antiquity. Of critical importance here is that Christian theologians recognized the value of Plato and of Greek learning, and for that reason they did not reject Hellenism per se, especially as there was much in Greek philosophy that, in their view, anticipated Christian theology. Basil of Caesarea (330–379), one of the fathers of Christian monasticism, and author of a small text entitled 'Address to Young Men on How They Might Derive Benefit from Greek Literature' (374), insisted that Christians could draw on the *chresis* (value) of Hellenism while ignoring its explicitly pagan religious content. He also recognized the need to produce complex theological treatises in a sophisticated language like Attic, rather than the much simpler medium Koine. Thus, whereas Hellenes were to be shunned, there were aspects of Hellenism that had to be salvaged for Christian use. Julian viewed the Christian use of Classical texts as utter hypocrisy. Therefore in 362 he banned the teaching of Greek Classics in Christian schools and the use of Attic for Christian theology.

It is difficult to underestimate the importance of *chresis* when considering the survival of the Greek literary heritage. The compromise implied in Basil's concept meant that Christians had dispensation not only to read but to cherish the writings of pagans. Hence, long after the disappearance of paganism, during the Middle Ages and the Modern era, Christians were determined to preserve the Classical Tradition, including works by Julian the Apostate himself.

THE LATE GREEK ROMAN EMPIRE (*C.*AD 395–527)

The year 395 marked a new phase in Roman history. Following the death of Theodosius I (379–395), the empire was formally divided into two halves, and while it remained united in legal terms the Greek and Latin halves now functioned with separate rulers, administrations, budgets and armies. Within a few years, the two empires were tested by 'barbarian' invasions. Since the 370s, the Huns, fearsome pastoral warriors from Central Asia, had been migrating into central-eastern Europe, forcing the Gothic peoples of the region into Roman territory. In 401, the Visigoths invaded Italy, and after 405 other Gothic groups, along with the Huns, also flooded the empire. During the course of the early fifth century, the Goths settled and gradually dismembered the West Roman Empire. In 476, the last emperor in the West was overthrown. The East Roman Empire also struggled to keep the invaders at bay, but it benefited from a more unified elite and a well-functioning state centred on Constantinople. Indeed the capital emerged as the key to imperial security. Under Theodosius II, the empire's longest reigning ruler (408–450), the city walls were rebuilt as a complex of fortifications. The main wall was 5 m thick and 12 m tall, and at 55-metre intervals were massive towers that stood 18–20 m in height. Not only did the Theodosian Walls keep the city safe from the Goths and the Huns, but they blocked access to the provinces that served as the state's tax revenue base: Anatolia, Syria and especially Egypt. At the very least, the eastern emperors could ward off the enemy with massive bribes. The walls allowed the East Roman Empire to weather the storm, and when the dust finally settled it had lost none of its territories.

As a more compact entity, the more populous and economically robust half of the Roman Empire entered a new phase of vitality not seen since the Pax Romana. After Theodosius II, the empire was bolstered by a succession of powerful and talented emperors, including Marcian (450–457), Leo I (457–474), Zeno (474–491), Anastasius I (491–518), Justin I (518–527) and Justinian I (527–565). These rulers sat at the apex of the world's most refined systems of state and provincial administration. That it sometimes worked out cheaper to pay off enemies than to challenge them in open war was really a measure of shrewdness and unmatched affluence. Certainly, the Mediterranean of Late Antiquity was poorer and weaker than it had been under the Pax Romana, but in relative terms the empire of Zeno and Justin was still the richest and most formidable power of the age – the fortunes left behind by Marcian and Anastasius (45,000 kg and 145,000 kg of gold, respectively) were astronomical by early medieval standards.

Divested of its Latin half, the truncated empire had also become *more* Greek. Latin remained the language of the imperial family and was used in certain aspects of the law and military administration. Otherwise, the East was a Greek-speaking domain. In communications between emperors and officials, in the running of everyday bureaucratic affairs, in all Church communications, ecclesiastical assemblies, and in communications between most of the emperor's subjects, the language was Greek. The *polis* also found a new lease of life in the East. Civic leaders were still expected to oversee municipal issues in the *bouleterion* – having a *bouleterion* was required of every self-respecting city. But what gave the city renewed civic vitality was its role within a large and expanding Church structure. Thus, an important *polis* now happened to be the seat of the bishop or archbishop. Locally, bishops were busy men who oversaw the construction and maintenance of church buildings, charity and welfare services, and most ecclesiastical and secular matters. Significantly, the bishop and his clergy assumed many of the roles once carried out by the local patricians – the higher clergy were normally of local patrician stock. How much influence a bishop could wield over his community no doubt depended on individual character or charisma, but it is clear that in any given city it was the sitting bishop that tended to be the focus of authority.

The revivification of the Greek city is confirmed by recent archaeological research on the fifth and sixth centuries. Extensive building activity was underway in every part of the empire, save for the upper Balkan provinces that bore the brunt of the Germanic and Hun incursions. For Greece, an important sixth-century document, Hierocles' *Synekdemos*, records the names of 80 *poleis* for the Peloponnese alone. A great deal of archaeological evidence points to the growth of construction, manufacturing and commercial activity in Corinth, Amphipolis and Thessalonica. At Athens, still a vibrant university town, construction efforts were often directed at restoring great buildings, such as the Library of Hadrian, while new building activity took up what remained of the classical city's open spaces. The Palace of the Giants, for example, which housed the family of Theodosius' wife, Eudokia, was a monstrous structure that took up most of the central area of the ancient *agora*. More commonly, room was made for the construction of large churches. As temples fell into disuse, civic leaders, often under the direction of the local bishop, oversaw the construction of impressive basilicas that appropriated *spolia* (materials) from old pagan sites. Occasionally, old buildings became churches. At Thessalonica, for example, the cylindrically structured Mausoleum of Galerius was converted to a church dedicated to St George. Fortifications were also deemed to be a distinguishing characteristic of a great city. Thus, the city of Aphrodisias in west-central Anatolia, which was tucked away in one the safest regions of the empire, appeared to have erected its impressive walls for largely symbolic reasons.

In recent years, historians have come to recognize the vitality of Late Antiquity. The Germanic invasions were quite destructive, but Christian contemporaries have left the false impression that civilization had been swept away by a tidal wave of barbarism. In fact, the imprint of Graeco-Roman civilization remained clearly visible throughout the West, much as it appeared to be almost intact in the East. But Late Antiquity was also a time of transition, when the ancient world was being reconfigured into something quite different, enough to warrant the label 'medieval'. The Latin and Greek halves of the empire moved gradually in different directions, thus generating distinct worlds defined not so much by language but by divergent Christian cultures. What eventually emerged in the East was a very different Greek world.

5

The Greek Roman Empire II (c.500–1200): The Triumph of Orthodoxy

> Our kingship is an imitation of yours, modelled on your good design, a
> copy of the only Empire. By as much as we follow you, so much we
> precede all other peoples.[1]

This much was conceded to the emperor Anastasius by the great
Ostrogoth King Theodoric (471–526). Although the ruler of a vast
Germanic kingdom that included the city of Rome, Theodoric gener-
ously acknowledged that the East Roman Empire was *the* empire, and
that he, at least in a nominal sense, was a mere viceroy. Until the rise of
the Carolingian empire of Charlemagne in the late eighth century,
western Christians, including the bishops of Rome, continued to accept
the emperor in Constantinople as the ultimate sovereign.

To understand the world of Late Antiquity, the period roughly from
the Age of Constantine to the Islamic conquests of the mid-seventh
century, the continuities of Roman history remain important. Even the
legacies of the Roman Republic retained a powerful resonance. It was
still necessary, to take one example, for an emperor like Anastasius to be
'elected' by acclamation, a role that was sometimes played by the Senate
or the soldiery, or better still the crowds of Constantinople, whose assent
was received in a vast stadium known as the Hippodrome. And yet, Late
Antiquity has also been described as the bridge to the Middle Ages.
Thus, there was no longer any pretence of the emperor being the *princeps* (first citizen). The *basileus*, as his Greek-speaking subjects
described him, was an autocrat whose right to rule was deemed a gift *ek
theou* (from God). Anastasius was God's primary representative on
earth, the key link between the heavenly and temporal realms, while his

subjects were 'God's Chosen', the 'new Israelites'. Constantinople itself had acquired a sacred aura, being the new Jerusalem as well as the new Rome.

Formally, the Roman Empire persisted for another millennium, but modern historians have dubbed it the 'Byzantine Empire' or 'Byzantium', for sometime between the third and eighth centuries it metamorphosed into something rather different. Certainly, Byzantium and its Greek-speaking elites continued to identify with the Graeco-Roman heritage, but what really set this dynamic and sophisticated society apart was its approach to Christianity. More specifically, Byzantium was defined by its preoccupation with doctrinal authenticity or *orthodoxia* (orthodoxy). In Byzantine minds, the empire's fortunes and adherence to strict orthodoxy were inextricably linked, which meant that God's favour depended on such things as whether the faithful adhered to correct Christology (the nature of Christ) or whether icon veneration was a divinely sanctioned practice.

The answers to such questions gave the empire a set of beliefs and cultural practices that the wider world came to recognize as 'Greek' Christianity or Greek Orthodoxy. From Anastasius through to the last emperor, who died defending his capital in 1453, Greek remained the language of the state and (crucially) the Church, while also being the most commonly spoken language on the street. Moreover, the Byzantines never relinquished their self-appointed role as keepers of the Greek literary tradition and continued to think that the Classical Greek heritage was *their* heritage. In many meaningful senses, therefore, the Roman/Byzantine world was also a Greek world: radically reconfigured, but authentic all the same.

THE SIXTH CENTURY

Justinian (527–565) was in many ways Byzantium's first medieval emperor, although in his own mind he was an uncompromisingly 'Roman' one. Born in 483 under the name Petrus Sabbateus, of Latin-speaking Illyrian stock, Justinian moved in his late teens to Constantinople, where his uncle Justin (Falvius Iustinus) had become an influential palace guard. Justinian worked behind the scenes to secure his uncle's succession in 518 and emerged as the most influential figure in his court. In 527 he assumed the throne, determined to leave a lasting legacy. The scope of his ambition was reflected in his legal reforms. In

529 he commissioned the codification of Roman law (*Codex Iustinianus*), a mammoth undertaking led by the extraordinary legal polymath Tribonian, followed quickly by the *Digest*, the *Institutes* and the *Novels of Justinian*. By the time these works had been completed in 534, the definitive version of the law codes, the foundations of European civil law, had been established.

Along with Augustus, Diocletian and Constantine, Justinian ranks among the few emperors whose name defined an era. Among his other feats was the transformation of Constantinople into a capital worthy of a universal empire. Although inaugurated two centuries earlier by Constantine, the city had been hampered by its lack of historical pedigree as compared to Rome and Alexandria. Building activity had proceeded in fits and starts, and mainly under emperors that resided in the city, such as Theodosius II. In 532, however, much of the city was ruined following the infamous Nika Riots, thus giving Justinian a golden opportunity to cast its lasting monumental shape. Within five years, the grandeur of the city's ceremonial centre had been radically enhanced. Most effort went into the construction of churches, with the Hagia Sophia, the world's largest church, being the crowning achievement.

Justinian also sought to reassert direct imperial control over what had been the West Roman Empire. In 533 a modest-sized military expedition led by the great general Belisarius recaptured North Africa and the city of Carthage from the Vandals. Buoyed by the expedition's rapid success, Justinian focused his attention on Italy, and by 535 Belisarius had restored Sicily and southern Italy to Roman rule. By the end of his reign the empire extended to the Alps, North Africa and a portion of southern Spain.

The question of whether Justinian's was a 'golden age' has always been a matter of conjecture, especially as the attempt to reclaim the West Roman Empire had greatly strained imperial resources and devastated the conquered regions. Moreover, Justinian's vision of an authentic Roman Empire was one that consciously rejected much of the Classical Greek heritage. Thus, Greek education, particularly philosophy, was purged to make the empire more Christian. In 527, he effectively closed the Academy, the school made famous by Plato. As noted in his *Codex Justinianus* (1.11.102), he believed the 'disease' of the Hellenes should not corrupt students: some of these Hellenes found refuge in the court of the Persian king. Procopius and John the Lydian, prominent literary figures who valued the classical heritage, were greatly disturbed at the relentless targeting of cultured men. Rather, this was an age dominated by theology and which belonged to chroniclers like John Malalas, whose approach to history had more in common with the Bible than with Thucydides.

There was much else about the age of Justinian that foreshadowed the medieval mode. The capital he left behind no longer featured a Graeco-Roman grid plan: the residential quarters were now characterized by winding streets and blind alleys. In art, we find a departure from figurative representations of the human form and an obsession with religious subject matter and motifs. The most famous case is the striking, but rather two-dimensional, portrait of Justinian and the Empress Theodora at San Vitale in Ravenna (Italy). Flanked on one side by clergymen holding a cross, the Gospels and incense, Justinian carries the patent for the bread of the Eucharist, while Theodora, facing the emperor from the opposite side of the apse, and with the Three Magi in her entourage, carries the chalice. The only features that distinguish the emperor and empress from the clergy are the halos and jewellery.

Halfway through Justinian's reign, the empire's fortunes changed. Ostrogothic resistance in Italy brought the impetus of imperial expansion to a grinding halt. Then, between 541 and 543, the Mediterranean world was ravaged by bubonic plague – recurrent outbreaks of it over the next hundred years may have reduced the Roman population by half. Justinian also changed: he lost interest in state matters and withdrew from public view, preferring to spend his time in seclusion or in the company of theologians. In his latter years he may well have suffered a mental breakdown. Procopius, whose writings betray both admiration and virulent antipathy, claimed the emperor would frequently lose all sense of self-awareness. His successor, Justin II (565–578), restored the empire's budget but incurred a reputation for ravenousness greed. Under his watch, another Germanic group, the Lombards, seized large parts of Italy, leaving only enclaves around Ravenna, Rome and Naples in imperial hands. Justin's troubles were compounded by the resumption of hostilities with Sassanid Persia and with the appearance along the Danube frontier of the Avars, a new pastoral power from the Eurasian Steppe. Along with the Slav peoples who occupied the region north of the Danube, the Avars penetrated the empire's northern defences and threw the entire Balkans region into turmoil.

Justin II and Tiberios II (578–582) had little success in recovering the Balkan provinces and keeping the empire's enemies at bay, but the situation improved markedly under Maurice (Maurikios) (582–602), an able military commander and strategist. After years of fighting, Maurice managed to push the Persians, Avars and Slavs back to, and even beyond, the original frontiers.

NEAR COLLAPSE: THE SEVENTH CENTURY

At the beginning of the seventh century, the empire emerged intact, but it had been shaken by invasions, financial stress and recurrent plague. While it is conceivable that Maurice's Roman Empire might have persisted as the great Mediterranean power for centuries to come, it remained vulnerable to simultaneous attacks along its northern and eastern borders. Worse still, the empire would show how susceptible it was to crippling internal divisions.

Maurice's wars required budgetary stringencies that made him unpopular among the underpaid soldiery and the crowds of Constantinople, who missed their free bread rations. In 602, troops stationed on the Danube refused orders to perform a military operation and marched on the capital instead, led by a centurion named Phokas. With the connivance of disgruntled elements in the city, Phokas' men entered its precincts. Maurice was eventually apprehended and executed. Phokas was installed as emperor, thus bringing to a close more than 200 years of (relatively) orderly dynastic succession.

Meanwhile, Khurso II of Persia denounced Phokas as a usurper and launched a major offensive that claimed Syria. Between 613 and 619, Khurso, now bent on avenging the destruction of the first Persian Empire by Alexander the Great, also reclaimed Egypt and set his sights on Constantinople itself. In the meantime, the Avars and Slavs sensed an opportunity to run amok in the Balkans. With Avar support, the Persians besieged Constantinople in 616. The empire seemed on the verge of collapse, but by that stage Phokas had been overthrown by the very capable Heraclius (610–641), one-time Byzantine governor of Carthage. Although much of his empire had been overrun, the Sassanids were overstretched and Heraclius could depend on the Church and its vast financial resources, especially as the Persians had reportedly committed vile acts against Christians and Church property. In 614, Heraclius' subjects were outraged when the Sassanids carried off the 'True Cross' from Jerusalem. In 626, the Byzantines lifted an Avar-Persian siege of Constantinople, after which the Avar threat faded. Heraclius then focused on the Persians, whom he defeated in a decisive battle in Mesopotamia (Nineveh) in 627. Khusro was toppled the following year and replaced by his son, Kavad, and Syria and Egypt were restored to Byzantine rule.

Heraclius had saved the empire, but having engineered one of Roman history's most astonishing comebacks he was soon confronted by an unexpected threat from out of the Arabian Desert. The Arab peoples had always been a familiar feature of the Roman Near East, but at no stage had they posed a serious challenge to imperial authority. In the 620s, the Arabs found unity under Muhammad and in the Islamic faith. Soon after Muhammad's death, his successor (caliph), Abu Bakr, led the Muslim faithful in a series of incursions into the Byzantine and Persian empires. Whether by design or not, the invaders were able to retain control of Syria and Iraq. Initially, the Byzantines viewed the Muslims as an exuberant heretical force that might be bought off or simply melt away, but the invaders had a vision for the world that they were determined to effectuate.

Islam had transformed the Arabs into an extremely coherent and motivated military force that out-fought the armies of both Persia and Byzantium. The Persian Empire collapsed and became part of the *dar al-Islam* (realm of Islam), while after a crushing defeat at the Battle of Yarmuk (636), Heraclius was loath to meet the Arabs again in open battle and withdrew his forces behind the Taurus Mountains, an effective barrier between the Near East and the cities of Asia Minor. Crucially, the Muslims consolidated their hold of former Roman territories by lightening the tax burden and by tolerating indigenous religious interests. Jews and non-Orthodox Christians such as the Monophysites were now free from official harassment. The Muslims also conquered Egypt in 641, although Alexandria held out until 646.

The sudden rise of the Islamic Empire or 'the Caliphate' shattered the Roman/Byzantine Empire. When Heraclius died in 641, the empire had been reduced to a rump consisting of Anatolia and Thrace, along with Calabria, Sicily, Sardinia and North Africa. The loss of Syria and Egypt forced the empire to survive on barely a quarter of its former revenues. Anatolia was now the empire's breadbasket, as well as its revenue and military recruitment base. The Muslim advance was halted at the Taurus Mountains, but the Byzantines could not stop the Arabs from using the mountain passes to conduct raids deep into Anatolia and from launching two fierce assaults on Constantinople in 674–678 and 717–718.

THE SEVENTH CENTURY 'DARK AGE'

The Islamic Conquests and the plague spelled the end of the *polis* and Graeco-Roman municipal culture. Arab raids transformed Anatolia into a vast region of military outposts that were meant to protect local villages. The original sites of such ancient cities as Ephesos, Sardis and

Pergamon were abandoned as the depleted citizenry relocated to nearby *kastra* (fortresses). Epidemics compounded the problem. Some cities, such as plague-riddled Aphrodisias, disappeared altogether. Meanwhile, the Byzantines had no choice but to concede the Balkans, where only a few fortified centres like Thessalonica and Monemnvasia in the Peloponnese were retained. In fact, by 700 the empire had only two cities worthy of the name. Aside from Constantinople there was Thessalonica, the city of St Demetrios, which stood alone in a region controlled by Slavic groups. Even the capital had barely survived this calamitous era, as its population plummeted to somewhere near 40,000, and large areas within its walled precincts reverted to farmland. Building activity was restricted to the maintenance of existing structures, and even something as important as the Aqueduct of Hadrian was left in disrepair.

Ironically, the Graeco-Roman city survived for several decades in the Islamic Empire. Under the Umayyad Dynasty (661–750), cities such as Edessa and Antioch flourished as in the past, although they would be overshadowed by Muslim-built cities such as Cairo, Mosul and Baghdad. The Umayyads also conducted government business in Greek, at least initially. In fact, Greek learning found a new lease under the patronage of a more open-minded ruling order, which valued 'Greek wisdom' and made a point of translating and mastering the Classical works. Muslim patronage did much to perpetuate the traditions of Greek learning when scholarship in crisis-ridden Byzantium was to all but disappear. John of Damascus (c.665–749), the greatest Greek theologian of the eighth century, as with many other writers, was free to produce innovative work under tolerant Muslim authority, as were Syrian Christian elites, who were inspired by the traditions of Greek learning and produced a vast body of literature.

Initially, Arab administration worked with Koine Greek and existing Byzantine systems, but with growing self-confidence came a desire to forge a distinctly Islamic civilization. By the beginning of the eighth century, Arabic had supplanted Greek and cities began to take on a distinctly Muslim appearance, with mosques and madrasas replacing churches and monasteries. If anything, the Caliphate was becoming more Persian, particularly after the Persian Abbasids overthrew the Umayyads in 750 and moved the capital of the Caliphate from Damascus to Baghdad. Indeed since having conquered the Sassanid Empire, the Arabs became captive to Persian culture. As a result, Islamic high culture and art became a synthesis of Persian and Arabic influences. As the modern historian Peter Brown has suggested, the Arab triumph also represented the ultimate triumph of Persia over Greece and Rome.[2]

Byzantium, in contrast, had descended into a 'dark age'. The archaeological data points to a steep decline in material conditions, and compounding the empire's security problems was the arrival in 679 of the Bulgars, the next in a long series of Turkic pastoral groups. They settled in Thrace and established their domination over the local Slav peoples, who had also since moved south of the Danube. Various Slav peoples, like the Drugubites, Sagudates, Berzetes, Baiunetes and Belegezites, had in fact settled in Greece itself. We know almost nothing about the political conditions in the area, except that most of the Greek mainland came under Slav domination, and that some sources refer to the disappearance of the Greek population. In modern debates between partisan nationalist groups, for whom bloodlines remain a vitally important matter, the fate of the Greeks is crucial in that it determines whether modern Greeks are *real* Greeks or re-Hellenized Slavs. For what it's worth, the extant evidence does not allow us to make any kind of definitive claims about Greece's cultural demography, except that there was extensive Slavic settlement in the region and that Greek communities predominated in Attica, the eastern Peloponnese and the islands. We also know that Greeks fled to Anatolia and southern Italy, and that many of their descendants were later repatriated to Greece.

As for the seventh-century Byzantine Empire itself, it had now become *more* Greek, at least in the sense that territories still under its authority tended to be Greek-speaking regions. Historians begin to describe a more inward looking polity that was obsessed by its fall from Grace and the search for redemption. That God had deserted his new 'Israelites' was deemed self-evident, but explanations varied. God's will was usually ascertained by the test of war. Muslims believed firmly that their own successes confirmed the veracity of Muhammad's revelations, while the Byzantines believed their woes were divine retribution for religious errors. To reclaim God's favour, they had to reinstitute the true Orthodox faith. Thus the military reverses suffered during the reign of Constans II (641–668) signified for many the worthlessness of Monotheletism, the emperor's favoured solution to the Christological impasse that proposed that Christ had two natures but one will.

On a more practical level, the Byzantine state recognized that survival required the reorganization of provincial society and administration along military lines. Over the course of this dark age, provincial units known as *themata* replaced the smaller, city-focused 'diocese' created under Diocletian. Each *thema* was ruled by a *strategos* who had his own standing force, also known as a *thema*. The *themata* in Anatolia could also call on the support of demobilized soldiers that had been resettled along the frontiers with land grants. The borderlands were thereafter guarded by hardy military folk who had a stake in defending the empire's territorial integrity and who were familiar with Arab and Bulgar combat methods. The empire therefore had expert provincial reserves that could be deployed expeditiously when required. However, there was at least one significant drawback. Regional military governors became powerful figures in Byzantine politics, and the more ambitious among them could unseat the emperor. Constans II, possibly the author of the military reforms, was definitely its first victim. He faced rebellion from the *strategos* of an eastern *thema*, but it was another *strategos* who assassinated the emperor in 668 and who then tried unsuccessfully to claim the throne. There followed a spate of palace coups between 695 and 717, many of which were led by military governors.

These changes greatly altered the nature of the imperial aristocracy. With provincial administration under military control, provincial social elites streamed to Constantinople, where they began to fill the Senate and the most important offices of state – it also appears that the established aristocratic lines had more or less become extinct. The most distinctive feature of this new imperial aristocracy was its dependence on the emperor and imperial favours. The average aristocrat now aspired to claim an office in state administration, with his salary being his main source of income. Byzantium therefore featured an all-powerful emperor and an insecure elite that competed ruthlessly for imperial offices and which was always implicated in dynastic intrigue.

THE FIRST AGE OF ICONOCLASM (717–775)

With the approach of the new century came a second wave of Arab expansionism. In 698, the Byzantines lost Carthage and North Africa, and by 711 the Caliphate had expanded into Spain and further into Central Asia. In 717, a massive Muslim force besieged Constantinople with the support of the Bulgars, but fortune this time favoured the Byzantines: that the Arab fleet was showered en route with volcanic rocks from Santorini was interpreted as a good omen. The Byzantines also had a secret weapon. A mysterious liquid substance known as 'Greek fire', which combusted upon contact with water, was used to decimate the Arab fleet. The Arab army was still determined to breech the city walls, but it was forced to endure an exceptionally harsh winter, as well as plague and attacks from their erstwhile allies the Bulgars. The siege was eventually lifted, and the general who led the defence, Leo the Syrian (Leo III, 717–741), was confirmed as emperor.

This Arab siege of 717 happened to be the last. Growing ructions within the Caliphate and the Abbasid takeover in 750 gave Byzantium time to recover and achieve military parity along the eastern front. Leo's dynamic son, Constantine V (741–775), further strengthened his military forces and the monarch's personal security by forming elite regiments under his direct authority. Known as *tagmata*, these regiments were stationed in or near the capital and became the core of the Byzantine army. Indeed, under Leo and the Isaurian Dynasty (717–842), the empire began to enjoy some semblance of normalcy. Emperors were able to attend to 'peacetime' activities, with Leo engaging in law reform and Constantine restoring public monuments and utilities like the main aqueduct. He also treated the capital to lavish imperial triumphs and repopulated its suburbs with settlers from Greece and the Aegean Islands.

However, the fact that the Isaurian emperors had engineered an imperial recovery was not enough to assuage their many critics. The surviving sources, in fact, are extremely hostile, with some likening both father and son to Lucifer. For Leo III and Constantine V are remembered for their attempt to abolish icon veneration, and for that all their other achievements counted for nothing.

The iconoclast controversy overshadows everything we know about Byzantium in the eighth and ninth centuries. The role of images in Christian worship, particularly portraits of Christ, was not new to theological discourse, but after the initial Islamic Conquests the issue assumed critical importance. Leo's basic objection to icon veneration can be gleaned from his correspondence with Caliph Umar II (717–720), in which he conceded that images had no support in Scripture, while Umar affirmed the link between Muslim military successes to the strict proscription of images. Back in Heraclius' day, the Byzantines had carried icons on campaign and nailed images of the Virgin to the ramparts, and yet they had suffered defeat after defeat. As with many of his contemporaries, Leo reasoned that icons were a liability. Since true ' odoxy' was the only insurance against bad fortune, icon worship eemed unorthodox and therefore banned: 'iconoclasm' literally 'the smashing of icons'. Modern scholars have also read Leo's an attempt to assert greater authority over the Church and the popular religion, particularly the cults of saints. By bringing devotional life under centralized control, the emperor might be better placed to prevent deviations from orthodoxy.

Iconoclasm found considerable support within sections of Byzantine society, particularly military circles, but for most Byzantines an icon was an intimate possession that could be found in most Christian households. Images of Christ, the Virgin and saints were regarded as the interface with the sacred, offering direct access to divine favour and protection. Its proponents claimed they were *representations* of the holy, but critics could see that they were treated as sacred objects in their own right. The empire was full of icons that were renowned for their miraculous powers: some were known to weep and bleed.

Leo's determination to move against icon worship was confirmed in 726, when another volcanic explosion at Santorini darkened the skies and pelted the Aegean with large pumice stones. In 730, he ordered his clergy to remove icons from churches, and our sources, all extremely hostile, depict a hellish phase of persecution. Of the emperor, one source reports that:

> The wild beast summoned all his subjects to a rally and roared like a lion in their midst as he belched forth from his angry heart fire and sulphur, pronouncing these grievous words: 'The making of icons is the craft of idolatry; they may not be worshipped.'[3]

Historians are reluctant to heed such biased material, especially as archaeological research does not support the claim of wanton destruction. Under Constantine V, however, priests and monks were persecuted, and there was at least one notable martyr. In 764, Stephen the Younger, founder of a monastic order and staunch defender of icon veneration, was tortured and executed.

THE TRIUMPH OF ORTHODOXY (775–843)

One could safely state that most Byzantines remained ardent 'iconophiles', including members of the royal household. It was only a matter of time before icon veneration was officially restored (787), but later military reverses against the Bulgars saw the pendulum swing back again. In 811, the armies of Krum, the Bulgar Khan, captured the emperor Nikephoros I (802–811) and used his skull as a drinking cup.

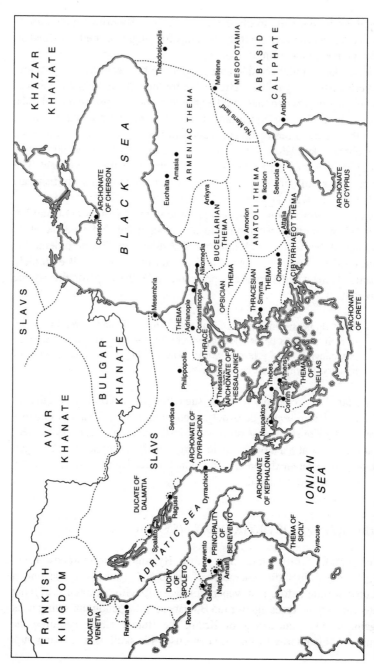

Map 6 The Byzantine Empire AD c.780

When the iconoclast Leo V (813–820) managed to turn the tables on the Bulgars, the official campaign to eradicate icons was resumed. Bouts of persecution followed, but this second phase of iconoclasm was characterized much more by robust debate and intellectual ferment. Whatever the merits of the rival arguments, the protagonists were inspired to read widely and mount impressive learned arguments. The revival of education in Constantinople also had to do with the arrival since the 790s of Christian scholars from the courts and monasteries of the Muslim East, where official attitudes for the moment had become less tolerant. Among the refugees was the chronicler George Synkellos, whose work inspired new interest in historiography. Education refocused again on the study of Attic Greek and Classical literature, including philosophy and science. We even find the term 'Hellene' being employed positively to describe individuals steeped in Classical learning. Thus, Leo the Mathematician (c.790–869), who was renowned for his teaching of ancient philosophy and mathematics, described himself as a Hellene, even though the term still had pagan connotations. Overall, the revival of Hellenism reflected a culture less overawed by Islam and more confident in its own heritage. The period is especially significant in seeing the transferral of classical works onto parchment, which is more durable than papyrus, and the invention of minuscule (joined cursive writing), which made it easier to reproduce texts.

The most telling impact of iconoclasm, however, was its role in defining 'Orthodoxy' as a distinct form of Christianity. In 838, Byzantine society was shocked by the Muslim sacking of Amorion, a town in central Anatolia and well inside the eastern frontier. Iconoclasm was discredited, and on 11 March 843, the formal restoration of icons was celebrated as the restoration of Orthodoxy. To this day, the event is commemorated on the first Sunday of Lent as the 'Feast of Orthodoxy'. In an important sense, however, Orthodoxy was not so much restored as remade, for the legacy of iconoclasm was to make images an essential part of Orthodox worship. Theologians such as St John of Damascus (c.665–749) and Theodore of Studios (759–826) had provided the intellectual arguments that claimed images to be a vital conduit between the temporal and the sacred. John of Damascus reasoned thus:

> How could God be born out of lifeless things? . . . The nature of God remains the same as before, the flesh created in time is quickened by a logical and reasoning soul. I honour all matter besides, and venerate it. Through it, filled with divine power and grace, my salvation has come to me.[4]

Icons were accepted as the interface with the sacred and were thus accorded a level of importance that rivalled the liturgy and the sacraments. For that reason, they came under much closer Church regulation. From the ninth century, icons were restricted to church interiors and homes, and stylistic conventions were strictly observed. The distinctly schematic 'Byzantine' icon, with its heavy lines and strong colours, became the exclusive standard. What had been a commonplace feature of popular devotion had been firmly appropriated by the Church.

The 'triumph of Orthodoxy' in 843 had lasting importance for another reason. In foreign eyes, icon-centred worship was what made Orthodoxy 'Greek'. It was *this* Greek Orthodoxy that was disseminated among the Balkan Slavs and the Russians in the ninth century. In fact, from this period one begins to see the formation of a series of 'Greek' Orthodox states, a commonwealth bound by a uniform doctrine and approach to religious practice. Clearly, the issue of language was comparatively unimportant. It was the celebrated Thessalonican missionary St Cyril (826–882) who invented Glagolitic (early Slavonic) script and launched Slavonic as a church language.

THE REVIVAL OF GREECE (800–1000)

The revival of Byzantine fortunes was accompanied by an improvement in material conditions. Archaeological data suggests population growth and rising agricultural productivity. Farming benefited from a warming climate and hence an extended growing season, and from greater security from foreign raiders. We again begin to see cities with more than 10,000 inhabitants, such as Adrianople, Ankyra, Ephesos, Trebizond, Nicaea and Smyrna. Another measure of prosperity was the reintroduction and mass circulation of imperial coinage. Revenues increased markedly because of growing tax receipts and a significantly expanded tax base, especially as the empire recovered more territory in Greece. Byzantium grew rich again, and Constantinople began to reclaim its former lustre. Information is scanty, but the resumption of building construction is suggested by ordinances prescribed by Leo VI (886–912), who noted the need for tougher regulation of building allotments and the demarcation of space between buildings. Another clue is the expanding trade in luxury items and growing evidence of lavish, conspicuous consumption among social elites.

Greece also began its slow recovery. The few southern Greek territories that remained in imperial hands had been organized as the *thema* of 'Hellas', with Corinth as its centre. Thessalonica served as the capital of another *thema*, while Crete and the Ionian Islands formed smaller *archonates* (provincial units). The reconquest of the rest of Greece began under Constantine V, but most of the work was done during the reign of Nikephoros I (802–813). Little is known about these campaigns, except that they were led by an obscure general named Skleros, who receives scant mention in the chronicles, perhaps because of the unglamorous nature of the campaigns and perhaps because the empire was preoccupied with its struggle with Krum, the Bulgar khan. The reconquest of Greece might have been a conscious attempt to redeem imperial territory or to deal with Slav groups that had been harassing burgeoning Byzantine towns such as Patras.

The work of Skleros set the stage for the regeneration of Greece. With reconquest came extensive land reclamation and the creation of new agricultural settlements. Imperial motives were obvious enough. By transplanting loyal Byzantines to the inland valleys of Macedonia, Thessaly and the western Peloponnese, the local Slavs were outnumbered and easily pacified. Interestingly, provincial subjects in Hellas were described from this period as *Helladikoi*, meaning 'people of Greece', rather than with the loaded term 'Hellenes'.

Not since the age of Justinian had Greece presented such a settled pattern of population growth and urban regeneration. The renewal of prosperity and urbanization in Greece had to do with the region's reincorporation into Mediterranean trade networks, if not the wider world – archaeologists have even uncovered a fragment of Chinese porcelain in excavations at Methone in the western Peloponnese. Since the seventh century, sea trade had been circumventing the Greek mainland owing to the collapse of its trading centres, save for a few fortified outposts like Monemvasia, but in the ninth century trade was being redirected *into* Greece, as witnessed by the boom in traffic coming through the Gulf of Corinth from the 830s, which then radiated inland through ports such as Patras, Naupaktos and Corinth. The growth of external trade is strongly suggested by the progressively larger yield of coins from excavations at Corinth, which passing pilgrims described as a reawakened city. Athens, Thebes, Patras and Corinth had again become wealthy manufacturing centres, and there was also a resumption of building construction. New churches and monasteries were to be found throughout the Peloponnesian and northern Greek landscape.

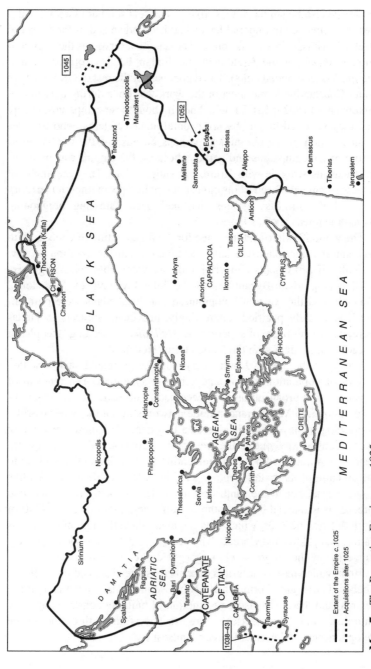

Map 7 The Byzantine Empire AD c.1025

Legend:
— Extent of the Empire c. 1025
······ Acquisitions after 1025

Labels on map:
1045
1052
Theodosiopolis
Manzikert
Trebizond
Edessa
Melitene
Samosata
Aleppo
Damascus
Tiberias
Jerusalem
Antioch
Tarsos
CILICIA
CYPRUS
Theodosia (Kaffa)
CHERSON
Cherson
B L A C K   S E A
Ankyra
Amorion
CAPPADOCIA
Ikonion
M E D I T E R R A N E A N   S E A
RHODES
Nicaea
Constantinople
Adrianople
Smyrna
Ephesos
CRETE
AEGEAN SEA
Phillippopolis
Nicopolis
Thessalonica
Servia
Larissa
Thebes
Athens
Corinth
Nicopolis
Sirmium
DALMATIA
Ragusa
Spalato
ADRIATIC SEA
Dyrrachion
Bari
Taranto
CATEPANATE OF ITALY
CALABRIA
Taormina
Syracuse
1038–43

120

IMPERIAL BYZANTIUM (863–1025)

The heartland of the empire was still Anatolia, but it continued to suffer disruptions from Muslim raiding parties from the emirates (Muslim principalities) that lined the eastern borders. Christian communities in the frontier zone of Cappadocia in east-central Anatolia had learned to withdraw into vast underground cities (near modern Goreme, Kaymakli and Derinkuyu) that were designed to accommodate thousands of inhabitants for long periods. These extraordinary subterranean complexes included all the facilities one might expect in a normal settlement, with churches, refectories, mills, storage facilities and wells. From the latter half of the ninth century, however, these elaborate sanctuaries fell into disuse. From 863, following a major victory over a Muslim army at Lalakaon in eastern Anatolia, the Byzantines not only managed to seal the frontier but also began regular raids into Muslim territories.

This turning of the tables marked a watershed in the empire's history. Byzantium was unique among early Medieval states in having a large bureaucracy and an efficient taxation system from which it received the bulk of its income. The aristocracy depended on office salaries that were funded by taxation. From the mid-ninth century, however, the abundance of war booty created a financially independent aristocracy along the frontier zone. Known later as the *dynatoi* (powerful), these new military elites forged regional power networks that often transcended imperial boundaries and created alternative centres of political power within the empire. Of particular concern to the imperial state was the fact that the *dynatoi* were accumulating landholdings at the expense of the peasantry, which diminished the imperial fiscal structure and the *thema* system as the chief source of military recruitment.

The rise of a financially independent aristocracy was to pose significant challenges to the emperor, but it was also the dynamic element behind the resurgence of Byzantine power. The 'Skleros' figure who reconquered Greece was among the first of an illustrious line of *dynatoi* that restored Byzantium's reputation as a great military power.

However, the revival of the Byzantine Empire cannot be measured adequately by territorial expansion. Indeed, until the reign of Basil II in the late tenth century, the state had been reluctant to acquire territories that might be difficult to defend or where most of the inhabitants were not Orthodox. Official ideology had it that the empire was universal, but it was a claim that was upheld in a symbolic sense. Thus in diplomatic dealings, Byzantine delegates always sought *recognition* of the emperor as the universal ruler (*pantokrator*). In practice, since the seventh century the empire had been conditioned mentally and militarily to defending its existing territories. Besides, even in this period of revival, imperial armies did not enjoy a decisive military edge over rivals. During the course of the ninth century, the empire lost Sicily to Muslim forces in a long and arduous struggle. And when the last Sicilian outpost fell in 902, the empire was struggling to survive a second Bulgar challenge led by Tsar Symeon (893–927).

It was only in the mid-900s that Byzantium re-emerged as the most powerful state in the Mediterranean. While its significant rivals, the Abbasid Caliphate and the Bulgarian and Carolingian empires, had either collapsed or faded, Byzantium began to develop a taste for territorial expansion. In 955, Constantine VII Porphyrogenitos (913–959), better known for his scholarly achievements, despatched his chief military commander, Nikephoros Phokas, to deal with Muslim military incursions from along the Syrian frontier. Nikephoros went on to claim much of Syria and Armenia and transformed these territories into military provinces. From this point the empire begins to expand. Cilicia and Cyprus were conquered in 965, the rest of Armenia by 967, and Antioch in 969. Nikephoros also used his position as imperial commander to claim the throne following the unexpected death of Romanos II in 963. His cousin and successor, John Tzimiskes (969–976), extended Byzantine rule into Lebanon and eastern Bulgaria and carried out raids into Palestine.

Since 867, the imperial throne had been in the hands of the Macedonian dynasty, but Nikephoros and Tzimiskes were of the Phokas family, the most powerful of the *dynatoi* clans. With Tzimiskes' passing in 976, the throne was meant to revert exclusively to Basil, the young son of Romanos II, but as Basil was still in his minority he was forced to defend his throne against two formidable generals: first Bardas Skleros and then Bardas Phokas. Basil II (976–1025) prevailed only after a long and destructive civil war, and largely because of generous support from Kievan Rus, a new power that had recently converted to Orthodox Christianity. It was Rus that supplied the emperor with the Varangian Guard, an elite corps of Russian and Scandinavian mercenaries that served as the imperial bodyguard.

Basil II stands out as the emperor who restored Byzantium as the superpower of the Mediterranean. He conquered Bulgaria and reduced Serbia, Croatia, Georgia and much of Syria to imperial protectorates. Under Basil, medieval Byzantium reached the acme of its power. In much later times, he was remembered as *o Boulgaroktonos* (the Bulgar-slayer) for having supposedly blinded 15,000 prisoners-of-war, sparing every tenth prisoner with one eye so the rest could be led back to Bulgaria. Nowadays, scholars agree that this story was almost certainly a later invention, but it did convey a ruthless disposition that the younger Basil developed whilst fighting for his throne. In fact, Basil had little taste for war, but he was determined to retain close control of his military forces, which partly explains why he spent much of his long reign on campaign.

For all Basil's military successes, Byzantium was still an empire that was primed for defence. For as with Justinian's imperial forays, Basil's conquests were costly. So too was his massive military payroll and the empire's method of diplomacy, which featured lavish distributions of gifts. These expenses were borne by the average taxpayer: the village peasant. The wars had predictably caused great social distress, and none of his special measures, such as a temporary abolition of state taxes, appeared to improve matters.

In fact, Basil's rather eccentric measure forced his cash-strapped brother, Constantine VIII (1025–1028), to demand rapid collection of the taxes that had been waived, causing even greater social stress. Financial problems continued under his successors, largely because of ongoing frontier warfare and the debasement of Byzantine coinage, which led to crippling inflation.

THE RISE OF THE KOMNENOI (1025–1095)

Byzantium's greatest challenge, however, came from a new set of aggressive foreign powers that converged on Constantinople from three different directions. The Pechenegs were a pastoral group that launched major incursions from across the Danube from the late 1040s. In the meantime, the Seljuks, a group of Oghuz Turks that had converted to Islam, had claimed control of a large region around the southern Caspian Sea, from where they conducted frequent raids into Byzantium's eastern territories. The third challenge emerged in the 1060s, when the Normans, a formidable feudal force that enjoyed the backing of the Papacy, claimed Byzantine territories in southern Italy. In military terms, the Pechenegs, Seljuks and Normans posed special problems. As pastoralists, the Pechenegs and Seljuks were master horsemen and archers, and as such they often had the better of the less mobile infantry-based armies. The Normans, on the other hand, were archetypal feudal knights who had no peers as heavy cavalry or in hand-to-hand combat. Not that the Byzantines were incapable of matching these groups in the field, for by this stage the empire had come to rely on foreign mercenaries that provided the same valuable martial skills. The typical Byzantine army of the eleventh century, therefore, included large numbers of Turkic horsemen and Latin knights, for with its strong tax system the empire was uniquely positioned to buy the best available military force.

As Basil II's military ventures showed, however, the fiscal system had its limitations. Whereas the Pechenegs and Seljuks were always capable of raising vast armies of horsemen very quickly and cheaply, Byzantine armies were massively expensive and imposed great strains on over-taxed peasantry. More to the point, the empire could not cope with simultaneous attacks, as happened in the 1070s and 1080s. In 1071, the Normans completed their conquest of Byzantine Italy and launched dangerous forays across the Adriatic. That same year, Romanos IV Diogenes (1068–1071) sought to bring the Seljuks to heel, but his army suffered a decisive defeat at Manzikert near Lake Van, and Romanos himself was captured.

Over the next 20 years, Byzantium was in complete disarray. The Seljuk sultan, Alp Arslan (1063–1072), released the emperor after receiving generous concessions, but in the meantime the Doukas family had seized the imperial throne with the support of the Varangian Guard. With Byzantium consumed by civil war, the Seljuks moved into Anatolia unimpeded and brought in vast numbers of Muslim settlers. From this early period, we begin to see the gradual 'Islamicization' of Anatolia, with Islam becoming the predominant religion along the central plateau.

Meanwhile, the great military families of the Anatolian marches competed for the imperial throne, but by the time the matter was settled all the provinces except Greece had been overrun. Alexios Komnenos had emerged as the unchallenged claimant to the throne in 1081, but he struggled desperately to finance new mercenary armies in order to save his empire. Fortunately, the Norman threat subsided in 1085 when its leader, Robert Guiscard (1015–1085), died suddenly during the campaign. The Seljuks became preoccupied with their own civil wars, while the Pechenegs were crushed in 1091 with the help of the Cumans, a rival nomadic pastoral group.

Alexios was given breathing space to repair the state's finances and consolidate his authority in Constantinople. He also saw the necessity of reconstituting the ruling order, given that aristocratic rivalries had brought the empire to the brink of collapse. Alexios' solution was to unite the leading families through a series of elaborate marriage arrangements. Thus the Komnenoi and the other *dynatoi*, especially the Doukas, Palaiologos and Melissenos families, came to form an extended imperial family that monopolized the highest offices and transformed the ruling order into a closed circle.

Alexios' other major task was to reclaim Anatolia, still the Greek Orthodox heartland of the empire and homeland of the Komnenoi. Alexios needed many more military recruits, hence in early 1095 he despatched an embassy to Pope Urban II (1088–1099), and whilst we do not know the contents of his correspondence it is likely that his request for mercenaries also featured appeals to the Christian brotherhood. Later that year, however, Urban used the emperor's request to proclaim a Christian crusade against the Islamic East and to reclaim the Holy Land. Urban had struck a chord, and within a short space of time thousands of armed pilgrims made their way for the Holy Land via Constantinople.

The emperor had unwittingly ignited the Crusades and a new threat to imperial security. As his position at home was never altogether secure, he could not risk the prolonged presence of armed contingents that might be exploited by ambitious relatives, nor could his ill-disciplined visitors be let loose in the city. Alexios' refusal to embrace fully the movement, however, gave the Crusaders cause for resentment and to doubt his fidelity. That he excused himself from personally leading the movement into the Near East did little to revive Byzantine claims to universal authority, although he did manage to secure oaths of fealty from its leaders, along with guarantees that all captured cities and lands would be transferred to imperial authority. In return, his Latin vassals expected military aid, supplies and intelligence.

BYZANTIUM AND THE WEST (1095–1180)

Until the First Crusade, Latin Europe barely rated in Byzantine and Near Eastern strategic thinking, although Norman forays into Italy and the Balkans had given the Byzantines a sharp taste of feudal military power. When the First Crusade succeeded in conquering much of Syria and Palestine, the eastern Mediterranean was suddenly exposed to an exuberant force that proved exceedingly hard to dislodge. Since the mid-tenth century, Latin Europe, which included all regions that came under the direct spiritual authority of the Bishop of Rome, had developed into an

Image 5 Imperial women: the Empress Zoe depicted with her third husband, Constantine IX; Zoe was instrumental in installing four emperors, and ruled jointly with her sister Theodora in 1042 (Hagia Sophia, Istanbul, Turkey) *(photo credit: Vanni/Art Resource, New York)*

ideologically coherent and more affluent world. The Latin Church or Papacy had also become a much more ambitious organization that sought to make good its claim as the supreme authority over all Christians. A parallel development was the equally striking rise of Europe's feudal aristocracies and their ability to amass formidable, if unwieldy, military retinues. The growth of Latin self-confidence was mirrored by a declining regard for Byzantium's moral authority, which was demonstrated by a more forceful insistence on Papal ecclesiastical supremacy and by the propensity of Latin monarchs to claim the Roman imperial heritage. With Papal support, the Ottonians in Germany began a process of *renovatio imperii Romanorum* (renewing the Roman Empire), which included the crowning in 1027 of Conrad II as 'emperor', and the creation of the 'Holy Roman Empire'.

The First Crusade, however, had a much more direct bearing on the future of the Byzantine Empire. Against all odds, the factious Crusaders survived the terrible trek across Anatolia and claimed control of much of western Syria and Palestine. As the emperor's support was considered too modest, the Crusaders felt less compunction about fulfilling their debts, particularly after Alexios had failed to aid the Crusaders trapped at Antioch in June 1098. When the vastly outnumbered and starving Crusaders put the Muslim besiegers to flight, Alexios' moral authority plummeted. He was deemed to have failed his duties as overlord, and for many Latins the siege of Antioch confirmed a widely held view that 'the Greeks' were disingenuous allies. That Alexios maintained diplomatic ties with the Islamic powers, a normal contingency in Mediterranean wartime diplomacy, was seen by Latins as yet another example of Greek treachery. When new Crusader states were created in Syria and Palestine, little heed was paid to the emperor's entitlements.

Yet Byzantines had long since become accustomed to dealing with such hazardous quandaries, and under Alexios, his son John II (1118–1143) and grandson Manuel I (1143–1180), the empire remained the single most powerful state in the Mediterranean. The later part of Alexios' reign saw the recovery of much of western Anatolia, while John II, the most able military emperor since Basil II, reasserted imperial authority over the entire Balkan region, while also reclaiming the rest of Anatolia, save for the semi-arid central plateau. By 1137–1138, after having improved the empire's security in the Balkans and Anatolia, John began intervening directly in the Crusader states' affairs, mainly with an eye to claiming Antioch, but also to securing Crusader recognition of his universal authority. Under Manuel I, the empire did not expand appreciably, but it maintained a strategic position through energetic political engagement on all fronts. Manuel's busy foreign policy record is too detailed to recount, but it included such typically 'Byzantine methods' as lending financial aid to the Lombard League to block German imperial expansion into Italy, and installing his son-in-law, Bela III, on the Hungarian throne in 1172. His most effective weapon was gold. Byzantium's incomparable wealth was used to reduce rivals into clients, for at one time or another imperial aims were realized with the flow of gold into Ottonian, Hungarian, Papal, Seljuk and French coffers.

THE KOMNENIAN GOLDEN AGE

The Latins venerated Manuel, but they did not necessarily think much of 'Greeks'. Along with the Romans of a much earlier age, the Latins, or 'Franks' as they were commonly known, regarded Byzantines as a debauched and treacherous people. The chronicler William of Tyre tells us that Manuel, who admired some Latin attributes, such as courtliness, and who employed many in his service, did so rely 'on [Latin] fidelity and ability that he passed over the Greeks as soft and effeminate and entrusted important affairs to Latins alone'.[5] In Latin minds, Byzantium's reliance on foreign mercenaries was telling, as was the Greek affinity for luxury and for learning rather than fighting. Needless to say, what appeared decadent to some was read as sophistication by others. Constantinople was beguiling to all comers, even the most blinkered Latin visitors. When the chronicler, Fulcher of Chartres, made his first visit in 1096, he was in awe of its size and splendour:

> Oh what a noble and beautiful city is Constantinople! How many monasteries and palaces it contains, constructed with wonderful skill! How many remarkable things may be seen in the principal avenues and even in the lesser streets! It is tedious to enumerate the wealth that there is of every kind, of gold, silver and robes of many kinds, of holy relics.[6]

Fulcher's effusive description was standard. More than a century later, Geoffrey de Villehardouin wrote that 'those who have never seen Constantinople before gazed very intently at the city, never having ever imagined there could be such a place in the world'.[7]

As noted earlier, Byzantium's majesty is not reflected so much in its territorial acquisitions or military record, but by its wealth and opulence, and nothing conveyed these qualities better than Constantinople. Under the Komnenoi, it had as many as 400,000 inhabitants, making it by far the largest city in Europe, rivalled only by Muslim Cordoba – Venice, with upwards of 80,000, was the largest Latin city. Pilgrims, crusaders and merchants were equally struck by its sumptuousness and cosmopolitan vitality. Anyone approaching the city centre via the main thoroughfare (the *Meze*) from the Golden Gate, or even the other route starting from the Gate of Adrianople, were entreated to relentless monumentality: grand churches, statues, forums, palatial residences, infirmaries, welfare institutions and much more. The centrepiece was still the Hagia Sophia, but there was also the Augousteion, the Hippodrome and the impregnable Walls of Theodosius. As with Hellenistic Alexandria and early Imperial Rome, the cityscape of Constantinople conveyed imperial pretensions as well as a superior level of cultural attainment. In this and in many other respects, twelfth-century Byzantium was still a 'classical' society: Byzantine notions of an ideal society continued to be imagined through visions of the ideal *polis*.

By the Age of Komnenoi, the empire had once again become a world of *poleis*. Thessalonica remained the second largest city with 150,000 inhabitants, but the standard sized city, such as Corinth, Ohrid, Monemvasia, Athens and Thebes, had upwards of 20,000. Greece figured prominently in this period. One Arab geographer claimed there were between 13 and 16 significant cities in the Peloponnese alone, and what made each centre significant was production and trade. Corinth and especially Thebes became major centres of silk and cloth making. Immigration was a sign of vitality. Jewish refugees from Fatimid Egypt brought expertise in glass and silk production to the Greek mainland: as many as 2000 Jews relocated to Thebes. Perhaps the clearest indication of ongoing urban renewal was the extent to which urban elites were prepared to invest in art and particularly in church construction.

There were other aspects of Byzantine civilization that impressed the Latins, such as bureaucratic government and the extraordinary reach of imperial authority. By medieval standards, the Byzantine Empire was an extremely centralized state: its influence extended directly into every locality. It could impose a single currency, along with a single standard for weights and measures. In many significant ways, therefore, Byzantium's was still a sophisticated ancient polity that also proved to be more cohesive and resilient than any of its counterparts in the medieval era.

The Byzantines were assiduous about preserving the Hellenic tradition in education. The standard curriculum had not much changed since Hellenistic times; the average Byzantine aristocrat was expected to have mastered Attic Greek and to be well read in the Classics. The twelfth century in particular witnessed a flowering of belles-lettres. Classical playwrights, poets and philosophers inspired new works and conscious imitations, and there was also an outpouring of critical scholarship. Typical was the *oeuvre* of Eustathios of Thessaloniki (1115–*c*.1196), who produced detailed commentaries of Homer, Pindar and Aristophanes. The age also produced a spate of learned studies on science, medicine, geography and many other secular topics, and could boast its own 'classics', such as Anna Comnena's *Alexiad*, a history that could be compared favourably with any of the great texts of antiquity.

Scholarship benefited from the existence of a literary 'scene' or something akin to a reading public. Anna Comnena and other rich elites patronized promising scholars and held court in circles that shared the patron's literary and scholarly tastes. While there were no Byzantine universities as such, Constantinople and other major Byzantine cities were full of private schools, while the state provided salaries to noted scholars in various fields of secular knowledge. Another striking aspect of medieval Byzantine was the fact that literacy was not exclusive to the social elites. After all, the imperial civil service was filled with literate functionaries from modest backgrounds, and it is clear that there were also readers to be found among middling social groups. The Komnenian era was distinguished by the flowering of Greek vernacular literature, particularly romances and satires: it is from this period that we date the first written account of *Digenis Akrites*, perhaps the best-known Byzantine epic. Certainly, the great bulk of Byzantine and medieval European literary output was still religious in nature (hagiography, theology and particularly works discussing heresy), but it was the relative importance ascribed to secular learning that offered the sharpest contrast between East and West.

It was the more keenly felt resonance of Hellenism, however, that really set Komnenian culture apart from earlier periods of Byzantine history and from contemporary cultural developments in the West. The reason why Hellenism had greater purchase had to do with the *barbaroi* (barbarians) who had inundated the Byzantine world, particularly the Franks (crusader knights, pilgrims and merchants), but also the Vikings, Turks, Slavs, Georgians and the many other peoples that served in the imperial army. Byzantine aristocrats sensed a greater urge to define

'Romanness', and for them the key was Greek heritage and education. In the ninth century, Hellenism was identified with certain individuals, like Leo the Mathematician, but by the eleventh and twelfth centuries interest was far more commonplace and pronounced. We begin to read of scholars claiming the Greek Classical heritage as 'our' heritage. In an oration to the Emperor John I, the court poet Theodore Prodromos (c.1110–1170) likened his enemies, the Seljuk Turks, to the Persians of Xerxes, and praised the emperor for having denied the Seljuk's earth and water from *kath imas Ellas* (*our* Greece).

That did not mean, however, that Komnenian elites began to describe themselves as Hellenes. Rather, it was one among a number of attributes that defined them as Romans: indeed Orthodoxy was infinitely more important in this regard. Hellenism does, however, assume an enhanced significance in the ensuing era, when the *barbaroi* seized the capital and divided the empire.

6

The Greek *Oikoumene* (1200–1700): Living under Frankish and Ottoman Rule

Soon after the death of Manuel Komnenos in 1180, the Byzantine court degenerated into a farcical display of court intrigue, murder and palace coups. The esteem enjoyed by the empire under the early Komnenoi dissipated quickly as Manuel's querulous successors allowed foreign armies to rampage through the provinces and the state to slide into bankruptcy. The Byzantine Empire finally collapsed. In 1204, Constantinople was seized and plundered by a Crusader army seeking to recoup outstanding debts; the provinces were broken up into a series of minor principalities.

In 1261, a Greek Orthodox potentate managed to reclaim Constantinople and declare the 'Roman Empire' restored. Within a short period, the remarkable Michael VIII Palaiologos also succeeded in re-establishing the empire as a significant regional power, but he had less success in normalizing the domestic front. Michael believed he could turn back the clock and reinstate the moral and political authority of the imperial monarchy and become an absolute ruler in the tradition of Constantine and Justinian. However, much had changed since the age of the Komnenoi. The Greek world (*oikoumene*) of 1261 had gained a greater sense of coherence because of the Latin invasion, but it was not as receptive to the traditional symbols of imperial unity. When Byzantine forces set out to reclaim the Peloponnese, they encountered resistance from local Greeks and Latins. Being 'Roman' no longer presupposed being a Roman subject.

What had changed? The extraordinary longevity of the Byzantine Empire had been a function of the unity forged between an autocracy and its Orthodox Christian subjects. That unity was symbolized above all by the emperor and his city. So long as Constantinople survived, so too did the empire. However, the Latin interregnum (1204–1261) had greatly weakened these associations. Certainly, since before the Komnenoi the Byzantine state had been combating the growth of aristocratic power and other centrifugal forces (city, monastic and regional), but the interregnum had fast-tracked this decentralizing trend. In the radically changed conditions of 1261, the Greek *oikoumene* regarded 'Orthodoxy' as the fundamental criterion of Roman identity. In places as far removed as Cyprus and Epiros, where Greeks lived sometimes contentedly under foreign suzerains, it was the Church rather than the emperor (and his city) that was the ultimate moral authority.

THE ROAD TO 1204

If one were to isolate the most significant factor behind the decline and fall of the Byzantine Empire, it would be the ruling elite's willingness to sacrifice imperial interests for private political gain. Its extraordinary capacity for self-immolation was starkly exposed following the death of Manuel I in 1180. From the outset, vicious court intrigue centred on the regency of Alexios II (1180–1183). His mother, Maria of Antioch, had survived a challenge from her stepdaughter, but it was one of Manuel's cousins and his greatest rival, Andronikos Komnenos (1883–1885), who claimed the regency by force in 1182. Although in his sixties, Andronikos carried the energy and ambition of a much younger man. In 1183 he felt secure enough to have both the empress and Alexios strangled and then wage a brutal campaign against all his potential rivals within the ruling clan. Many Komnenoi sought refuge in foreign courts, where they begged for intervention against Andronikos. In the meantime, frontier defences were neglected and the provinces were overrun. When news came of the Norman seizure of Thessaloniki in 1185, Andronikos was deposed and tortured by mobs, which then dragooned Issac Angelos, a marginal member of the ruling clan and one of the few left in Constantinople. For the next ten years (1185–1195), Isaac had mixed success in restoring imperial power in the Balkans, but he was burdened by a fast depleting treasury and repeated challenges from clan members.

In the meantime, Byzantium had come to be seen internationally as a soft target. In 1189, the armies of the Third Crusade were allowed to plunder Macedonia and Thrace unchecked, while nothing was done to

stop Richard the Lionheart from claiming Cyprus in 1191. By the time
Isaac had succumbed to a plot masterminded by his older brother,
Alexios III Angelos (1195–1203), the Latins had ceased to bother with
diplomatic decorum. When the Holy Roman Emperor, Henry VI
(1190–1197), demanded money and men for his projected crusade,
Alexios III humiliatingly complied by introducing a new tax, the infamous *Alamanikon* or 'German tax'. Meanwhile, Pope Innocent III
(1198–1216) saw no reason to temper the Papacy's frustration with
Byzantium's disingenuous support for the Crusades:

> For you ought most zealously to attend to this as human energy allows so
> that you might be able to extinguish or feed the fire in distant regions lest
> it be able in some measure to reach all the way to your territories.[1]

The standard view among modern scholars is that Byzantium's rapid
demise after Manuel's death was the result of deep-seated structural
problems. One could point to the decline of state tax revenues as aristocrats continued to accumulate landholdings, along with tax exemptions
and privileges. There was also the state's failure to maintain regional
defence systems and to keep up with the crushing costs of warfare. Much
is also made of the growing estrangement between Greek and Latin
Christians. Particularly grating to Latin leaders was Byzantium's refusal
to accept Papal spiritual supremacy and its readiness to cultivate links
with Muslim powers. There were certainly enough Latins who believed
the Greeks were no better than infidels, and that Byzantium itself was a
legitimate target of holy war.

Alternatively, one could argue that the only structural problem that
mattered was one that was shared by all medieval monarchies: the struggle to contain the growth of centrifugal power. Most of Europe was in
turmoil by the beginning of the thirteenth century: the Holy Roman
Empire had been plunged into civil war in the late 1190s, while
England's King John faced a crisis that led to Magna Carta. Tellingly, no
reigning monarch participated in the Fourth Crusade. The growth of
power decentralization was especially acute in the Balkan–Anatolia
zone, where empires had once ruled the entire region (Bulgarian, Seljuk,
Byzantine), but where monarchs were now forced to fend off incessant
challenges from rival family members and nobles. Underlying the rise of
political instability in this period was the growing financial dependence
of monarchs and lesser potentates on booty, and the greater need to
prosecute wars. The era was therefore an exceptionally volatile one in

interstate politics: the historian Angeliki Laiou found it useful to convey the nature of interstate relations in this period by invoking chaos theory.[2]

Another critical development in this period was Byzantium's deteriorating relations with the Mediterranean's most significant maritime power: Venice. Once an imperial dependency, Venice had grown rich on its lucrative eastern trade, and by the eleventh century its emporia and merchant communities could be found throughout the eastern Mediterranean. Meanwhile, Byzantium had come to depend heavily on Venetian naval power. When Venice helped to neutralize the Norman threat in 1082, it was rewarded with extraordinary tax exemptions. By the twelfth century, Venice and other maritime Italian powers such as Genoa and Pisa had also secured similar privileges from the Crusader states, and together they dominated Mediterranean seaborne trade. Inevitably, Byzantine merchants and state officials came to resent the advantages enjoyed by their Italian counterparts. In 1171, the Venetians were expelled from Constantinople, and in 1182 the Genoese and the Pisans were set upon by city mobs. It was only a matter of time before the Italians would try to secure their commercial interests through military means. The Crusade of 1204 offered such an opportunity.

THE FOURTH CRUSADE (1204)

The Fourth Crusade began inauspiciously. Its main problem was meeting the costs of maritime transport set by the Venetians (84,000 silver marks). Despite great opposition from within the ranks, Crusader leaders agreed to stop first in Constantinople and install Alexios Angelos, the son of the recently deposed Byzantine emperor, in return for 200,000 marks of silver and 10,000 Byzantine troops. When the Venetians and Crusaders arrived outside the city walls on 24 June 1203, the reception was hostile. Guided by the octogenarian Venetian Doge, Enrico Dandolo, who knew Constantinople intimately, the Crusaders stormed the sea walls near the Blachernae Palace, its most vulnerable point. The sitting emperor took flight, and on 1 August Alexios IV took his place. His immediate problem was to settle accounts with the Crusaders, but the state was bankrupt. Partial payment was made through pillaging Church treasures, but once that source was exhausted open conflict became inevitable. On 9 April 1204, the Crusader assault began, and by the 12th they broke into the city. Military resistance crumbled almost immediately.

The exceptional martial skills of the Crusaders was revealed in 1204, but it also exposed the pitiable state of the Byzantine ruling order. The Varangian Guard was prepared to fight, but the new emperor and the great political families had already taken flight, leaving the rest of the population to its fate. A killing spree ensued, although it was brought to a halt within a day. It may be that as few as 2000 Constantinopolitans were slain.

As it happened, the Fourth Crusade was the moment that marked the permanent break between the Orthodox and Latin Christian worlds. Previous difficulties, such as the schism of 1054, were ecclesiastical disputes that could be resolved through debate and compromise, but the outrages committed in 1204 remained etched in Orthodox Christian memory. Far more shocking than the looting and slaughter were the reported acts of sacrilege, particularly those committed within the Hagia Sophia. The Byzantine chronicler Choniates reported the following:

> For the sacred altar, formed of all kinds of precious materials and admired by the whole world, was broken into bits and distributed among the soldiers . . . a certain harlot, a sharer in their guilt, a minister of the furies, a servant of the demons . . . insulting Christ, sat in the patriarch's seat, singing an obscene song and dancing frequently.[3]

Modern historians point out that the Crusaders were far more restrained in Constantinople than they had been after capturing Muslim-held cities, but the desecration of churches had a traumatizing effect on the Orthodox world. Constantinople, moreover, was not just another city. Even in Western eyes it was still 'the City of Constantine', while for Orthodox Christians it was a holy city: the centre of Christendom, the seat of the patriarchate and home of the world's greatest collections of holy relics, including the True Cross. The lasting effect of 1204 was to demonize the Papacy and the Latin Church in Orthodox Christian eyes. Being Orthodox now also meant being anti-Latin. Innocent III himself feared the situation had become irretrievable: the Greek Church 'has been beset with so many afflictions and persecutions that she sees in the Latins only an example of perdition and the works of darkness'.[4]

THE LATIN INTERREGNUM (1204–1261)

On 9 May, one of the Crusader leaders, Baldwin of Flanders, was elected emperor (Baldwin I, 1204–1206), but his realm was limited to

Constantinople and its environs. The provinces were carved up into a series of feudal states, with the commander of 1204, Boniface of Montferrat, awarded a sizeable kingdom centred on Thessaloniki that encompassed much of western Macedonia and Thessaly. The Venetian price for financing the Fourth Crusade was high: control of the Hagia Sophia, the Patriarchate and the city's commercial quarter. Venice also claimed Crete, along with a list of smaller islands and mainland ports that lined the sea route between the Adriatic and Constantinople. With its naval and trading power radically enhanced, Venice was the real winner of 1204.

Some of Byzantium's remaining mainland provinces were claimed with little resistance. In Thrace, Macedonia and Thessaly, the 'Franks', as they were generally known, were welcomed by some provincials who believed the Byzantine ruling elite was corrupt and had got its just deserts. Further south, the Franks overcame some initial resistance from Greek *archontes* (warlords), such as Leo Sgouros in the Argolid and Leo Kamateros in Lakonia, to create a separate feudal state. The Peloponnese, now under the authority of the 'Prince of Achaea', was subdivided into fiefdoms that controlled each locality from a series of fortresses. Although countless outrages were committed against churches and monasteries during the initial stages of conquest, the Peloponnese soon settled into its normal rhythms. The Greek *archontes* were absorbed into the principality's power structure, while local peasants enjoyed much firmer protection from highland pastoralists. The principality also made an effort to meet the interests of the Greek Church and its clergy. Managing religious sensitivities was essential for social stability, and quite tellingly the era witnessed a great deal of Greek *and* Frankish church construction. The potential for discord was further diffused when the Greek clergy were allowed to retain key tax privileges.

Similar patterns of accommodation allowed for the consolidation of Frankish rule in Attica (the Duchy of Athens) and the Cyclades Islands (the Duchy of Naxos). Cyprus was another Frankish success story. The Lusignans of Poitou managed a stable monarchy from 1197 through to the mid-fourteenth century. The most fragile principality was the so-called Latin Empire of Constantinople. Here, Latin clerics tried to force their Greek counterparts to accept Papal supremacy. In 1206, the Greeks were refused permission to replace the deceased Orthodox patriarch, and in 1214 the papal legate Pelagius forced the closure of all Orthodox churches. These hamfisted measures did nothing but ensure that the memory of 1204 remained a festering wound.

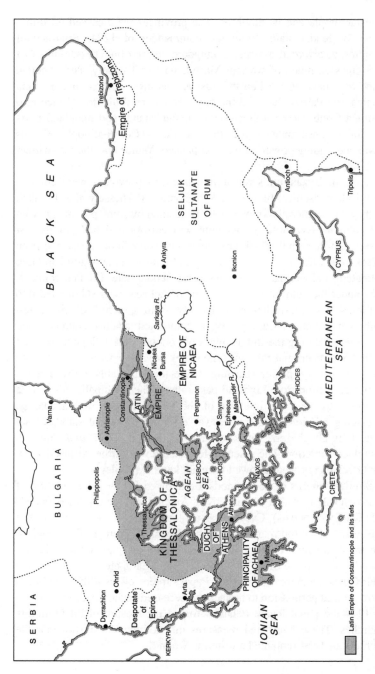

Map 8 The Latin Interregnum, AD c.1214

Labels on map:

BLACK SEA

SERBIA

BULGARIA

SELJUK SULTANATE OF RUM

EMPIRE OF NICAEA

Empire of Trebizond

LATIN EMPIRE

KINGDOM OF THESSALONICA

DESPOTATE of Epiros

DUCHY OF ATHENS

PRINCIPALITY OF ACHAEA

AEGEAN SEA

IONIAN SEA

MEDITERRANEAN SEA

Trebizond
Antioch
Tripolis
CYPRUS
Ankyra
Ikonion
Sarkaya R.
Nicaea
Bursa
Pergamon
Smyrna
Ephesos
Maeander R.
RHODES
Varna
Constantinople
Adrianople
Philippopolis
LESBOS
CHIOS
NAXOS
Thessalonica
Athens
Mistra
CRETE
Ohrid
Dyrrachion
Arta
KERKYRA

Latin Empire of Constantinople and its fiefs

Meanwhile, material conditions in Constantinople deteriorated rapidly as its population plummeted from 400,000 to something closer to 50,000. The Latin Empire had a radically restricted fiscal source base, while the city was starved of the private incomes of the Byzantine elites that absconded in large numbers to the provinces. The Latin emperors were forced to tour Christendom and beg for men and money, but their plight had little emotional pull in European courts. Indeed, it was the Latin Empire's insolvency that led to the *real* crime of the Fourth Crusade. The city was stripped of its riches, as thousands of artworks and holy relics were exported for a price. Even the lead from the royal palace rooftops was removed and sold. Riches that had been accumulated over centuries had been ransacked. Among the more significant items that were stolen were the four bronze horses in the Hippodrome, which nowadays guard the entrance to St Mark's in Venice.

LITTLE BYZANTIUMS

From the outset, the Latin states were counterbalanced by the rapid emergence of new Orthodox powers, each claiming to be the surrogates of Byzantium. These included the so-called 'Empire of Trebizond' on the eastern Black Sea littoral of Anatolia, and the 'Despotate of Epiros', which covered much of the western Greek mainland. Its founding ruler, Michael Doukas, a cousin of the emperor Isaac I Angelos, later went on to claim much of Thessaly (1212) and the Venetian controlled ports of Corfu and Dyrrachion (1214). His successor and half-brother, Theodore Angelos (1215–1230), came close to restoring the empire when he recaptured Thessaloniki (1224) and then Adrianople (1228), but he was defeated and held captive by the Bulgarians until 1237. In the meantime, his relatives continued to rule as *basileis* over most of northern Greece.

The most powerful successor state was the so-called 'Empire of Nicaea', which emerged in western Anatolia under Theodore Laskaris (Theodore I Laskaris, 1204–1222), son-in-law of Alexios III. The city of Nicaea became the new home of the Constantinopolitan aristocracy, its higher clergy, educators, scholars and merchants. Significantly, the Nicaean emperors demonstrated the abiding efficacy of Roman/Byzantine institutions, which appeared to function with considerable efficiency in fresh hands. Theodore even managed to restore the old *thema* provincial system, but his most valuable state instrumentality was the Byzantine fiscal system. Unlike the indigent Latin Empire, the 'Laskarids' had the means to hire numerous squadrons of Latin mercenaries and to maintain a sizeable naval fleet.

The Nicaean Empire thrived under a series of able rulers, who presided over a stable political order and a vibrant economy. It also played an important role in the history of Greek culture. Since the ninth century, Latin Christians had come to believe that *they* were the true Romans, and Byzantines always took offence when Latins described them as *Graikoi* (Greeks). After the Fourth Crusade, however, the Byzantines singled out the Greek heritage as the factor that, in cultural terms, made them superior to the Latins. We even begin to see the term 'Hellene' used as an ethnic self-ascription. The evidence is admittedly limited but striking nonetheless. The surviving correspondence of the Nicaean Emperor John Vatatzes (1222–1254) shows a habit of using 'Hellene' as a synonym for 'Roman'. His son and successor, Theodore II Laskaris (1254–1258), makes the clearest claim that he is of Hellenic ancestry. In one of his letters he claims Nicaea is the new Hellas: 'the same air that was then, is now ours too: the Hellenic language is ours; and we are drawn from their blood'.[5] The Patriarchate had also begun to see itself as a 'Greek' institution, showing markedly less interest in Slavs and other Orthodox peoples. Patriarch Germanos II (1223–1240) talked of the ethnic purity of his Greek flock and was prepared to acknowledge the semi-independent status of the Bulgarian Church.

Of the Greek successor states, it was the Empire of Nicaea that had the most convincing claims to being the legitimate surrogate of Byzantium. Significantly, Nicaea became the temporary seat of the Orthodox Patriarchate. It also had the most prestigious schools of Greek learning. All the while, the Laskarids saw the recapture of Constantinople as its highest priority. The historian Niketas Choniates promoted the idea that Nicaea was the 'New Zion', but it was also expected that Constantinople would be returned to the 'Chosen' once they had atoned for their sins.

The Laskarids bided their time. What they feared most was Frankish retaliation in the form of another crusade, and there were also the rival ambitions of the rulers of Epiros. Matters came to a head in 1259, when Michael II Angelos, in alliance with Greece's Frankish potentates, clashed with the Nicaeans at Pelagonia in northern Greece. The then Nicaean emperor, Michael Palaiologos, won a decisive victory that cleared the way for the repossession of Constantinople. However, before Michael had made any substantive preparations, the city was delivered to him in quite bizarre circumstances. A contingent of 800 Nicaean soldiers happened to be in the vicinity of the city when they were informed that the entire Latin garrison was on expedition. On 25 July 1261, the soldiers were ushered in through a gate and reclaimed the city. Michael formally entered Constantinople on 15 August and was crowned Michael VIII Palaiologos (1261–1282). The Byzantine Empire was formally restored.

BYZANTIUM REDUX (1261–1282)

The challenges facing Michael VIII were immense. Constantinople had been stripped bare. Its buildings were in a deplorable condition; even the Blachernae Palace was declared uninhabitable. Repopulating the city and rebuilding its physical environment would prove a major undertaking. The most pressing concern, however, was the reaction within Western Christendom. Retaliation was inevitable. The last Latin emperor, Baldwin II (1228–1261), joined forces with the Venetians and William of Villehardouin, the prince of Achaea (1246–1278), but Michael despatched three military expeditions that nullified this threat and in the process netted a series of islands and Peloponnesian fortresses. In the meantime, Michael also enjoyed successful military campaigns against the Despotate of Epiros and the Bulgarians, while also driving Seljuk Turks out of the Maeander River basin in Asia Minor. In 1269, a new anti-Greek crusade had been organized by Charles of Anjou, the ruler of Sicily and Naples, but it was diffused when Michael suddenly opened negotiations with the Papacy on ecclesiastical union, which was ratified at the Council of Lyon in 1274. Charles's second attempt to launch a crusade was foiled by the so-called Sicilian Vespers in 1282, perhaps the greatest mass revolt in the island's history. There were strong suspicions that Byzantine money may have played a role.

The outlook for the Byzantine Empire in 1282 looked promising. At the end of his busy reign, Michael had seen off threats on all fronts, expanded the empire and re-established Byzantium as a major political force. Even Constantinople was beginning to take on the appearance of an imperial capital. With some reason, Michael VIII saw himself as the 'New Constantine', but in Byzantine eyes his reputation was sullied by his dealings with the Papacy. For that, he shared the same fate as the early Iconoclast emperors. The rapprochement with the Papacy might have saved the empire from a major military assault, but it caused great distress within Orthodox communities, where the mere talk of union with the Papacy was anathema. Brutal state retaliation against protesters in Constantinople merely made things worse. When Michael died in 1282, the Church refused him final rites and he was buried on unconsecrated ground.

Michael's chief domestic problem, therefore, was the enhanced moral authority that the Church hierarchy had acquired during the Latin interregnum. In fact throughout the Greek *oikoumene*, there had been a vital shift in thinking about the role of the emperor. Under the Empire of Nicaea, the emperor had been redefined as the 'servant' of the people and the Church, while in 1261 Patriarch Arsenios had actually gone so far as to excommunicate Michael for having usurped the Nicaean throne in a nefarious fashion. Later, the recalcitrant despots of Epiros and Trebizond could justify their defiance of Michael's authority on the basis that he had been excommunicated. The shift in the balance between imperial and Church power was put unequivocally by Arsenios himself:

> Given that the lesser must obey the greater, the Church is the greater, for it has Christ as its head and the patriarch as His image. The latter sanctifies and anoints the emperor who stands in need of such grace. He therefore should in gratitude serve the Church and its leader who spiritually bears the image of Christ.[6]

THE CATALANS AND THE HOUSE OF OSMAN (1282–1328)

With his exceptional military and diplomatic talents, Michael had nevertheless restored Byzantium to a respectable position within a hostile international environment. It did not last. In the deeply unstable political conditions of the fourteenth century, every state in the eastern Mediterranean world led a precarious existence, and in the hands of Michael's markedly less talented son, Andronikos II (1282–1328), the empire slid rapidly back to the precipice.

Encouraged by the relative lull in interstate hostilities that greeted his investiture, Andronikos resolved budgetary difficulties incurred from his father's military campaigning by reducing the size of the army and abolishing the navy. Given the empire's strategic vulnerability and the predatory nature of interstate relations, these were astonishingly short-sighted measures. Inevitably, frontier problems resumed, and during the 1290s the empire was to suffer vast territorial losses on three fronts. The Serbs had seized northern Macedonia and Albania, while the Venetians, with no Byzantine navy to contend with, captured more Aegean islands. Meanwhile, the Turks now sensed that they could occupy, rather than merely raid, the empire's rich Anatolian provinces. Andronikos' military responses were ineffectual, initially because of poor generalship, but later because of want of money and men. By the end of his reign, Anatolia was almost entirely in Turkish hands. Government incompetence played a role, but there were also long-term structural problems to consider, most of which were related to the general trend towards power decentralization. Of great significance here were the costly tax exemptions granted since the eleventh century to the Church, monastic institutions, aristocrats, cities and regional power brokers. Under Michael VIII and Andronikos II, immunities and privileges were distributed on an unprecedented scale, as were the number of *pronoia* (hereditary land grants) issued in return for military service.

The overall effect was greatly to diminish the state's fiscal base and its ability to raise mercenary armies. Andronikos fielded armies that often numbered less than 2,000, and there was the additional problem that mercenaries could be treacherous when they smelled weakness. In 1303, the Catalan Grand Company offered the services of 1,500 cavalry and 5,000 infantry at a price that was possibly greater than the state's annual revenue, but Andronikos was desperate. The Catalans went on to enjoy considerable success against the Turks, but they also attacked and plundered the Greek population and inevitably turned on their cash-strapped employer. For several years, the company ran amok in Byzantine Anatolia, Thrace and then Macedonia. The empire was plunged into disarray. As a consequence, the Turks occupied more territories in Anatolia, while the Genoese seized control of many port cities and islands. The pressure had abated by the 1310s, but by then all that was left of the empire was Constantinople, Thrace, the region around the Sea of Marmara and a few enclaves in Greece.

It was around the time of the Catalan fiasco that a small warrior band of Oghuz Turks, led by Osman, founded the Ottoman emirate a short distance east of Nicaea and the Sarkaya River. In 1302, flooding caused damage to imperial defences along the Sarkaya, thus allowing the Osmanlis to conduct *gaza* (holy war) in Byzantine territory and bring in large numbers of Muslim settlers. Under Osman's successor, Orhan (*c*.1324–1262), the Ottomans captured the last significant Byzantine cities: first Proussa (1326), then Nicaea (1331) and finally Nicomedia (1337).

Ottoman military strength depended on the number of retainers it could attract with promises of land and slaves. The earliest Ottoman armies therefore included many Christian warriors, although Osman's core-following appeared to be Turkic warriors from Central Asia. As with traditional pastoral armies from that zone, the earliest Ottoman armies were potent but not particularly sophisticated. They were composed of horseback archers whose forte was mobility and surprise attacks. They were reluctant to meet disciplined Byzantine armies in open battle, and their only siege tactic was to starve a city into submission. And yet by this stage Byzantium did not have the means to keep the countryside clear of these lethal mobile warriors.

CONTRASTING FORTUNES (1328–1354)

Owing to the lack of primary documentation, we know very little about the internal dynamics of the Ottoman emirate in these early years, but we do know that its growing influence was not solely the result of its military might. Rather, what can be gleaned from a variety of Greek and Turkish sources is that the House of Osman had an exceptionally versatile approach to state building and imperial expansionism. Its resourcefulness was demonstrated most clearly in its willingness to break with Turkic and Islamic conventions where necessary. Although ideologically committed to war against the infidel, the Ottomans found it prudent to seek alliances with Christian powers and consolidate these links through marriage arrangements. Thus, early Ottoman rulers often had Christian mothers and wives. They also appeared more successful than their rivals in retaining the loyalties of warrior retinues. Indeed, throughout the Balkans and Anatolia, maintaining bonds of solidarity among nobles and other leading warrior figures was crucial to the survival of any ruling figure. The rise of Serb power in this period can be explained by the solidarity forged among the *bojars* (nobility). In minimizing their own internal divisions, the Ottomans were well placed to exploit domestic divisions within rival powers.

Meanwhile, Byzantium's demise was not a foregone conclusion. Under the energetic rulership of Andronikos III (1328–1341) and his loyal and gifted chief minister, John Kantakouzenos, Byzantium again began to reveal its innate strengths. The younger Andronikos was an able military commander who re-established Byzantine dominance over the southern Balkans. By restoring control over Epiros and Thessaly, his empire now included a thick stretch of territories from Constantinople to the Adriatic, much of it constituting rich farmland and hence a solid fiscal base. Ottoman expansion in Anatolia was well advanced, but the Frankish lords of southern Greece, including the Catalans, who had seized control of the Duchy of Athens back in 1311, were forced to acknowledge Andronikos' suzerainty, while the Serbian empire builder, Stephen Dushan, who had proclaimed himself the 'Tsar' of all Orthodox peoples, was successfully kept at bay.

For a short period, therefore, Byzantium demonstrated that it could function as a respectable middling power, but it all came to nought when Andronikos died suddenly in June 1341. By all accounts, John Kantakouzenos had been the talent behind the throne, as shown by the fact that in the immediate aftermath of Andronikos' passing, he dealt quickly and successfully with a series of major frontier crises. However, civil war soon broke out over the regency. Andronikos' son was a minor, and the empress, Anna of Savoy, backed by the patriarch and the Grand Duke Apokaukos, moved quickly to neutralize Kantakouzenos' political power. After a series of provocations, such as inciting mobs to ransack his family properties, Kantakouzenos retaliated.

The most damaging feature of this civil war was that the protagonists enlisted foreign powers that inevitably expected great rewards in return, including Byzantine territories. Kantakouzenos initially used Serb forces, but he became increasingly dependant on Umur, the Turkish emir of Aydin, with whom he established a form of brotherhood, and Orhan, the Ottoman emir, who became his son-in-law. These ties appeared to have been based on genuine emotional bonds – Umur refused Kantakouzenos' daughter's hand in marriage since they were indeed 'brothers': the daughter in question married Orhan instead. Familial ties did not mean, however, that Kantakouzenos' allies resisted taking advantage of Byzantium's troubles. By 1346, after Kantakouzenos had won the civil war and became emperor (John VI), most Balkan territories were in Serb hands. Stephan Dushan laid claim to being emperor of the Serbs and Greeks. Then, in 1354, a natural disaster in southern Thrace sealed the empire's long term fate. In March, residents of Gallipoli, a fortress town on the European side of the Dardenelles, were forced to evacuate when an earthquake destroyed their city. The Ottomans quickly occupied the ruins with Muslim settlers, rebuilt its defences and refused to hand it back to their erstwhile ally. Suddenly, the Ottomans had a beachhead on the European continent, and Thrace was there for the taking.

Within a decade of claiming Gallipoli, the Ottomans had seized most of the province, including the ancient city of Adrianople (Edirne), which became the new Ottoman capital. That Constantinople survived at all owed everything to the Walls of Theodosius, still impregnable unless approached from the sea. Almost 150 years earlier, the Crusaders had breeched the sea walls with Venetian support, but the Ottomans still lacked naval strength. In these early years, they hesitated attacking the city because they also feared Latin Christian retaliation. Ottoman caution allowed Byzantium to linger for another century.

OTTOMAN VASSAL (1354–1451)

The early Ottoman state was unique in that, unlike all regional powers, it developed the means to accumulate power and territory. What is even more remarkable was that it achieved unassailable power over the Balkans, where the vast majority of the population was, and would remain, Christian. Certainly, the early Ottomans had been committed ideologically to perennial war against Christian powers, but in practice they saw the necessity for accommodating Christian interests and intermarrying with Christian monarchies. There is some evidence to suggest, for example, that Bayezid I (1389–1402) was even interested in creating a syncretic Muslim-Christian religion that might unify all his subjects. Crucial for the consolidation of Ottoman authority was an ability to absorb Christian elites into the new political order. The conquest of the Balkans and Anatolia was achieved mainly with the support of vassals, both Christian and Muslim, most of whom were given a stake in the fast-expanding imperial system.

Other vital developments were the formation of an absolute monarchy and a standing army that owed exclusive loyalty to the ruler. Murat I (1362–1389) created a massive private army of slaves known as the Janissaries, an elite force composed of boys requisitioned from Christian families, who were raised as Muslims and trained in state institutions. Later, in the early fifteenth century, problems of dynastic succession were resolved with the emergence of 'unigeniture': the new ruler's siblings were executed to counter the possibility of future challenges. The Ottomans also introduced quite effective state institutions and practices by adapting older Turkic, Persian, Islamic and Byzantine traditions. Thus, the quasi-feudal *timar* system of non-hereditary land grants, designed to support a cavalry force dependent on the ruler's favour, was inspired by Byzantium's similar *pronoia* system.

The story of Byzantium after 1354 could not be more different. Within ten years, the capital was completely surrounded by the Ottomans. Imperial revenues and manpower reserves were trifling, and yet the Palaiologoi could still manage to stage a series of civil wars – first between John V and Manuel Kantazouzenos during the late 1350s and another between John and his eldest son Andronikos IV (1376–1379). There was further conflict between John and his second son Manuel on the one hand, and Andronikos' son, John VII, on the other. In each of these conflicts, the Ottomans learned to play off the rival Byzantine camps.

Despite its proclivity for civil conflict, the Byzantine imperial elite had few illusions about the Ottoman menace. Given its pitifully small army and tiny resource base, Byzantium's only real hope lay, ironically, in another Latin crusade. In 1369, John V went so far as to convert to Roman Catholicism in an elaborate public display in St Peters in Rome, but this great act of humility did little to raise Byzantine stocks in the West, and it completely alienated public opinion back home. After visiting many royal courts, he returned to Constantinople in 1371 empty handed. When the Ottomans soundly defeated the Serbs later that year, John followed Serb leaders in seeking vassalage. Henceforth, the Byzantines were required to provide the Ottoman ruler, now a sultan, with military assistance when required. In 1390, they were required to participate in the siege of Philadelphia, an isolated Christian outpost in Anatolia that had somehow retained its independence.

On assuming the throne, Manuel II Palaiologos (1391–1425) refused to be treated as a mere vassal and thus provoked a direct Ottoman attack on Constantinople and the Peloponnese. Sultan Bayezid had been planning to stamp out the surviving Christian outposts, but he was suddenly confronted by the arrival of the Mongols, who won a crushing victory at Ankara (1402) and left the fledgling Ottoman Empire in disarray. Byzantium was able to reclaim Thessaloniki, which had been in Ottoman hands since 1387, and long stretches of the Thracian coastline. Manuel also gave generous support to the eventual victor of the ensuing Ottoman succession struggle, Mehmet I (1413–1421). As a result, the two states coexisted amicably until Manuel's son, John, alienated Murat II (1421–1451) after backing a pretender to the Ottoman throne. Murat went to war against the Byzantines, and by 1424 all that was left was Constantinople and the Peloponnese.

Byzantium's final years featured more attempts to lobby Western support. The efforts of John VIII (1425–1448) led to the Council of Florence (1438–1445), which proclaimed the union of the Latin and

Greek Churches on Papal terms. Needless to say, most Byzantine subjects preferred the Sultan's turban to the Papal tiara, but the rapprochement did pave the way for another crusade, and the intervention appeared timely. Murat was forced to deal with a major revolt in Anatolia and to secure the succession he abdicated in favour of his 11-year-old son, the precocious Mehmet. On hearing the news, the Byzantines decided to release Orhan, a pretender to the Ottoman throne. The resulting turmoil produced panic in Edirne, the Ottoman capital, where fires broke out. Muslims began to flee to the safety of Anatolia. At this point, Murat was forced to make peace with his Anatolian adversaries and return with his army to the Balkans. He destroyed a large Crusader army at Varna (Bulgaria) in 1444 and then reclaimed the throne from his ineffectual teenage son. The Byzantines were again punished for their treachery, but Murat had no stomach for further military conflict. The next siege of Constantinople had to wait until after Murat's death in 1451, when Mehmet, keen to redress the humiliations of his first reign, set his sights firmly on making Constantinople his own.

THE GREEK *OIKOUMENE* IN THE FIFTEENTH CENTURY

As the Byzantine Empire slid towards extinction, the *oikoumene* assumed greater significance. It is worth recalling at this point that, since 1261, the majority of Greeks had been living outside the empire. The *oikoumene* included other Greek states (the Archontate of Morea and the Empire of Trebizond) and extended across Frankish- and Venetian-ruled territories, such as Cyprus, and Turkish Anatolia. Despite the steady contraction of Orthodox population in Anatolia, quite sizeable Greek communities could still be found in almost every part of this vast region, including the central plateau (Cappadocia), where surviving Orthodox communities spoke Turkish.

The Greek communities that fared best during the initial Ottoman conquests were those that submitted peacefully, as was the case with Thessaloniki in 1387. By all accounts, the city enjoyed a short period of renewed vitality: when it was temporarily restored to Byzantine rule in 1402, visitors were struck by the marvellous condition of the monasteries. When the Ottomans returned in 1422, however, its citizens resisted and the city suffered a long blockade until the walls were breached finally in March 1430. Mass looting, rape and enslavement followed. Having failed to adequately repopulate the city with Muslim settlers, however, the Ottomans ordered the return of the surviving Greeks, including the 7000 that had been enslaved. The city retained its slim Greek majority until the end of the fifteenth century, but Christians and Muslims alike were eventually to be outnumbered by Jews that had been expelled from Spain. By 1519, Jews constituted over half of the population.

During the first half of the fifteenth century, the one part of the *oikoumene* that showed real vitality was the Despotate of Morea, a Byzantine territory that functioned as an autonomous territory. During the course of its history (1349–1460), the Despotate expanded at the expense of the region's Latin principalities and it became the focus of Byzantium's last age of cultural efflorescence, the so-called 'Palaiologan Renaissance'. The capital, Mistra, with its schools and libraries, became a beacon for Greek scholars from throughout the *oikoumene*, drawing such luminaries as Bessarion of Trebizond (*c*.1399–1472) and Gemistos Plethon (*c*.1360–1452), a native of Constantinople and the greatest intellectual figure of his time.

Inevitably, Morea fell to the Ottomans (1460), as did the grandiosely named 'Empire of Trebizond' the following year. Trebizond's survival to that point can be attributed to the Pontic Ranges, which acted as a barrier against incursions from central Anatolia. Indeed throughout the long history of Byzantine–Islamic relations, the Pontus region had been spared from the frequent raiding and attendant disruptions. Hence in contrast to the rest of Anatolia, Pontus remained largely Greek Orthodox for quite some time after 1461: in 1520, the Pontic Greek population amounted to about 86 per cent of the population. The region survived the Ottoman takeover virtually intact because its last Greek ruler submitted without resistance. Its monastic institutions also played an interesting role. They enjoyed the patronage of significant figures within the Ottoman court, including Maria (later Gülbahar), wife of Bayezid II and mother of Selim I. As a result, the Pontic monasteries retained control of large inland valleys and the local Christian villages, and under the watchful eyes of the monks these valleys remained pockets of Greek Orthodoxy for centuries.

THE FALL OF CONSTANTINOPLE (1453)

As 1453 approached, the people of Constantinople sensed that the end was near. Prophetic traditions did not bode well, although some residents, such as the future patriarch, Gennadios Scholarios, believed the fatal year would be 1492. The Ottomans too regarded the seizure of Constantinople as providential. Mehmet II had his astrologers hard at work. The young sultan's grip on power had been tenuous and he was aware that his reputation and political survival depended on whether he could claim the ultimate 'imperial' city. Preparations were therefore meticulous, and no expense was spared. The Ottoman army he assembled outside Constantinople in the spring of 1453 was massive. Estimates vary, but there were perhaps as many as 60,000 infantry, 40,000 cavalry and thousands more in auxiliary roles. Mehmet's armoury included the world's largest canons and 30,000 stockpiled canon balls. The Byzantines inside were forced to defend seven km of walls with fewer than 5000 local troops and 2000 foreign allies, mainly from Genoa.

Despite pitifully small numbers, Constantinopolitan resistance was fierce. Initial Ottoman casualties were high, and by the end of May there was some concern within the Ottoman camp that they were not fated to succeed. Constantine rejected an offer to cease hostilities in return for an annual tribute of 70,000 ducats, an astronomical figure. A final assault was ordered for the early hours of 29 May. The canons breached the walls near the Blachernae Palace, where the attackers poured into the city precincts and through its suburbs. The Byzantine soldiery fought to the last man, including the last emperor, Constantine XI, whose body was never recovered.

The city was pillaged for three days. As expected, most of the inhabitants were either enslaved or put to the sword. Plundering appeared frenzied, but it was systematic and thorough. Panicked Constantinopolitans either hid in their homes or made their way to churches to seek divine intervention; but even the Hagia Sophia was no sanctuary. Ottomans beat down its doors, removed the huddled crowds and pillaged anything that could fetch a price. Some defenders escaped, including the Genoese who seized Ottoman ships that had been abandoned by crews seeking a share of the spoils, and a contingent of Cretan soldiers who were so hard to dislodge from their fortified posting that Mehmet gave them permission to leave unharmed. For the rest, the city had become a hellish death trap.

The final fall of Constantinople did indeed mark the termination of the Byzantine Empire, but 1453 was not quite the watershed it appears to be. It is certainly true that Constantinople suddenly became the capital of an Islamic Empire, and the Hagia Sophia a mosque. Paradoxically, the Palaiologoi continued to wield power, as did many Byzantine noble houses. All three of Constantine's nephews, his natural successors, were taken under Mehmet's wing. We know something about two of these boys: one would later become Mesih Pasha, Admiral of the Ottoman fleet and then Grand Vizier (the Sultan's chief minister), and the other we know as Murat Pasha, another major figure who led the assault on Rhodes in 1480. In fact, the Ottoman elite was full of converted Serb, Bulgarian, Albanian and Greek aristocrats, many of whom remained intimately linked to their Christian relatives. There were also many victims. The Grand Duke Loukas Notaras, the man who coined the famous phrase 'better the Turkish turban than the Papal tiara', and perhaps Byzantium's highest ranking noble in 1453, was deemed insufficiently trustworthy. After toying with the idea of making him the city prefect, Mehmet had Notaras and his sons executed in June.

However much they might have lamented the demise of the Byzantine Empire, former subjects, both rich and poor, could now prosper under a powerful new order that was able to impose peace: a 'Pax Ottomanica'. Unlike the Byzantine emperors, the Ottoman sultans could enforce laws, protect peasants from the abuses of greedy elites and put an end to destructive military conflicts. Some Christians enjoyed a spectacular improvement in their fortune. The expansion of Ottoman power saw the dramatic revival of Greek merchant shipping. The Ottomans were keen to promote their own subjects and bring an end to Italian domination of the seas. According to registers from the Black Sea port of Caffa, dated to 1487–1490, the Muslim captains numbered 41, Greeks 21 and Italians only four. Much of the merchandise carried between Ottoman ports was now in Jewish and Greek hands, as was a growing portion of the empire's external trade. By the sixteenth century, Greek families were engaged in international trade and banking. Later dubbed the 'Phanariots' because they were concentrated in Constantinople's Phanar/Fener district, these new Greek elites emerged as a highly influential element in the life of the capital.

The Orthodox clergy also found that there were benefits to be had from Islamic overlordship. Mehmet, in fact, was especially keen to be seen as protector of the Orthodox, if anything to retain local Christian support against the Latin West. The Church hierarchy was therefore granted extensive authority over the empire's Orthodox subjects, and it was allowed to rebuild the ecclesiastical structures of Anatolia. Along with the Armenians and the Jews, the Orthodox were recognized as a community that functioned like a 'state within a state', with its own leaders and laws.

LATIN GREECE

The Ottoman Empire did eventually develop into a naval power, but it could never dominate the seas in the same way as it could the mainland. The Italians therefore retained a substantial presence in the Aegean. The Venetians controlled many islands and seaside fortresses on the Greek mainland, while the Genoese held the Anatolian town of (Old) Phokaia and New Phokaia until 1455, the island of Lesbos until 1462, and the mastic producing island of Chios until 1566. Another Latin force in the Aegean were the Knights Hospitaller of St John, a monastic military order that had been evicted from Syria and transferred its operations to Rhodes and nearby islands in the early fourteenth century. These Hospitallers withstood a series of Ottoman assaults, but finally succumbed in 1522. The Latin Kingdom of Cyprus was another Frankish state that persisted long after the fall of the Holy Land. Lusignan monarchy and its landed nobility enjoyed untrammelled power through to the middle fourteenth century, and the kingdom's economy thrived because of high European demand for Cypriot sugar. Cyprus became a Venetian protectorate in 1473 and was formally annexed in 1489.

Venice was the only Latin Christian power that could not be ejected completely from the eastern Mediterranean. Whilst it fought a losing battle against Ottoman encroachment, Venice was powerful enough to draw out that process and grow rich on its seaborne empire. The *stato da mar* (state of the sea) included Cyprus until 1571, Crete until 1669 and Tinos until 1710, while the Ionian Islands and Kythera (Cerigo) were only relinquished when Venice itself was seized by Napoleonic France in 1797. For various lengths of time, the *stato da mar* also featured a string of coastal forts like Lepanto (Naupaktos), Modon (Methoni), Coron (Koroni), Navarino (Pylos) and Monemvasia: the latter four protected the long passage linking the Adriatic to the Aegean. At the end of the sixteenth century, the Venetian empire contained just under half a million Greek subjects, which represented perhaps as much as 20 per cent of its total population. Inevitably, subjects flocked to the imperial centre. Venice became home to a sizeable Greek-speaking community that grew in scale and influence. It eventually overcame official Catholic intransigence to open an Orthodox parish church (*San Giorgio dei Greci*) in 1573. Between 1478 and 1580, the Greek community in Venice, the largest in Italy, had grown from 4000 to 15,000.

HELLENISM BETWEEN ISLAM AND THE RENAISSANCE

By the sixteenth and seventeenth centuries, therefore, the Greek *oikoumene* was distributed across the Ottoman and Venetian empires. The great majority of Greeks lived under the Pax Ottomanica, which provided Greek social elites with many significant benefits, particularly in the economic sphere, but Venice offered at least one vital advantage. Along with the rest of Italy, it had rekindled its love for Greek art and learning.

The Ottomans, however, had developed a far more exclusive attitude to subject cultures, and certainly showed no interest in Hellenism. By the sixteenth century, by which time it had expanded to incorporate the Muslim Near East and the holy cities of Mecca and Medina, the Ottoman Empire had become a more Islamic polity. Access to the ruling order was restricted to Muslims, and educational institutions (madrasas, the *devshirme*) were tailored to meet the specific needs of a Muslim polity. Within this milieu, other forms of learning were consciously restricted. The Greek Church was permitted a seminary, but for secular learning and the training of doctors and lawyers, wealthy Greeks were forced to send their sons to Italy and sometimes as far as Paris and Oxford.

As one door closed, another opened. The rise of Ottoman power coincided with the Renaissance, a movement that was defined by the renewed appreciation of the Classical heritage. Italian interest certainly predated the fall of Constantinople, but the flow of Greek scholars and manuscripts to Italy did serve as a vital stimulus to Renaissance scholarship and artistic creativity. Greeks arrived as copyists (transcribers of manuscripts) and teachers. Of particular value were manuscripts of Classics in the original Greek, especially for producing more accurate translations of well-known texts. For such purposes, Greek scholars performed an invaluable service as translators and as teachers of Attic. The first Chair in Greek was established at Padua in 1463, and many of its occupants were from the Greek East, including the well-known Cretan humanist Markos Mousouros (1503–1509). As for Gemistos Plethon, his famous lectures on Platonism in Florence in 1439 helped to re-establish Plato in Western education and encouraged Cosimo de Medici to invest in the Platonic Academy. Plethon was such a luminary that after the Ottoman conquest of the Peloponnese, a special Italian expedition was despatched to retrieve his body.

The old theory that the influx of Greek scholars to Italy provided the spark that ignited the Renaissance, and therefore the birth of modernity, has little to commend it, but the impact of Byzantium's scholars cannot be underestimated. The myriad of Renaissance artworks that depict scenes from Greek mythology, or particular masterpieces, such as Raphael's *The School of Athens* (*c*.1510), which portrays the greatest philosophers of the Classical and Hellenistic eras, pay explicit homage to the Hellenic heritage. Of even greater significance is the recovery of the Classical approach to art and learning. With the works of great masters such as Leonardo da Vinci and Michelangelo, we again see the human body as the object that defines beauty. The nakedness and muscularity found in such works as Michelangelo's *David* (*c*.1500/4) were more 'Greek' than anything that had been produced in Byzantine times.

It was not just scholars and texts that flowed to Italy. Orthodox clergymen that were prepared to embrace Papal primacy were often accepted into sees and dioceses. Some rose to the highest echelons. Bassilios Bessarion of Trebizond, once the titular head of the Diocese of Nicaea, later became a cardinal. In Rome he served as a patron of other Greek émigrés in Italy. Other clergy found a home among the Greek-speaking communities of Calabria, which was still much a part of the Greek *oikoumene*. One Cretan named Petros Philarges ended up as Pope Alexander V (1409–1410), although he did not begin his vocation as an Orthodox clergyman. Like many children from elite Greek families, however, Philarges was sent to Italy to be educated. (He studied at Padua and Oxford and lectured at the University of Paris.) Indeed throughout the early modern period, Greeks in Ottoman territories and the *stato da mar* would send their young to Western universities.

The Venetian Greek community was responsible for a specific innovation that would have immense long-term significance for Greek culture. Modern scholars have come to recognize the role of the printing press and the book trade in fashioning new transnational communities. From the late fifteenth century, a Greek 'print culture' did emerge, whereby a widely dispersed *oikoumene* found an added source of coherence as a reading public. For reasons that are not clear, the Ottomans placed a complete ban on printing until 1729. It was therefore in Italy where the Greek book trade began. The first book printed in Greek, a work on grammar, was actually produced in Milan in 1476, but it was a Cretan named Zacharias Kalliergis who started the first Greek printing press in Venice in 1499. More presses would emerge in Venice and other centres to meet the demand for books, and while most were religious works an increasing proportion appealed to secular academic and popular interests. Significantly, much popular material was published in vernacular Greek, particularly epics and romances in verse. Especially appealing were works such as *Apokopos*, *Belisarios*, *Apollonios* and *Rimadha of Alexander*, each of which were to be printed in several editions between the sixteenth and eighteenth centuries.

The extent to which the Renaissance reshaped Greek culture can be gleaned from the literary and artistic efflorescence under way in the cities of Venetian Crete. By the sixteenth century, the Venetian ruling caste had adopted Cretan Greek and had more or less assimilated with the local society; visiting dignitaries from Venice were bemused at the local nobility's lack of fluency in the mother tongue. What had emerged in Chania, Candia (Iraklion) and Rethymnon was a hybrid society that shared an appetite for Renaissance art forms, but wished to experience these works in Greek. Cretan painters such as Michael Damaskinos (*c*.1530–*c*.1591) and Domenikos Theotokopoulos, better known by the name El Greco (*c*.1540–1614), managed to move between Byzantine and Renaissance styles and find ways to blend elements to produce highly original work. The Cretan Renaissance, however, was best known for literature. Particularly striking were the variety of plays, epic romances and poems that were written during the last century of Venetian rule. As in Classical Greece and sixteenth-century Italy, Cretan audiences were treated to mature and highly original plays that served as commentaries on social life.

The Ottoman conquest of Crete brought a sudden halt to the island's literary output, although copies of local masterworks, such as Vitsentzos Kournaros' 10,000-line romance *Erotokritos*, would still be read with pleasure throughout the Greek *oikoumene*. But Crete also happened to be the empire's last significant territorial acquisition. Within a few years, its armies suffered a rare defeat during the siege of Vienna (1683), which turned out to be the first of many against European Christian armies. And during the course of the following century, as the balance of world power shifted decisively in Christian Europe's favour, the Ottoman Empire was transformed from the continent's greatest power to its weakest. As its standing diminished, Greeks and other Ottoman Christians began to envisage a future without Muslim overlords.

7

The Making of Modern Hellas (c. 1700–1910): Ethnicity and State Building

The Ottomans came to appreciate their dire predicament only belatedly, when the empire was dealt an uncharacteristically devastating defeat in the Russo-Turkish War of 1768–1774. The Russians attained access to the Black Sea and posed a direct threat to Constantinople. Subsequent wars had further revealed the Ottomans lacked the capacity to resist further encroachments. In fact, the empire's fate was now a problem to be resolved by Christian European powers, and one that was to be revisited many times over: it came to be known as 'the Eastern Question'. That the Ottoman Empire survived as long as it did was a function of the balance of power that was arranged between Christian states, which seemed to depend on keeping the 'Sick Man of Europe' alive.

For the empire's Christians subjects, the ramifications of Europe's ascendancy were far reaching. The welfare of Armenians, Serbs and Bulgarians became a matter of international scrutiny, but it was the Greeks who received special attention. After all, the eighteenth century was also the Age of Enlightenment, yet another era of intellectual ferment that took its cues from the Classical tradition. The Greeks therefore enjoyed a special place in the Western imagination, especially as Europe came to see Classical Greece as *its* cultural birthplace, with educated Frenchmen, Germans and Britons believing that they too were 'Greeks'. As with the Romans of Hadrian's era, however, modern Europe, from its position of power, had its own vision of Hellenism that it dictated to the Greeks, telling them who they 'really' were and setting the terms for what a 'reawakened' Greece should look like.

When Greece did become a nation-state by the 1830s, it only managed to do so under European Great Power patronage, and it was European statesmen who determined the nation's borders, constitution and head of state. The revived 'Greece' therefore began largely as a European contrivance – or an aspect of European modernity. Needless to say, the new Greece quickly took on a life of its own.

THE WORLD OF THE GREEKS IN THE EIGHTEENTH CENTURY

What did 'Greekness' mean before the age of nationalism? Who were the Greeks of the latter phases of Ottoman rule? There are no straightforward answers to these questions, but there are at least three perspectives that ought to be considered. The first, and the most important in the long run, was the European or Western perspective, which understood the world as a collection of sharply defined ethnic groups. The written accounts of Western travellers refer to a multitude of Ottoman ethnicities. It was a 'Turkish' empire, but one that contained 'Greeks', 'Bulgarians', 'Arabs' and many other groups to whom such labels meant almost nothing. In most cases, however, these ascribed labels would later form the basis of national identities.

Westerners understood Greeks to be Orthodox Christians that spoke Greek. These *ethnic* Greeks were concentrated in areas we normally associate with the historic Greek heartland: the Peloponnese, central Greece, Attica, the Aegean and Ionian Islands, Cyprus and Crete. It is worth noting, however, that none of these 'homeland' territories were exclusively Greek. Central Greece and the Peloponnese also had large numbers of Orthodox Albanians and Vlachs, while Muslim Turks were concentrated in towns. There were also Greek-speaking Jews (Romaniotes), whose ancestry could be traced as far back as Roman times, and Greek-speaking Muslims in places like Crete, the descendants of Christian converts. Frankish and Venetian rule had also left a series of Greek-speaking Catholic communities in the Cyclades and the Ionian islands.

In northern Greece the population was far more heterogeneous. Greek might have been the language of the majority in Epiros, Thessaly and along the Macedonian coastline, but further inland and northwards it appears that ethnic Greeks were restricted to towns. The plains and hills were thickly populated with various Muslims and Slavic peoples, while Albanians and Vlachs dominated the steep highlands. Some Balkan centres like Larissa and Serres were essentially Muslim cities, but the

Image 6 Ottoman Greece: to westerners, Athens seemed no different from any other part of the Islamic 'Orient', as shown in this watercolour by Edward Dodwell (c.1805) (*courtesy of the Benaki Museum, GE 23059*).

rest featured a dense mixture of faiths and languages. Greeks were also a significant minority in Thrace and Constantinople.

Beyond the Balkans and the islands, the Greek *oikoumene* was spread more thinly. During the course of the eighteenth century, the diaspora could be found throughout Europe, in cities as far apart as London and St Petersburg. Another kind of Greek dispersion was formed by the remnants of Byzantine Anatolia and Italy. There were still numerous 'Greci' villages in southern Calabria and in central Apulia. The largest group in Anatolia were the Pontic Greeks, whose villages lined the alpine areas and the shoreline of the Trebizond region. The rest of Anatolia was overwhelmingly Turkish-speaking and Muslim, although parts of the interior contained scatterings of Orthodox communities, particularly in the environs of Kayseri (Caesaria), Konya (Iconium) and Ankara (Ankyra). Greek could still be heard in some rare cases. Located somewhere between Kayseri and the Syrian hinterland was Pharasa, where an archaic Greek dialect survived into the early twentieth century. Along the Aegean coast and around the Sea of Marmara, however, Greek was common because of ongoing contacts and migration from the islands. At the beginning of the nineteenth century, Greeks formed roughly 20 per cent of Smyrna's population, and figured strongly in towns like Foça, Kios, Aydin and Bodrum.

The second perspective was the standard Ottoman perspective, and what mattered here was faith. In the eighteenth century, if a Greek were to be asked his identity, the answer would either be 'Christian' (*Hristianos*) or 'Roman': (*Rum* in Turkish, *Rhomios* in Greek). Being Roman, however, meant being Greek Orthodox Christian. Hence it was a term applied to all Orthodox peoples, those whose mother tongue could also be Albanian, Bulgarian, Serb, Vlach, Georgian or Arabic. Only in Church matters was 'Romanness' specifically associated with Greek as the language of liturgy and the Bible, and it particularly came to the fore in disputes with the bishoprics and parishes that used Slavonic.

The third and final perspective referred to Greekness as a form of high culture. Throughout the Orthodox Christian world and especially in the Balkans, where the Orthodox formed a majority, Greek language and education was standard among the upper classes and the upwardly mobile. Thus, as in Hellenistic and Roman times, Greek culture was social capital. Balkan elites could become Greek with a Greek education or at least by adopting Greek ways. In Belgrade, for example, polite society spoke Greek and subscribed to Greek fashions until the 1840s. Greek also happened to be the medium of Balkan commerce and trading associations, hence places like Bucharest, Philippopolis (Plovdiv), Ohrid and Monastir were Hellenized cities. In some important senses, therefore, the Greek Roman Empire described in earlier chapters had not altogether disappeared.

Many of the leading figures in the Greek *oikoumene*, some of whom became important figures in Greek national lore, were often people from homes where different tongues were spoken. Two major intellectual figures of the eighteenth century, Iospos Moisiodax (1725–1800) and Rhigas Velestinlis (1756–1798), were Vlachs who could also claim a Greek identity. Moisiodax acquired Greek at school and adopted a Hellenized name: 'Moisiodax' refers to the classical name of his Rumanian birthplace, Moesia (Cernavoda). The most telling indication of the cultural power of Greek could be found in the court of Ali of Tepelen (or Ali Pasha, *c*.1750–1822), a Muslim Albanian potentate who effectively ruled the western Balkans in the late eighteenth and early nineteenth century. Ali's court in Ioannina (Yanina) featured a significant number of Greek elites that served in various ministerial and advisory roles, but particularly striking was the fact that he made Greek the language of his court. Ali also set about promoting Greek education and arts within his domain, and ensured that the schools of Ioannina were staffed with good teachers. As someone who had ambitions to rule the Balkans as an independent sovereign, Ali recognized that Greek and Greek culture were essential.

GOVERNANCE AND AUTONOMY

How was the Greek world organized at the grass roots level? The Ottomans preferred to engage with corporate bodies, and in the Greek world each locality had its *koinotita* (commune). The *koinotita*, a vestige of the ancient *polis*, was a formal institution that had limited revenue-raising powers and served judicial functions, operating initially with Roman Law, but increasingly with common law. Most communes were probably dominated by local strongmen, the village priest or men of influence (*archontes*). In the regions that the Ottomans found difficult to control, such as the various *agrafa* villages of the Pindus Mountains or the autonomous Zagorachoria of Epiros, the *koinotita* acted more or less as an independent government.

At the broader regional level, matters were somewhat more complicated. The empire was essentially held together by an agglomeration of special arrangements between the region and the Ottoman state. The Peloponnese, for example, appeared to possess significant autonomy. It had a 'senate' that dealt with administrative and taxation issues, and its delegates were drawn from the *koinotites*. The senate occasionally sent delegates to Constantinople to raise problems before imperial officials. Different kinds of political arrangements obtained between the Ottoman state and such places as Mani (Peloponnese), the Zagorachoria, Mt Pelion (Thessaly), Mt Athos, the monasteries of Pontus and most Greek islands, although each involved significant tax concessions and self-rule.

There were vast regions of the empire that neither the state nor the provincial governors could effectively control. The rugged alpine regions of the Balkans were the domain of Christian pastoralists and brigands, known as *haiduks* in the north and *klephts* further south. In essence, the *klephts* preyed on highways and lowland village communities, stole sheep and waged vendettas. As with other bandit groups in the Mediterranean, however, the *klephts* acquired the image of dashing and free-spirited outlaws. The heroic feats of *kapetanioi* (captains) were the subject of stories that were circulated throughout the mountain villages. Theodoros Kolokotronis, a *kapetanios* who achieved great prominence in the Greek revolt of 1821, claimed that being a *klepht* was a means to achieving honour: 'the name *klepht* was a boast … The prayer for a father for his sons was that he might become a *klepht*'.[1] Behind the romantic sheen, however, was simply another power structure that Ottoman authorities somehow tried to control or accommodate. One particular Epirot *kapetanios* named Stournaris controlled 120 villages, had a standing force of up to 400 men, and his clan owned something like half a million sheep and goats.

GREEK LEADERSHIP UNDER THE OTTOMANS

The Orthodox Church became more 'Greek' under the Ottomans. The power of the Patriarchate of Constantinople had been enhanced by the fact that all Orthodox sees were placed under its jurisdiction, including the ancient patriarchates of Alexandria, Antioch and Jerusalem, and the Balkan Patriarchates based at Ohrid and Pec. The closure in 1766 of the Serbian Patriarchate (Pec), followed by its Bulgarian equivalent a year later, was driven in part by the Greek hierarchy's determination to maintain its dominance. The Greek Church also took it upon itself to open new schools in northern Greece in order to counter the use of Bulgarian

Boundary of the Ottoman Empire, c. 1638

Map 9 The Ottoman Empire AD *c*.1683

or Albanian. In 1770, the firebrand preacher, Kosmas of Aetolia, toured the villages and offered listeners some additional incentives: 'Let those who promise not to use Albanian at home rise and say so, and I shall absolve them from all of their sins'.[2]

Under the Ottoman system, the Patriarch of Constantinople was the head of the *Rum* community. It was ultimately the Patriarch's responsibility that his community remained loyal and paid its taxes. It was left to bishops and abbots to collect the taxes, and they often used janissaries as enforcers. Peasants therefore regarded the higher clergy as oppressors, and this was particularly the case during the seventeenth and eighteenth centuries, when the Orthodox were taxed heavily to subsidize the higher clergy's mounting debts. Upon each election, the successful candidate for the Patriarchate (and indeed every important bishopric) was expected to upstage his predecessor with a larger payment to the sultan and his officials. So lucrative was this money source that the sultan's court engineered a rapid succession of patriarchs: during the seventeenth century there were 58 elections, making the average reign less than two years. In 1730, the Patriarchate's debts were in the range of 7000 kg of gold.

The other group positioned at the apex of the *Rum* community were the Phanariots of Constantinople. This set of highly refined and cosmopolitan families, some being among the richest in the empire, came into its own by the eighteenth century. Phanariots were invaluable to the sultan for their expertise in medicine, finance and banking, but in the eighteenth century they were indispensible for their knowledge of European languages and cultures. Thus Phanariots usually served in the role of 'dragoman', the sultan's translator, and played important roles in diplomatic missions and in brokering treaties. They also served as *hospodar*s (regents) in the autonomous Christian principalities of Moldavia and Wallachia (modern-day Rumania), where they earned notoriety as brutal rulers.

The Phanariots took pride in being loyal servants of the Ottoman state, but the mere fact that they remained Christian also suggested a level of detachment. For as with most Orthodox Christians, the Phanariots believed that Ottoman rule was transitory. In typical Byzantine fashion, they believed that Muslim suzerainty was a form of divine retribution for past sins, but that redemption for God's Chosen was also part of His divine plan. All classes remained obsessed by prophecies and were deeply familiar with the words of such diviners as Leo the Wise and Agathangelos. The future Greek revolutionary leader, Theodoros

Kolokotronis, noted in his memoirs that prophecies played a major role in his own religious upbringing, and it is clear that many of his contemporaries were encouraged to revolt in 1821 because they were anticipating the final reckoning. That meant the overthrow of Muslim suzerainty and the restoration of the Roman (Byzantine) Empire. The standard line had it that the *Rhomioi* would reclaim Constantinople and its empire, and that the faithful would see the return of the 'marble emperor', Constantine XI, who fell during the fighting in 1453. Another popular prophecy referred to the coming of the *xanthos genos* (fair-haired peoples), who were widely assumed to be the Orthodox Russians.

The pervasive influence of such prophecies pointed to what was the underlying weakness of the Ottoman Empire. As an Islamic polity, it practised a form of tolerance that worked well as long as the empire remained powerful on the international stage, but by refusing to confer equality to non-Muslims it could not depend on their loyalty once the empire began its decline. Rather, the Ottoman ruling order and Muslim subjects expected non-Muslims to accept political and social subordination in perpetuity, or otherwise convert to Islam. Subordination was manifested in various everyday restrictions, such as the proscriptions against carrying arms and riding horses, and with dress codes. In practice, many of these proscriptions were not observed, but there were others, such as taxation and legal inequalities, that did have a way of reinforcing the point. The precarious position of the patriarch and the occasional execution of the uppity Phanariot also reminded Christians that their well-being depended on Muslim sufferance.

BACKGROUND TO THE GREEK REVOLT (c.1770–1820)

It was not until the latter decades of the eighteenth century that Greek elites began to give serious thought to the question of political emancipation. The turning point was the Russo-Turkish War of 1768–1774, which demonstrated clearly that the great European powers enjoyed a decisive military edge. Balkan Christians sensed they could challenge the Ottoman state provided they received substantial European aid. The earliest rebellions that erupted in the Peloponnese and Crete in 1770 were backed by promises of Russian money and military support.

The precipitous decline of Ottoman power in relation to Christian Europe serves as the essential historical backdrop for the emergence of modern Greece. As European states became more centralized, the

Ottomans and the other great Islamic powers (Mughal India and Safavid Persia) had been moving in precisely the opposite direction. Over the course of the seventeenth and eighteenth centuries, the Ottoman state had gradually conceded enormous powers to *ayans* (regional magnates), who were entrusted with the responsibility of resolving problems such as rural indebtedness and tax extortion. Some *ayans* became well ensconced and developed the means to challenge the empire, as was the case with Muhammad Ali Pasha (1769–1849) of Egypt and his less successful counterpart in the Balkans, Ali Pasha. Many parts of the Balkans were also under the thumb of Christian warlords known as *koçabasis*. It was a Peloponnesian warlord, Panayotis Benakis of Kalamata, who headed the failed revolt of 1770. Russian observers found that his rebellion not only lacked popular support but, crucially, the support of other Peloponnesian *koçabasis*.

The decentralization of state power made it difficult for the Asian empires to maintain military parity with the Europeans, whose ascendancy had to do with technological and tactical innovations, as well as a far greater capacity to mobilize resources and finance military innovations. Since the previous Russo-Turkish War of 1735–1739, the Russians had achieved greater mastery of mobile firepower and more disciplined regimental formations. The Ottomans, on the other hand, had come to rely on the *ayans* to raise manpower that was ill equipped and inadequately trained. The Ottomans were slow to respond to Europe's challenge, and it would take more than a century of state, provincial and military reforms, starting from the reign of Selim III (1789–1807), to begin the process of bridging the gap.

The impact of Europe's economic ascendancy would also have enormous ramifications for non-Muslim groups. Over the course of the century, Ottoman towns became much more engaged in external trade networks and credit operations. France was the empire's most significant trading partner, but Greek ships using various European flags carried much of the trade with the British, Russians and Dutch. After the outbreak of the French Revolutionary Wars, the Greek merchant marine supplanted not only the French but also outstripped its Venetian and Maltese competition. Between 1786 and 1813, the Greek fleet doubled in size and individual merchants made vast fortunes.

A good portion of these accumulated fortunes was used to revitalize Greek education. Contrary to later Greek nationalist mythology, which had it that children were forced by the Ottomans to meet in secret locations in the dead of night, the Greek *oikoumene* had educational facilities that were better funded and organized than their Muslim counterparts. In the lead up to 1821, the enthusiasm for schooling within the Greek *oikoumene* was noted by visitors. In his highly detailed *Researches in Greece* (1814), the British topographer William Martin Leake reported that:

> there is not a Greek community in a moderate state of opulence, either in Greece or in other parts of Turkey, or in the Austrian dominions, or in Russia, that does not support a school for teaching their children the ancient Greek, and in many instances the other principal branches of polite education.[3]

With the growth of the Greek mercantile marine came the expansion of the diaspora, particularly in major Mediterranean/Black Sea commercial centres such as Trieste and Odessa. Here, Greek merchants, intellectuals, students and professionals formed various kinds of associations, many of which took an interest in the Greek *oikoumene* and reflected on its prospects. From a distance, the overseas Greeks came to develop a greater sense of ethnic self-awareness, and were best placed to appreciate the plummeting stocks of the Ottoman Empire. It was within these social circles that the very first plans for an emancipated Greek *oikoumene* were first mooted.

From the French Revolution (1789) onwards, many European 'nations' were dreamt up by similar kinds of associations. When considering the emergence of nationalism, modern historians have highlighted the importance of 'critical publics' for conceiving a new form of state based on liberal ideals and institutions, which in turn would supplant the established systems of monarchy by divine right and aristocratic privilege. These critical publics emerged during a generic crisis in governance that came to a head with the Revolution and with the spread of its radical political influence across Europe (1789–1815). Greek thinkers in the diaspora and the Balkans were swept up in this maelstrom. Between 1790 and 1800, Greek publications on secular themes began to exceed religious studies (192 as opposed to 128), with many more books now on philosophical topics. In major diaspora centres such as Vienna, Greeks had access to their own journals. The most influential publication during the Revolution period was *Efimeris*, which ran between 1790 and 1798. It was with *Efimeris* that many Greek readers were kept abreast of developments in France and their reverberations across Europe.

ARTICULATING MODERN GREECE

There was no Greek consensus, however, regarding what self-rule might mean. Existing power brokers, such as the *koçabasis*, were interested in enhancing their personal power and autonomy. Others were guided by ideals. The Revolution promoted ideas that were especially attractive to upwardly mobile merchants and professionals, who expected to share power in any ruling order based on merit. The violence of the Revolutionary Era in Europe, however, confirmed in the minds of more conservative Greeks that if the Ottoman state was to be overhauled some form of Christian Orthodox *ancien régime* should take its place.

The broader European context is important for another reason. For Europe's rise to global mastery inevitably fostered a great deal of introspection and re-evaluation of itself and of its attitudes towards the Muslim world, including the enfeebled Ottomans. By the late eighteenth century, European scholarship and literature had created a self-serving view of the Islamic states as weak, despotic, cruel and backward, if only to set up an antithetical Western self-image. In the meantime, the idea of Greece as the birthplace of European/Western civilization was reinforced in order to explain genealogically its genius for artistic and scientific invention. It was Shelley who proclaimed in his rhapsodic *Hellas* (1821) that 'We are all Greeks'.

Shelley's contemporaries did not share his passion in equal measure, but Europeans had long since begun to see contemporary Greeks as their own kind, or as relatives who had fallen on hard times. Hence the Greeks and their political fate was a matter of intense public interest. The pivotal moment was the failed Peloponnesian revolt of 1770, which generated a flood of fictional and non-fictional publications that took up the cause of Greek freedom, including Voltaire's *Ode Pindarique a propos la guerre presente en Grece*:

> I want to revive Athens,
> Let Homer sing your combats
> Let the voices of a hundred Demosthenes
> Revive your hearts and your arms.[4]

Unsurprisingly, contemporary Greeks were also infected by this European passion. This was certainly the case among the educated, for whom the most pressing issue was the need to teach fellow Greeks about their heritage. The figure most closely associated with this imperative was Adamantios Koraïs (1748–1833), a major classical scholar in his own right who lived most of his life in Paris. One of his most significant contributions to the renewal of the Greek *oikoumene* was the 'Hellenic Library', with its translations of Greek Classics that were specifically tailored to educate his Greek contemporaries. In his firm view, the regeneration of the Greek people would come about through re-engagement with the glories of antiquity. It was Koraïs who fostered the development of a form of 'high' Greek based on a mixture of Attic and contemporary demotic. *Katharevousa*, the 'clean language', later became the established register of the Greek state and education.

One of its virtues was to bring a much richer and useful vocabulary to modern Greek communication. The very fact that it was named 'the clean language', however, suggested a certain inferiority complex about contemporary Greek culture. Common Greek, so the line went, was ridden with impurities by infiltration of extraneous borrowings that diminished *real* Greek and ought to be expunged. Along with many other Westernized Greeks, Koraïs was particularly keen to sideline the clergy, a group that he believed were responsible for keeping the Greeks in a state of cultural backwardness. Rather, Koraïs believed that the Greeks should look to their Western counterparts, for European civilization was much more faithful to the Greek heritage. Paris, he claimed, was the new Athens:

> Imagine a city larger than Constantinople, with 800,000 inhabitants, with various academies, libraries, where science and art have been developed to perfection . . . all these blessings no longer exist in Greece.[5]

Thus to become more 'Hellenic', Greeks had to be more European. Ottoman history and culture was a major liability. The new Greece had to reject the decadent and Islamic-dominated East and 'rejoin' the rising West.

Another important Greek luminary was Rhigas Velestinlis (1757–1798), otherwise known as Rhigas Pheraios. Unlike the retiring Koraïs, Velestinlis was an intrepid political activist who engaged with conspiratorial circles and wrote important revolutionary tracts. His background was more typical of anti-Ottoman activists in the lead-up to Greek independence. He was educated at Ambelakia in Thessaly, became a schoolteacher and served as secretary to the Phanariot Alexander Ipsilandis in Constantinople. Inspired by events in Revolutionary France, he tried to raise the banner of revolution in the ιns and Anatolia. His vision was for a republic of peoples that ιded all ethnicities and confessions, including Muslims, but which ι ιnd unity in Greek education and language. In the 1790s he produced a series of political tracts, including *The New Political Constitution of the Inhabitants of Rumeli, Asia Minor, the Archipelago, Moldavia and Wallachia*, of which 3000 copies were printed and distributed throughout the Greek *oikoumene*. In Article 7 he calls for an *Elleniki Demokratia* (Hellenic Republic) of 'sovereign people [to] include all the inhabitants of this kingdom (the Ottoman Empire) without exception to religion and language: *Hellene*, Bulgarian, Albanian, Vlach, Armenian, Turks and every other people'.[6] In 1798, he was betrayed to the Austrian authorities and was handed over to the Ottomans. He was strangled en route to Constantinople.

After Velestinlis' execution, many more individuals and groups dedicated their lives to the removal of the Ottoman yoke. There were also more political tracts, but it was not until 1814 that a coherent movement was formed. The *Philki Etereia* (Friendly Society) was a secret movement formed in Odessa, and it included merchants, professionals, scholars and students. In 1818, it moved its headquarters to Constantinople, where it planned the overthrow of the Ottoman order. The critical problem with such underground movements was that they could not succeed without first inciting popular uprisings. The most influential Greek of his era, Count Ioannis Capodistrias (1776–1831), a senior minister in the Russian imperial court during the 1810s, dismissed the movement's aims as reckless and irresponsible, and it was a view shared by most Greek elites at the time. The movement itself never had more than 1000 members, but it had some success in galvanizing interested parties, particularly among *klephts* and *haiduks*, *koçabasis* and sympathetic bishops. By 1820, the *Eteraia*'s plans for a coordinated insurrection were well known among Greek elites. Simultaneous attacks were planned for various parts of the Ottoman Empire and its bordering territories. Once the flag of revolution was raised, the conspirators expected the discontented masses to rise up in revolt and sweep the old regime away.

THE GREEK REVOLT (1821–1825)

As it happened, conditions appeared to be ripe for social upheaval. While the Napoleonic Wars had been a boon for Greek shipping, the cessation of conflict in 1815 inevitably led to a sudden collapse in

Western demand for Ottoman raw materials. In the immediate post-war years, piracy and banditry were rife, and local commerce and manufacturing suffered greatly in these deteriorating conditions. Therefore, once the banner of revolt was raised in Greece, there was substantial mass involvement. The much more significant threat to the Ottoman state, however, was posed by *ayans* such as Ali Pasha. The 'Lion of Yanina' had used the war years to shore up his power in the Balkans, and by 1819 it was widely believed that he could muster as many as 40,000 men. In 1820, the sultan's chief advisor, Halet Efendi, who had been responsible for bringing other *ayans* to heel, made his move against Ali. Loyal Balkan *ayans* were ordered to levy troops and to march on Epiros.

The resulting war seemed a good opportunity to raise the banner of Greek liberty. With thousands of Ottoman troops tied up in the western Balkans, the *Philiki Etereia* planned a coordinated uprising in the Danubian provinces, Constantinople and the Peloponnese. The revolt in Moldavia and Wallachia was led by the *Etereia*'s newly appointed leader, Alexander Ipsilantis, a Phanariot who had been the aide-de-camp of Tsar Alexander I. On 8 October 1820, Ipsilantis led an army of patriots, the so-called 'Sacred Legion', a motley force of 5000 men with little fighting experience, who were expected to join forces with a much larger Rumanian army (of 65,000 men) led by Tudor Vladimirescu. Once these armies were mobilized, it was assumed that the 'enslaved' peoples of Rumania and the Balkans would rise up against their oppressors. When the Sacred Legion finally moved into Moldavia the following March, however, the masses were unmoved. Rumanians had suffered greatly under the harsh rule of Phanariot *hospodars* and hence were never likely to support a Greek cause. Ipsilantis and Vladimirescu were therefore left to face the inevitable Ottoman onslaught. Ipsilantis' army made a brave, if hopeless, stand at the Battle of Dragatsani on 19 June, and he was later captured and executed. Predictably, the suicidal uprising planned in Constantinople, where Greeks formed a vulnerable minority, did not take place, but the community suffered mass reprisals regardless. The patriarch, as leader of the *Rum* community, was hanged on 10 April, as were other prominent Greeks.

In the predominantly Greek Peloponnese, however, revolt was a much more realistic proposition. In March 1821, the *kapetanoi* moved against the Ottoman gendarmerie and massacred the Muslim communities of Nafplion, Kalamata and Tripoli. (When news of the Greek revolt reached Constantinople, retaliatory action was taken against Greek communities in the capital, Smyrna and Chios.) The south-west of the Peloponnese came under the authority of Petrobey Mavromihalis of Mani, while Theodoros Kolokotronis extended his control over the central Peloponnese. Other leaders also sensed the time had come to reject the sultan's authority. On 25 March at Kalavryta, near Patras, following a meeting of Peloponnesian notables, the local bishop Germanos proclaimed a *epanastasi* (general insurrection). On 28 March, Mavromihalis issued a proclamation declaring independence from the Ottomans, and in May he led the formation of a government in Kalamata.

The situation further north was slightly more complicated. Here, Ali Pasha was losing the war against the empire. Christian brigands had either been fighting for or against him, although some sat back so as to intervene at the most opportune moment. As news of the success of the Peloponnesian insurgency filtered through, however, many *kapetanoi* in Central Greece moved against the Ottomans, as Odysseus Androutsos did in Boeotia and Giorgos Karaïskakis in Messolonghi. The Ottomans also lost control of the Aegean, as Greek sea captains, led by Konstantinos Kanaris of Psara and Andreas Miaoulis of Hydra, used their piratical skills to harass Ottoman shipping. Greek domination of the seas made it much harder for the Ottomans to send troops to the rebellious territories and keep their supply lines open. Within a year of the proclamation at Kalavryta, the rebels had liberated southern Greece and the islands. The defeat of Ali Pasha on 24 January 1822 had freed up Ottoman forces, but by that stage southern insurgents were well ensconced. For the moment, it appeared that the Greek revolt had succeeded.

It soon transpired, however, that the rebels did not necessarily share the same objectives. The political principles advocated by the *Philiki Etereia* seemed all too abstract to the *kapetanoi*, who were only vaguely familiar with 'Greece' as a concept; but there was recognition that statehood was necessary if the insurgency was to succeed. In November 1821, there were three separate governments (Peloponnese, western Greece and eastern Greece), but by January 1822 a provisional constitution was drawn up at Epidauros, making Greece a republic with a senate, legislature and an executive. All delegates agreed in principle for centralized administration, but the captains and *koçabasis* were reluctant to forfeit their personal power. In practice, the strongmen who dominated the localities before 1821 continued to do so during the revolt.

As a consequence, there was no coordinated war against the Ottomans. Indeed most of the fighting between 1822 and 1824 took place between the *kapetanoi*, as petty conflicts raged throughout the Peloponnese and Central Greece. In 1823 there were at least two governments, and by mid-1824 the two were at war. Meanwhile, the Ottomans reluctantly sought the assistance of Mohammad Ali, the *ayan* and effective ruler of Egypt, who was promised Crete in the bargain and the Peloponnese for his son Ibrahim. A well-drilled army of 17,000 Egyptians was despatched in early 1825 and quickly subdued most of the Peloponnese. In the meantime, Ottoman troops led by Reshid Pasha moved against the *kapetanoi* in central Greece. Despite some successes, including a spectacular victory led by Makryiannis near Argos in late June, the Greek revolt had been effectively suppressed. By 1827, all that was left in Greek hands was Nafplion and Corinth.

THE INTERNATIONAL CONTEXT (1825–1833)

In the meantime, Europe's Great Powers had been watching intently from afar. There was much nervousness about the response of Russia, which was expected to intercede on behalf of its Orthodox co-religionists. There was also public opinion to consider. European society was overwhelmingly pro-Greek, and numerous philhellenes had been quick to join the fight for Hellas, including Lord Byron, who contributed a small fortune to the cause and died (April 1824) during a military campaign. There was some disquiet regarding the reluctance of European governments to intervene. Back in 1821, Byron's friend Shelley had put it bluntly:

> The apathy of the rulers of the civilized world to the astonishing circumstance of the descendants of that nation to which they owe their civilization, rising as it is from the ashes of their ruin, is something perfectly inexplicable to a mere spectator to the shows of this mortal scene. We are all Greeks.[7]

What really mattered in the courts of Europe, particularly after the tumult caused by the French Revolution and the Napoleonic Wars, was the maintenance of the international balance of power, which meant keeping the Balkans, Constantinople and the Near East out of Russian hands. Between 1821 and 1825, the 'Greek Question' remained the hottest diplomatic issue in an otherwise quiet period of international diplomacy. The Great Powers had little appetite for more open conflict,

Image 7 Hellenism, Orthodoxy and Nationhood: the Greek revolt is launched after warrior chief's swear an oath in the Church of Aghia Lavra on 25 April 1821 (by Theodoros Vryzakis) (*courtesy of the Benaki Museum, (GE 8970)*).

and they initially followed the lead of Austrian statesman Klemens von Metternich, whose approach was to stall Russian action until the Greek revolt was stamped out. However, the very idea that the freedom-seeking Greeks might be left at the mercy of bloodthirsty 'infidels' was unconscionable in many influential circles. It was during the Egyptian invasion of the Peloponnese that the practical interests of the Great Powers were overtaken by public opinion. Rumours were circulated that Greece, the cradle of European civilization, was to be repopulated by Africans. When Britain decided in the autumn of 1825 that it would work with Russia to impose a resolution on the Ottomans, Greek autonomy was inevitable. Ottoman recalcitrance was finally overcome following the Battle of Navarino in 1827, when an Ottoman-Egyptian fleet was destroyed within four hours, leading to the Egyptian evacuation of Greece. While French troops were sent to occupy the Peloponnese, a Russian army led by Tsar Nicholas I crossed the Danube. By August 1828, with the Russians within striking distance of Constantinople, the Ottomans sued for peace, having already agreed to British and French terms for Greek independence.

Modern Greece was therefore the product of a diplomatic solution that served the interests of the concert of Europe. The matter was formalized in three stages: the Treaty of Adrianople (1829), the London Convention (May 1832) and the Treaty of Constantinople (July 1832). In the meantime, the Greeks had recruited Ioannis Capodistrias to take up the role of president in January 1828. An eminent statesman who was well known in diplomatic circles, Capodistrias was also a conservative who gave the Greeks a veneer of respectability in a continent ruled by reactionary monarchies. He immediately oversaw various reforms, ranging from land redistribution to the formation of a state army. His greatest problem was overcoming the insubordination of *kapetanoi* and *koçabasis*, and from growing dissent from disenfranchized liberals. On 9 October 1831, he was assassinated in Nafplion, the provisional capital, after having alienated the powerful Mavromihalis clan of Mani.

As the country descended again into chaos, Greece's fleeting experience with constitutional government was brought to an abrupt end. The Great Powers saw fit to impose a more authoritarian system of government that was not unlike other restoration regimes in Europe. After some searching, the Powers settled on Prince Otto (Otho) of Bavaria as the first 'King of the Hellenes': the Greeks would know him as 'Othon'. Since Otho was a minor when he assumed the role, his father, King Ludwig I of Bavaria, appointed three regents to rule Greece in his stead

POST-INDEPENDENCE GREECE

The question of the kingdom's borders was also subject to extensive deliberation. The Peloponnese, Attica and Central Greece formed its heartland, and many of the nearby islands were also included, namely the Cyclades and Saronic Islands. However, Crete, Samos, Chios and the Dodecaneae Islands, each of which had played substantial roles in the independence struggle, were restored to Ottoman suzerainty. Otho's Greece was therefore roughly one-third of its present-day size, and it contained a minority of the empire's Greek-speaking Christians. Population levels had fallen since the pre-war period, slumping from 766,470 in 1821 to roughly 600,000 in 1828, although from 1838 we begin to see an impressive recovery (1838: 752,000; 1843: 915,000; 1853: 1,042,527). Slightly over half the population (53 per cent) in 1833 lived in the Peloponnese (397,500), 25 per cent in Central Greece (187,500) and 22 per cent were found among the islands (165,000). The kingdom was also home to large numbers of Vlachs and Orthodox Albanians.

The new Greece was launched in inauspicious circumstances. Industry was virtually non-existent, shipping had been in a depressed state since the end of the Napoleonic Wars, and much of the country's built environment had been reduced to rubble. An early visitor to Athens noted the absence of roofing. Just before Otho's arrival, Christopher Wordsworth, the nephew of the great poet William, reported in his *Athens and Attica* (1837) that the ancient ruins appeared in better shape:

> The town of Athens is now lying in ruins. The streets are almost deserted, nearly all the houses without roofs. The churches are reduced to bare walls and heaps of stones and mortar. There is but one church in which services are performed. A few wooden houses, one or two of more solid structure, and the two lines of planked sheds form the bazar [sic] are all the inhabited dwellings that Athens can boast.[8]

Similar stories were told of Patras, Kalamata and other towns. The villages too were in dire condition: as many as 662 lay in ruins. Most of the country's olive groves had been destroyed, while livestock numbers (sheep and goats) had been reduced by 90 per cent.

Reconstruction was therefore a monumental challenge for the new monarchy. Another was land redistribution. The broad aim was to create a contented population of independent proprietors by reallocating lands abandoned by Muslims. The best arable land had in fact been in Muslim hands, but since the beginning of the revolt it had already been occupied by squatters. Another problem was property boundaries. Greece lacked a proper cadastral survey, and since independence the courts had been overwhelmed with property demarcation disputes. Capodistrias launched a survey but it caused enormous friction with Greek landholders and squatters. The state's belated resolution to the country's land question was the so-called 'Donation' law of 1853. It effectively restricted the average parcel of land to under four hectares, and the state claimed an additional six per cent tax on the purchase price that was to be paid over a 36-year period. As a consequence, the average peasant family could not feed itself and pay its state mortgage debt. As these properties varied radically in soil quality and water access, many peasant families were locked into a spiral of debt. Peasants were forced to take up craftwork, work seasonally on larger estates, join the merchant marine or find work in places like Alexandria and Smyrna. Land reform, therefore, did little but perpetuate poverty and foster the age-old Greek tradition of migration.

The one positive development since independence was the revival of the Greek merchant marine. During the 1830s, the Greeks reclaimed their share of Mediterranean trade and became the chief carriers of Russian grain to the rest of Europe and the Middle East. The period also saw the emergence of Chiot shipping dynasties, such as the London-based Rallis Brothers and the Rodocanachis family. Greek shipping did much to stimulate the growth of Greek ports like Patras and Ermoupolis. The latter had a population of less than 200 in 1821, 12,000 in 1840 and perhaps as many as 25,000 in 1860. By the middle of the century, Patras served as the chief outlet of Peloponnesian agricultural products (chiefly currants), and it grew to be the kingdom's second largest city. Greater exposure to foreign interests and diaspora networks transformed Patras into a cosmopolitan city, noted for commercial schools that specialized in European languages. A clear sign of commercial prosperity were its many *archontika* (neoclassical mansions) and the fact that the city could support many local newspapers and magazines.

In 1834, Athens was chosen as the kingdom's capital by virtue of its historical prestige. The Peloponnesians tried to keep it in Nafplion or have it transferred to Corinth, Tripolis or Argos, but Otho's regency was mindful of the place Athens held in the Western imagination, and the importance of retaining Great Power support. It had never been a sleepy village, as modern historians have a habit of claiming. In late Ottoman times it had a population above 10,000, with 36 parishes, mosques, a *tekke*

Map 10 Modern Greece

(dervish convent) and a regular stream of Western visitors. There was broad agreement, however, that Athens must no longer *look* like an Ottoman town. As the capital of new Hellas, it had to appear more European. The chief designer, a German architect named Leo von Klenze (1784–1864), confirmed that the 'design of Athens was a European affair'.

A new city was to be built slightly to the north of Plaka and Monastiraki and to be focused along the axis between present-day Syntagma, Omonia and Theseon. The lack of state funds meant progress was slow, but by the 1870s the morphology of modern Athens had become apparent. The city now featured boulevards (Panepistimou, Akadimias, Sygrou), squares (Styntagma, Omonia), the Academy, National Library, the Royal Palace (Zappeion), the Grand Bertagne Hotel, as well as parks and squares. Private benefaction was crucial, and it was wealthy Greeks of the diaspora that funded the city's notable structures. Among them were Rumanian-based Evangelos Zappas (1800–1865), who also first mooted the idea of reviving the Olympic Games, and Giorgos Averoff (1815–1899), a major cotton merchant in Alexandria, who was responsible for the Panathenaic Stadium, where the first modern Olympics would be staged in 1896.

THE REIGN OF OTHO (1832–1864)

The new Greece had an absolute monarchy that subscribed to the divine right of kings. As with most of Europe's ruling regimes after 1815, it rejected constitutional governance and yet accepted the need for the kind of efficient bureaucratic administration that had been instituted during the Napoleonic Era. Otho's regents therefore removed the complex provincial arrangements that obtained under the Ottomans and divided the kingdom into ten *nomarchies* (departments) and 47 *eparchies* (subdepartments). All authorities within these subdivisions were state appointees. Traditional local government (*koinotites, demarchies*) was retained, but candidates for local offices were subjected to scrupulous state vetting.

Otho's reign was troubled from the outset. Although he could trace his lineage back to the Komnenoi, being Catholic he found it difficult to earn public trust. Particularly galling were the measures that infringed on the Church, including the dissolution of monasteries and the sale of religious treasures. His regents ruled in an arbitrary fashion and quarrelled incessantly. It was the *koçabasis, kapetanoi* and other social elites, however, that posed the greatest challenge to the regime. Athens was a seething hotbed of disenfranchized notables and university students that resented the new order and who scrutinized the state's every decision and failing. By the end of the 1830s, and under considerable British pressure, the regime was forced to appoint some Greeks into the ministry.

The only issue of common agreement between the state and society during Otho's long reign was irredentism: the reclamation of territories that, on historical and ethnic grounds, ought to have been included in the new kingdom. Visions of this 'Greater' Greece featured Epiros, Thessaly, Macedonia, Crete, the Ionians, Smyrna and Constantinople, along with many other territories. To most minds, the nation as it was in 1832 was incomplete. The most powerful Greek notable of the Othonian period,

179

Ioannis Kolettis (1773–1847), argued against making Athens the capital when the 'natural' centre of the Greek world was Constantinople. It was Kolettis who first coined the *Megali Idea* (Great Idea), according to which the Greek nation was meant to channel its energies towards reclaiming *the* city and its empire (Byzantium). Significantly, the *Megali Idea* resonated at all social levels, largely because it corroborated prophetic traditions regarding the redemption of Constantinople by God's Chosen.

What was the purpose of nation's like Greece? Why the need for a nation-state? In Europe, the nation had been initially dreamt up as a means to creating a just social order, but under the restoration regimes it appeared to have no purpose other than to bolster the power of the state. And as with many new nation-states that came into being during the course of the nineteenth century, Greece found its meaning in irredentism. It existed to pursue an imperial foreign policy. For the more influential 'political' classes, irredentism was the nation's *raison d'être*, and governments were judged in accordance with how well they prosecuted the noble dream.

In practice, the Megali Idea proved to be a dangarous, high-stakes mission that could not succeed without substantial Great Power support. In military terms, Greece was not a match for the Ottoman Empire. Political elites nevertheless persisted in fanning public expectations. Over time, the failure to meet these expectations had the effect of eroding the state's legitimacy. The power of public opinion was first demonstrated with the onset of the Ottoman–Egyptian crisis in 1838 and a Cretan rebellion in 1840. Otho, who by this stage had dismissed his regents and ruled in his own right, was pressured to take action in pursuit of the *Megali Idea*, but he lost face when a bandit leader beat him to the punch: one Ioannis Valentzas led an incursion into Ottoman Thessaly. The Great Powers quickly intervened, however, and further humiliated Otho by threatening to withhold state loans if the attack proceeded. In September 1843, a group of army officers had his palace surrounded. Fearing that the country might be plunged into chaos, or that Russia might secure an Orthodox nominee to replace Otho, the other Great Powers assented to the demands of the conspirators. Greece became a constitutional monarchy, with legislative powers transferred to a constituent assembly.

Once the new constitution was promulgated in March 1844, Greece appeared to have one of the most progressive political systems in Europe. All adult males over the age of 26 had the right to vote, and governance appeared to be in the hands of elected officials. In reality, political power was transferred into the hands of a few powerful figures. Wealthy individuals like Kolettis were now able to accumulate personal power by trading votes for jobs, protection and other favours, and thereby create large networks of political clients. Between 1844 and his death in 1847, Kolettis commanded the largest client network, and with it he was able to run the parliament like a dictator. Meanwhile, Otho suffered further political setbacks, but as the monarch nominated by the Great Powers he managed to survive until 1862, by which time his stocks with the Powers had evaporated. After another exhaustive search, the Powers settled on George, the second son of Prince Christian of Denmark. George I reigned as King of the Hellenes from 1863 to 1913.

GEORGE I AND THE AGE OF TRIKOUPIS (1863–1893)

With the new dynasty also came a new constitution that set a new compromise between monarchy and representative government. The king retained enormous powers. He enjoyed the right to dismiss governments and ministers, to declare war and sign treaties, and he remained the head of the armed forces. Governments were now formed by political coalitions that could muster a parliamentary majority. In practice, however, forming government coalitions required a great deal of wheeling and dealing between political patrons and potential clients. The result was a rapid succession of coalition governments and political turmoil that ultimately prompted excessive intervention from the monarchy – there were 23 governments during the first 11 years of the new king's reign.

As elsewhere in Europe, however, the state failed to keep in step with changes in society. As the political elite remained focussed on the *Megali Idea* and constitutional matters, the real challenges would arise from accelerated population growth and urbanization. At the very end of Otho's reign, the population stood at 1,096,864 (1861), but by 1870 it had grown to 1,457,894, and by 1896 to 2,433,806. The period witnessed impressive urban growth. By the 1890s, over 31 per cent of the population was urbanized or semi-urbanized. Athens-Piraeus combined jumped from a population of 47,750 in 1860 to 150,000 by 1890; Patras doubled in size, from 26,190 in 1870 to 50,154 in 1896; and Trikala in Thessaly grew from 1100 to 30,387 over the same period. The foundation of this period of population growth was the dramatic expansion of agricultural productivity and exports. The late 1860s and 1870s saw a boom in currant exports following the devastation of French, Italian and Spanish vineyards by a phylloxera epidemic. For the first time, the kingdom had an agricultural commodity that enjoyed strong external demand. In 1881, the agricultural sector was expanded through acquisition of Thessaly, with its vast and well-watered plains.

Social change in Greece followed the general European trends. With the expansion of manufacturing and industry came the growth of working-class communities and associations. Between 1867 and 1889, the number of large factories increased from 22 to 145. Over the last quarter of the nineteenth century, the population of Volos expanded by 80 per cent as a result of industrial growth. With economic modernization, however, came new kinds of social problems, such as urban over-crowding, sanitation and crime. A large proportion of newcomers to urban centres, particularly Athens, were male youths with honour codes and a disposition for violence. Visitors were struck by the fact that every male sitting in cafes seemed to be carrying a gun. The result was a homicide rate that by international standards was extraordinarily high: between 1870 and 1900 there were 79 murders per 100,000 as compared to 21 per 100,000 on vendetta-ridden Corsica.

By the end of the century, we also begin to see the expansion of the Greek middle class (shopkeepers, clerks, bureaucrats, professionals) and the development of typically bourgeois pursuits and forms of sociability, such as organized sports, vacationing and promenading. The typical middle-class adult was a voracious reader of magazines and romantic novels. Foreign observers were most impressed by their intense interest in politics and eager consumption of newspapers. According to one commentator writing at the turn of the century: 'The answer to the question "What does a Greek read?" must be "First and foremost, newspapers". There is no other country where the press plays such an important part in the life of its people'.[9] The rise of the middle classes actually posed the most significant challenge to the state, which was now beholden to a 'public' that developed very high expectations as to what the nation ought to be and what it should achieve. From the latter decades of the nineteenth century, an expanding and more assertive public kept the state on its toes. With every failure of state, whether real or apparent, came the threat of public demonstrations and street violence.

The first major shift in thinking regarding the purpose of the state occurred in the mid-1870s when Harilaos Trikoupis (1832–1896) began the first of his many periods as prime minister. He argued that the noble quest for a *Megali Ellas* (Greater Greece) must begin through domestic development. It was in the 1880s and the first half of the 1890s that the first great infrastructure schemes were set in train, such as a national railway network, road building schemes and the Corinth Canal (1881–1893), a monumental feat that was completed by a Greek company belonging to Constantinopolitan banker Andreas Syngros. When Trikoupis first came to power there was only one line of track, a mere 12 km long, linking Athens with Piraeus. By the beginning of the twentieth century, there was well over 1000 km of railway linking Athens with the Peloponnese, Central Greece and Thessaly, and the extensions to the track continued as national borders expanded after 1912. By 1892, 4000 km of roads had been constructed, with almost 1000 km more under construction. By 1893 there was almost 9000 km of telegraph wire and 186 telegraph offices. Other state-directed nation-building exercises included the expansion of the public school system. Student numbers at university, tertiary and primary levels enjoyed a massive increase, particularly primary schools for girls, in which numbers increased ten-fold between 1860 and 1900 (from 8,000 to 82,000).

For Trikoupis, therefore, nation-building had to with national development, but it came at a cost. Infrastructure and other nation-building projects were paid for largely by foreign loans and a national deficit that ballooned to unmanageable proportions. Taxes were raised significantly to service the interest payments, but in 1893, by which time the French vine crop had recovered and the price for Greek currants had collapsed, Greece was in effect bankrupt. Trikoupis suffered his final electoral defeat in 1895, and he died the following year. With his approach to nation-building somewhat discredited, Greek public opinion focused more squarely on irredentism as the more direct and glorious approach.

MASS POLITICS AND INSTABILITY (1890–1910)

Between 1890 and 1910, Greece had some of the hallmarks of a 'mass society'. It had frequent elections, a vibrant critical press, and it was among a handful of European states that could claim to have universal male suffrage. What counted for 'public opinion' was united in the cause of irredentism as much as it was about the central importance of Classical Greek heritage. Thus, countless numbers of regions, towns and villages were renamed by their Classical designations if current names were thought to sound too Slavic, Albanian or Turkish. Islands that had been known for centuries as Tzia and Tzirigho (Cerigo) were renamed

Kea and Kythera, respectively. Historians beginning with Konstantinos Paparrigopoulos (1815–1891), the Father of modern Greek history, wrote and taught histories of Greece that asserted a genealogical link between Classical, Byzantine and modern Greeks.

An indication of the critical importance of classical antiquity in modern Greek consciousness was the so-called 'language question': whether *katharevousa* or demotic should be the standard register for Greek public life. Indeed, anything to do with the Greek language was likely to lead to mass rioting and even bloodshed. In November 1901, central Athens was shattered by the *Evangelika* incident, when the publication of the Bible in demotic (common Greek) caused a violent backlash by the purists. The upshot of the ensuing mayhem, which involved tens of thousands of demonstrators and several fatalities, was the fall of the then government of Giorgios Theotokis. In November 1903, supporters of *katharevousa* rioted when Aeschylus' *Oresteia* trilogy was performed in demotic:

> students marched out in defence of Aeschylus, a riot took place, in which an innocent onlooker from Alexandria was killed, and the Rálles Ministry, in order to prevent worse disorders, forbade further performances of the offending trilogy.[10]

If political discourse was any guide, then matters relating to poverty and social injustice were unimportant, which suggested that labour organizations were not large enough to impress their concerns in the public domain. What really mattered in the 1890s was nationalism and the *Megali Idea*, and the partisan press played an important role in fanning prejudices and injecting a great deal more heat into public disputation.

In the lead up to 1896, the public mood for national regeneration through irredentism had reached fever pitch. In April that year, Athens was the setting of the first modern Olympics, an event that made Greece a centre of worldwide attention. The occasion appeared to make the public more acutely aware of the Classical heritage, including the values of competition and sport. The country was swept up in the cult of athleticism, which journalists likened to the 'true' Greek spirit of strength and struggle. According to the editorial of *Akropolis* in March 1896:

> Where we observe strength, we can also find will, courage of decision, action. Those who will not dare are condemned to flee . . . What happens to individuals happens to nations . . . Oh, if only Greece had ten times ten thousand bodies.[11]

The conflation of muscular athleticism with the *Megali Idea* was irresistible. When the games were staged in April, King George in his opening speech spoke on behalf of the 'liberated part' of Greece, and soon after the games streams of volunteers flowed into Ottoman Macedonia and Crete to fight the Turks. The Ottomans protested against the state's sponsorship of these irregulars and threatened war, and by April 1897 war did indeed break out.

The then prime minister, Theodoros Deliyiannis (1845–1905), the one-time opponent of Trikoupis and arch exponent of irredentism, was prompted to intervene in Crete where sectarian conflict was out of control and Ottoman intervention appeared imminent. Fearing the conflict might encourage the Russians and the Balkan states to set upon the Ottomans, the Great Powers moved quickly and imposed a political solution that favoured the Christian Cretan majority: autonomy under nominal Ottoman suzerainty. In the meantime, a Greek army was sent into Macedonia; but here the outcome was disastrous. Although the state and the political classes had developed an appetite for war, military preparations were woefully deficient. The Greek army had not been tested in decades: in fact, it was hardly adequate for policing duties and suppressing banditry. The Ottomans prevailed in two battles and won the war within four weeks. But for Great Power intervention, the rest of Greece was there for the taking.

As it happened, territorial losses were modest, but the Ottomans were owed a large indemnity, and Greece endured the added humiliation of having its finances placed under the supervision of an international finance body (i.e. the International Finance Commission). To the wider region, the ignominious defeat of 1897 revealed Greece to be militarily weak and overly dependent on the patronage of Great Powers like Britain. Domestically, it shattered public morale and public regard for the state and politicians, who were seen as too corrupt and consumed in petty politicking. In other words, the state had failed the nation.

THE RISE OF VENIZELOS

Interest in the *Megali Idea* subsided, but the lull did not last. The issue that refocused public attention was a looming crisis in Macedonia, and fears that this prized territory might be seized by Bulgaria and Serbia. Needless to say, the days when Balkan Orthodox elites aspired to be Greeks had long since been forgotten. Several developments since the

1840s had fostered separate nationalist movements among Serbs and Bulgarians, including the transformation of Serb and Bulgarian into literary languages and the ongoing attempts by Greek bishops to impose Greek on Bulgarian parishes. Since 1878, Serbia and Rumania had been independent states, and Bulgaria was autonomous. Like Greece, each of these states was dissatisfied with its territorial allocations and expected restitution through irredentism.

Greece's most direct competition for Macedonia was Bulgaria. Since the 1890s, agents of Greek and Bulgarian nationalism had been waging a campaign to win the hearts and minds of the Orthodox peasantry; but from 1904 the contest had degenerated into a violent struggle between rival militias. Villagers came under intense pressure to declare their national loyalties, and often found it expedient to bend with the prevailing wind. As one peasant put it: 'Our fathers were Greek and none mentioned the Bulgarians. We became Bulgarians, we won. If we have to be Serbs, no problem. But for now it is better for us to be Bulgarians'.[12] Evidently, language was not a sure indication of national allegiance. Numerous Slav-speaking Macedonians, mostly itinerant workers, found themselves stranded in Athens following Bulgarian attacks on their home villages, and many lobbied the Greek state to intervene.

In Greece, stories of the *makedononmachoi* (Macedonian fighters) evoked memories of the heroic revolutionary past and did much to rekindle national pride. Few, however, had any faith in the Greek state supporting the heroic *makedononmachoi*. Few indeed believed the politicians were capable of governing. The rapid succession of governments and regular public unrest over such matters as the language question gave the impression of a political system in disarray. Matters came to a head following the Young Turk Revolution in 1908, which saw the restoration of constitutional government after a long hiatus and the promise of equality for all subjects, including Ottoman Greeks. The revolution promised to rejuvenate the Ottoman Empire, and within Greek circles it signalled a setback to Greek aspirations in Macedonia.

In May 1909, officers that had formed the *Stratiotikos Syndesmos* (Military League) demanded reforms that might improve Greece's preparedness for war. After being rebuffed a number of times, the *Stratiotikos Syndesmos* seized power on 28 August. It transpired that the officers had no intention of retaining power, but they refused to hand it back to the established political parties. A solution soon appeared, however, in the form of a Cretan politician who had earned a considerable reputation during the Cretan struggle for autonomy. Eleftherios

Venizelos (1864–1936) had never been part of the political scene in Athens, but he had a proven record for political action, and he captured the public mood with his talk of *antikommatismos* (anti-partyism). In a speech in September 1910, he set himself apart from the political establishment by claiming: 'I do not come here as the leader of a new political party. I come simply as the bearer of new ideas'.[13] Rather, he spoke the language of national rejuvenation through *epanastasi* (revolution) and *anorthosis* (regeneration).

In other words, Venizelos presented himself as the man to save the nation from the state. On 8 August 1910, the established political parties won only 218 of the 362 seats in the parliament. The king offered him the prime ministership, but Venizelos sensed the political momentum was running in his favour and called another election. On 28 November, his hastily organized Liberal Party won decisively with 300 seats. His victory ushered in a new group of politicians, and a very different era in Greek politics.

8

·······

Greece in the Twentieth Century: The Age of Extremes

In 1900, the great majority of Greeks inhabited a domain that could hardly be described as 'modern'. The average person lived in a village or hamlet, where the typical family dwelling was nothing more than a single room with few amenities, and where everyday life followed time-honoured social preoccupations and cultural traditions. Since time immemorial, annual social events were fused with the religious calendar, particularly Lent and the various saints' day commemorations. Popular devotional practices revealed an obsession for the supernatural, the healing powers of saints and angels, and the malign presence of demons. All believed in the power of the 'evil eye'. The priest was usually a figure of influence, as were the handful of *archontes* who dispensed patronage and dominated the offices of the *koinotita*. Behaviour was also governed by values centred on female fidelity and male moral worth to uphold honour and avert shame. There was also grinding poverty. Farming techniques and technologies were primitive and yields were low. For the average peasant, *zoi* (life) was a euphemism for travail, a journey laden with personal sorrows and dominated by the ceaseless struggle to stave off ruin. As a moral community, the village could certainly provide comforting familiarity, but it was also seen as a dead end. As ever, the solution was emigration, and in 1900 the most likely destination was Athens or America.

By the year 2000, however, this 'traditional' world had all but vanished. Gone was the peasantry, and aside from students matriculating at European and American universities, Greeks saw little need to move abroad. Nowadays, the average Greek enjoys a standard of living not unlike his or her counterpart in Western Europe. The twentieth century had witnessed the most dramatic societal change in Greece's long history, but what makes this transformation all the more remarkable is that it occurred in a century of horrific war, brutal foreign occupation, famine and authoritarian oppression. As for much of Europe, Greece's twentieth century was an age of extremes.

BELLE EPOQUE GREECE

Cities were the harbingers of modernity. For the neighbouring villages of rural Attica, Athens was another world. Here, new social formations with new aspirations and ideologies were beginning to take shape. In 1900, other cities like Volos and Patras were also on the make. In 1907, the kingdom's population was about 2.6 million, with just over 32 per cent living permanently, or for part of the year, in urban centres. With industry came the making of working-class communities and unions, although it would be decades before labour was sufficiently organized and had the numbers to impact directly upon Greek politics.

Rather, it was the middle classes that were shaping the new Greece, and it was Athens that symbolized its aspirations. Aside from the usual problems that plagued all the burgeoning cities of Europe, such as over-crowding, crime and poor sanitation, belle époque Athens also had its elegant districts that spoke of bourgeoisie tastes and sensibilities. The main thoroughfares (e.g. Athenas, Akadimias, Philellinon, Stadiou) and squares (Syntagma, Omonia) were lined with planted trees and benches, and each was designed for promenading and outdoor cafes. It was during the first decade of the twentieth century that the first gas streetlights, electric trams and public toilets were introduced, and that uniformed cleaners were employed by the city council to keep the main thorough-fares clean.

What was especially 'modern' about belle époque Athens, however, was the way women had claimed a share in its public spaces. The paintings of such well-known artists as Pavlos Mathiopoulos (e.g. *Panepistimiou* of 1900) depict a modern city in which mature women can be seen sitting in cafes and going about their daily business in the background. Western attire was another mark of bourgeois distinction. Athenian women of *kales oikogeneiyes* ('good' families) were fond of brightly coloured frocks and gloves. They liked to chat about balls, vacations and chance meetings with other good families at New Phaleron, a seaside resort that Athenians could access readily by tram. The *kalos cosmos* (good society) also loved to promenade and to use this distinctly middle-class activity for matchmaking. Chaperoned youths could catch a glimpse of prospective love-matches, which led to letter exchanges, serenading, secret rendezvous and, if necessary, elopement.

The Greek bourgeoisie was also a transnational phenomenon, with ties to such buoyant commercial centres as Alexandria, Bucharest, Odessa and Smyrna. Alexandria, for example, was home to a particularly prosperous Greek community that dominated the cotton export trade and cigarette production, whilst also playing a prominent role in cement, brewing, soap manufacturing and paper making. (They also introduced the city's first chocolate and aerated-water factories, and its first lithographic studio.) In Smyrna (Izmir), the Ottoman Empire's second city and the focus of its external trade, the Greek community formed the largest single cultural group. Smyrna's Greek bourgeoisie boasted an even greater diversity of commercial and manufacturing enterprises, from pastirma wholesaling to banking, from food processing and woollen cloths to shipping and mining. The city was also full of Greek institutions and organizations. Its 'Greek Directory' for 1920 (*Ellinikos Odigos*) provides the addresses of every conceivable type of service, including cinemas named 'Phoenix', 'Star' (Astir), 'Pallas' and 'Parisian', along with several newspapers, a Greek hospital, several Greek banks and an orphanage.

During the first decade of the twentieth century, a very different part of the Greek *oikoumene* was taking shape on the other side of the Atlantic. Between 1896 and 1907, 111,500 Greek subjects migrated to the United States, along with another 128,780 Greeks from outside the kingdom. By 1917, almost half a million subjects had passed through Ellis Island and settled in New York or industrial towns such as Lancaster (Pennsylvania) and Lowell (Massachusetts). Many did return to Greece with their savings, but the general tendency was to establish permanent residency and facilitate the migration of family members and villagers from the *patrida* (homeland). Much effort, in fact, went into creating *nees patrides* (new homelands). Even in such remote locales as Salt Lake City, Greek migrants organized themselves into *koinotites* and they raised money to build a church. Overseas Greeks were particularly passionate about *remaining* Greek, hence these communes were also responsible for running Greek language classes and regular social functions, such as balls and picnics. Community life also developed around other cultural spaces, such as Greek-owned *kafeneia* (cafes), 'diners' and even pizzerias. Meeting the tastes of the host society was key. In Australia, a much smaller Greek community appeared to dominate the nation's 'fish and chip' shops and its milk bars.

The expansion of Greek communities across North America, Brazil, Argentina and Australia marked the beginnings of a global diaspora, but to the homeland it was a mixed blessing. Greece lost much of its able-bodied youth to American factories and service sector, yet it also bene-fited enormously from remittances: as much as five million dollars per year between 1903 and 1914 from American expatriates. By 1910, the year that Venizelos formed his first government, the remittances played an important role in the improvement of national finances and the imple-mentation of far-reaching reforms.

BALKAN 'CLEANSING' AND GREECE DIVIDED (1910–1918)

The most striking feature of Venizelos' first tenure as prime minister was its frenetic legislative agenda. There were 53 constitutional amendments covering all areas of public life, many of which were designed to depoliticize public offices and the judiciary, while some were meant to make government more efficient. His *Phileleftheron* (Liberal) party, a loose coalition rather than a 'party' in the British sense, pushed through many significant civil rights reforms that included the right to hold public meetings, trial by jury and protections against arbitrary arrest. Much needed reforms relating to workplace conditions and pay were also awarded to women and children.

It might have seemed that Venizelos heralded the transformation of the state into a sector that served society, but as elsewhere in Europe early welfare policy was designed to mollify social disquiet and to regu-late social behaviour. Rather, Venizelos needed a reliable workforce at home so that his government could pursue the *Megali Idea* more effec-tively than any previous regime. In that respect, he was a traditional politician. The main focus of expenditure was on the military sector. The armed forces were dramatically strengthened through the reorganization of the officer corps and by increasing the size of the army to just over 148,000 men. The Greek navy was also upgraded and expanded.

Venizelos' haste can be explained by the deteriorating international position of the Ottoman Empire. By the summer of 1912, Bulgaria, Serbia, Greece and Montenegro had arranged a coordinated invasion of Ottoman Balkan territory, but what really ensued was a scramble for territory. The First Balkan War commenced on 18 October and the Balkan armies made short work of Ottoman forces. Having captured much of southern Macedonia, Greek forces made haste for Salonica/Thessaloniki and arrived on 8 November, only hours before the Bulgarians. Crete was finally annexed, as was Epiros and all the islands of the northern Aegean. A second phase of the war (the Second Balkan War, June–July 1913) between Bulgaria and all its neighbours brought additional territories in central Macedonia.

With relatively little effort, Greece almost doubled in size and population, but the Balkan Wars merely whetted the appetite for more territory, especially as it now seemed that Greeks were fated to fulfil the dream of the *Megali Idea*. When George I was felled by an assassin while strolling near Thessaloniki's White Tower on 18 March 1913, his successor, Constantine I (1913–1917), was touted as the incarnation of the last Byzantine emperor, Constantine XI Palaiologos. However, success also bred doubt. It was soon after the occupation of Thessaloniki that some in 'Old Greece' began to question the value of territories that seemed somewhat un-Greek. A few months after the initial euphoria, an Athenian writing home to his wife reported his personal misgivings:

> 14 May 1913: I am totally fed up. I'd prefer a thousand times to be under the canvas on some mountain than here in the gaudy city with all the tribes of Israel.
> 19 May: How can I like a city with this cosmopolitan society, nine-tenths of it Jews. It has nothing Greek about it, nor European. It has nothing at all.[1]

A census conducted in 1913 found the Greeks of Thessaloniki formed less than 40,000 in a population of 157,889, which included 45,867 Muslims and 61,439 Jews. Greece now possessed the world's largest Jewish city, and Muslims formed a large proportion of the rural population.

However, the war had also given Balkan states a golden opportunity to resolve partially such 'problems'. Under the cover of war, and with the complicity of local militia groups, the Serb, Bulgarian and Greek armies had driven tens of thousands of Muslim communities from their homes. As many as 400,000 Muslims were evicted from the Balkans: just under a million people in the region were 'unmixed' between 1912 and 1914. The Ottomans retaliated in kind. In fact, Greek Christians had begun to evacuate Anatolian and Thracian towns and villages from 1912. In 1914, the Ottoman government drove a further 115,000 Greeks out of eastern Thrace, and 40,000 more from Çesme and its environs. Altogether, over a million Christians had evacuated Anatolia and eastern Thrace before formal population exchange was signed in 1923.

The First World War promised further territorial spoils. Venizelos argued forcefully for active support for Britain, France and Russia, but King Constantine, who enjoyed very close ties with the German royal family, and who also believed the Central Powers were likely to win, used his monarchical prerogatives to insist on neutrality. On 6 March 1915, Venizelos resigned from office, and although he was re-elected with a clear majority in June, the monarchy refused to accept his election as a mandate for intervention. At the same time, Britain and France refused to respect Greek neutrality, particularly given its strategic significance. When a new pro-German government was installed in Athens, the Entente powers were given an excuse to move troops to Thessaloniki. In October 1916, Venizelos followed and set up an alternative government, thus splitting the nation in two. Britain and France then set up a blockade of 'Old Greece', a move that caused much suffering and diminished Venizelos' support base. By June 1917, Constantine had been forced into exile, allowing Venizelos to return to Athens and declare war against the Central Powers.

The most damaging aspect of the *Ethnikos Dichasmos* (National Schism) was that it enveloped much broader sections of society than any previous political crisis. Constantine had become a rallying point for Greeks who had opposed Venizelos' liberal reform agenda, and for those who began to question the value of shedding Greek blood for the *Megali Idea*. The most dangerous precedent set by the Schism, however, was the politicization of the armed forces. The military naturally took an interest in the question of intervention, but here too opinion was sharply divided and factions were formed. It did not take long before allegiance to either group became a crucial factor in promotions and appointments. The other damaging precedent was the practice of political recriminations. Venizelos' supporters conducted a wholesale purge of pro-Royalist elements in education, the military, the law and public service, thus launching a pattern in Greek public life that would recur with every regime change.

Meanwhile, a much greater tragedy was unfolding in the Anatolian countryside. Once the Ottoman Empire had entered the war on the side of Germany and Austria-Hungary in October 1914, groups thought to be a security risk were removed from militarily sensitive areas. Communities near coastal areas were deported into Anatolia's interior, and many were to perish from exposure and Muslim militia attacks. The Pontus region suffered most because the Russian advance had transformed it into a war zone. Pontic militias fought alongside the Russians, which meant that Pontic communities were vulnerable to reprisals when the Russians pulled out in 1917. Researchers have noted that Pontic Greeks were among several groups in eastern Anatolia that were targeted for mass killings.

THE ASIA MINOR CATASTROPHE (1918–1922)

In 1918, Greece emerged on the winning side – and it expected spoils. In August 1920, it was awarded nearly all of eastern Thrace. Most of Anatolia was divided into Italian, French and British occupation zones, with Greece allocated Smyrna and its environs. The question of sovereignty in the Greek zone was to be resolved by plebiscite after five years.

In fact, Greek troops had already been given permission to occupy Smyrna and the surrounding region on 15 May 1919, but bringing order to the region proved much more difficult than had been the experience in Macedonia. After all, the population of Anatolia was overwhelmingly Muslim, and there was the further problem of the *chettes* (bandit militias), who had dominated the countryside throughout the war years. The Greek army quickly became mired in a vicious guerrilla campaign that led to mass atrocities against Muslim civilians. During the summer of 1920 and again in 1921, the Greek army moved inland and occupied a territory more than three times the size of its original allotment. The aim was to deal a killer blow to Turkish resistance, but, after two major offensives that brought them within range of Ankara, the Greeks found themselves overcommitted and their position unsustainable. The Greek army was further weakened by a regime change in November 1920, which ushered in an anti-Venizelist government. In the midst of a difficult and brutal military campaign, Venizelist officers were sent home and replaced by their anti-Venizelist counterparts. All the while, a coherent Turkish nationalist movement led by former Ottoman officers, including Kemal Mustafa, had been building its strength in central Anatolia, waiting patiently as the Greek occupation weakened by the day.

On 26 August 1922, the Turks broke through enemy defences, and the Greek army, lacking a retreat strategy, fell into disarray. Greek troops fled back to the Aegean coast, burning and pillaging all before them, and committing ghastly atrocities against Muslim civilians. As news spread of the military defeat, Christian communities feared the worst and began to follow the soldiers to the coastline. By 6 September, the first Greek soldiers had arrived in Smyrna, with their Turkish pursuers not far behind. The army was evacuated in time, but most of the civilians were left stranded on the Smyrna quayside. When the Turks entered the city, they targeted the Armenian community for systematic killings. Greek civilians huddled along the harbour were also attacked in full view of British, French, Italian and American warships that were there as neutral observers, and under strict orders not to intervene. One particular Turkish soldier provided the following eyewitness account:

> all [the] seaside [is] full of gavur [infidel] carcasses. Our soldiers have killed them all with bayonets. There were seven fleets across Pasaport. English, French, Greek fleets. All the Greek gavur are throwing themselves into the sea. They are yelling 'help'. Even the fleets couldn't save them . . . The Armenians and the gavurs didn't give up their houses. The irregulars burnt all those houses. Bombs were exploding, rifles were fired. Most of the gavurs and Armenians burned alive.[2]

As stated by this source, Smyrna was set ablaze to flush out the city's infidel population. It is estimated that as many as one hundred thousand people might have perished in the inferno.

Greek Smyrna disappeared in the fire, and with it went the *Megali Idea*. In Turkish lore, the inferno is remembered as a cleansing agent that relieved the country of a seditious minority. In Greece, the inferno came to symbolize a national tragedy, marking the end of the irredentist dream and almost 3000 years of Greek life in Asia Minor. The broader meaning of Smyrna, however, must surely be associated with the darker side of modernity. Historians have identified the twentieth century as an age when the search by nations for ethnic exclusivity produced genocides and mass expulsions on an unprecedented scale. Smyrna 1922 was the ugly climax of the local chapter in this larger story.

THE REFUGEE IMPACT

In January 1923, a new treaty was signed at Lausanne. The Republic of Turkey, which had effectively replaced the Ottoman Empire, secured the entire landmass of Anatolia and eastern Thrace as far as the Evros River. Greece was left with what it has today, save for the Dodecanese Islands, which were granted to Italy as post-war spoils. Turkey and Greece also agreed to a compulsory population exchange. About one million Greek Orthodox Christians had already departed from Turkish territory before the Treaty was signed, but another 200,000 awaited removal. There were some 300,000 Muslims still in Greece, including Greek-speaking groups. Under the auspices of the newly formed League of Nations and its principal agent, the Norwegian scientist Dr Fridtjof Nansen, a methodical exchange was undertaken that was to serve as a model for later internationally supervised population transfers.

The social consequences of the exchange were enormous. From the state's perspective, the resettlement of refugees in Macedonia and the eastern part of Greek Thrace supposedly improved the nation's security, with indigenous minorities now swamped by settlers whose primary loyalty was not in doubt. At the everyday level, however, the incomers were seen as unwanted competition for scarce land and jobs, and as a consequence local Greeks were prepared to question their ethnic credentials. Hostility towards the refugees was palpable: in early December 1923, for example, refugees encamped in Syntagma Square were confronted by crowds shouting 'Down with the Turks! Down with the Turks!' Open conflict between indigenous peasants and newcomers erupted occasionally in rural Macedonia, where the absence of land surveys had encouraged indigenous Christians to claim Muslim properties earmarked for refugees.

The greatest challenge facing the Greek nation and the Refugee Settlement Commission set up by the League of Nations was how to accommodate the estimated 1.2 million refugees in Greece, including 117,633 Greeks expelled from Bulgaria. About 60 per cent of the refugees were settled in Macedonia, mainly on land vacated by Muslims and Slavs. Precisely 1381 rural settlements were created, while thousands were also settled in Thessaloniki, giving the city a large Greek majority. Whereas just under half of Macedonia (47.4 per cent) was non-Greek in 1912, by 1926 non-Greeks formed just 11.7 per cent. One of the political ramifications of the settlement of refugees in rural Macedonia was that disgruntled Slav Macedonians flocked to the Communist movement and rallied to the cause of an independent Slav Macedonia.

Further south in Old Greece, where there was little land to spare, refugees were concentrated in the greater Athens area, where they built new suburbs with Anatolian names (e.g. Nea Ionia (New Ionia), Kesariani (Caesaria)). Whereas rural resettlement processes were successful on the whole, Greek authorities and the Refugee Commission were less resourceful when it came to assisting the urban refugees. It would take many years before proper housing replaced the makeshift camps and shanty towns that blighted the outskirts of Athens, Piraeus and Thessaloniki. The refugees also needed jobs. Historians have assumed plausibly that the injection of Anatolian labour and entrepreneurs had long-term benefits for the Greek economy, and that over the short term it fostered industrial expansion. Some industries did indeed thrive because of Anatolian expertise, such as carpet and cigarette making, but in general the industrial and manufacturing sectors did not have the capacity to absorb the refugee labour pool. In fact, the influx put downward pressure on labour costs. Local commentators were struck by the overabundance of pedlars and self-employed craftsmen trying to ply their trades and competing for scarce drachmas.

INTERWAR TURMOIL (1922–1940)

The political fallout from the Asia Minor catastrophe was immense. Not long after the Turks entered Smyrna, on 26 September, Venizelist officers led by Colonel Nikolaos Plastiras carried out a *coup d'état* in Athens The monarchy was forced into exile, while Demetrios Gounaris, the then prime minister, along with other leading politicians and generals, were summarily tried and executed. Predictably, anti-Venizelists were removed from public service and military postings. A failed counter coup by anti-Venizelists in October 1923 resulted in more extensive purging, and the more radical Venizelists insisted on the abolition of the monarchy. A referendum on 13 April 1924 had 70 per cent of voters in favour of a republic.

As elsewhere in interwar Europe, Greece's ruling elite struggled unsuccessfully to create a stable political order. Unprecedented economic turmoil in the early 1920s and throughout the 1930s made it impossible for liberal democratic regimes to meet public expectations regarding employment and welfare. Greece, of course, had its unique problems. The most obvious was the split between Venizelists and anti-Venizalists, which cut even deeper following the execution of Gounaris. Another was the absence of a state ideology to replace the defunct *Megali Idea*. When Venizelos returned to power in 1928, his government proclaimed a new kind of *Megali Idea* focused on domestic regeneration; but as with all schemes that required large government outlays, it foundered with the onset of the Great Depression. As elsewhere, Greece was also beset by the growth of social unrest. Peasants and workers were much more likely now to express their grievances through social protests and by joining unions. Between 1917 and 1928, Greek union membership had grown from 44,230 to 167,509, and from 1924 the Greek Communist Party (KKE) provided a disciplined and well-organized movement that was capable of articulating workers' grievances and mobilizing its membership. Union subscriptions and agitation increased significantly during the Depression, and by the mid-1930s, the KKE was a noticeable presence in the parliament.

In the meantime, most Greek politicians remained wedded to the view that state governance was essentially about high politics (i.e. foreign policy and constitutional issues), and that popular dissent was a security matter. Venizelists and anti-Venizelists were agreed that the answer to social unrest was brutal repression. During the interwar years, the police force grew into a larger and more sophisticated institution, and in contrast to other public policy concerns police pay and welfare were matters that did receive special state attention. Popularly known as *i batsi* (the truncheons), the police were preoccupied with harassing unionists and bludgeoning demonstrators. Killings were not uncommon.

Political violence had become a fact of life throughout Europe during the Depression years. So too was the paralysis of parliamentary rule and the rise of dictatorships. In Greece, growing disenchantment with the established political parties facilitated the return of the Greek monarchy in November 1935, but only after a patently rigged plebiscite. In the ensuing months, the parliamentary system became unworkable as the leading parties were unable to form a government without the support of the KKE, which they refused to contemplate. In April, the parliament voted to allow General Ioannis Metaxas (1871–1941), a man widely known for his ultra-conservative views and his detestation of politicians, to rule by decree. In August, Metaxas persuaded George II (1922–1924, 1935–1947) that a Communist takeover was imminent and that the constitution should be suspended. Greece therefore succumbed to a broader European pattern. With monarchical assent, Metaxas was given licence to create a dictatorship.

Metaxas was typical of interwar dictators who were clearly inspired by Mussolini and Hitler, but who were much more conservative in outlook and temperament. Aside from smashing the unions, he also abolished press freedom and clamped down on all manifestations of cultural decadence, including Turkish-sounding music like *rembetika*. As a military man, Metaxas naturally believed in regimentation. He organized a vast youth movement that was clearly inspired by Italy's Ballila and the Hitler Youth. He gave the police and the secret services unfettered powers, which in turn were focused on rooting out Communists: 30,000 were arrested and incarcerated on islands like Kea and remote Aghios Efstratios. As with many interwar dictators, Metaxas sought the assent of all classes, hence he broke new ground in social policy: one of his most significant measures was the introduction of the five-day working week and set wage rates. His main weapon, however, was political repression, and under his watch Greek society remained deeply polarized.

GREECE UNDER THE AXIS POWERS (1940–1945)

On 28 October 1940, Mussolini ordered Italian troops stationed in Albania to invade Greece. With Germany having recently defeated France but still at war with Britain, Mussolini hoped to conquer new territories while Hitler was still preoccupied. He ordered the attack on Greece without adequate preparation, and as it happened the Greek army pushed the Italians deep into Albania.

For a short period, Greek society appeared to be united in the face of enemy aggression, but direct German intervention was now inevitable. On 6 April, Germany invaded Greece via the Bulgarian border. Greek and British forces failed to follow a coordinated strategy and were quickly overwhelmed by Germany's *blitzkrieg* assault. By 26 April, the Germans were raising the swastika over the Acropolis. Stiffer resistance awaited on Crete, where a desperate battle raged between May and June. In the meantime, the king and many politicians escaped to Egypt and set up a government in exile. It was left to General Giorgos Tsolakoglou, a commander who had earned distinction in Albanian only months earlier, to come to terms with the Axis powers. He was subsequently tainted by the humiliating terms of the surrender and by the fact that he now led a puppet regime. All of Greece was now occupied territory, with most of the country placed under Italian administration. Germany retained direct control of Athens and Thessaloniki and the strategically sensitive border regions. Bulgaria supported the invasion and received eastern Macedonia and much of Thrace. Within a short space of time, 100,000 Greeks were 'ethnically cleansed' from these territories.

Wary of Germany's experiences during the First World War, Hitler's government set out to build an empire without burdening the German homefront, hence occupied territories like Greece were looted with

Image 8 Patriotism: national solidarity is depicted here in a propaganda poster that appeared following the Italian invasion in October 1940 (Gennadius Library, Athens, Greece) *(photo credit: Snark/Art Resource, New York).*

frightening efficiency. By the second half of 1941, the occupiers had induced famine in the cities and islands. A British naval blockade served to exacerbate the situation. Between 1941 and 1943, as many as 300,000 civilians died of starvation. Much of the early relief during the spring of 1942 came from Turkey, but so dire had the situation been that the warring powers agreed to allow shipments of food to be distributed by the Red Cross and its Swedish personnel. Islanders quickly exhausted local resources, and as fishing was forbidden starvation was rife. On Syros, for example, the annual death toll between 1939 and 1942 had risen from 435 to almost 3000 people.

With war came rampant inflation and a flourishing black market. A loaf of bread was 10 drachmas in 1940, but by the middle of 1944 it was 34,000,000 drachmas. In the meantime, the puppet regime was obliged to serve the interests of the Axis authorities and could do little to protect its citizenry. Eventually, the leadership vacuum was filled by voluntary groups and workers' organizations, and during the course of 1941 a national movement emerged. On 10 October 1941, the Workers' Liberation Front (EAM) was formed, and it came to attract supporters from all classes and occupations. Its main priority in the initial stages was food relief and rationing, but it also provided welfare services. Activists such as Maria Manthopoulou, for example, led the organization of childcare services in central Greece. In the countryside, the most pressing need was to organize village communities to manage their own resources, and to requisition food and materials to support relief efforts elsewhere. By the end of 1942, EAM cells could be found throughout the country, and for the most part the movement seemed to be popular.

ORIGINS OF THE GREEK CIVIL WAR (1943–1946)

EAM's appeal had much to do with its progressive political ideals, but many also noticed that barely concealed behind its rank-and-file was the KKE. Although EAM's grass-roots membership was drawn from all walks of life, its leadership consisted largely of KKE members, and its structure and culture of discipline clearly bore the party's imprint. Therefore, in politically conservative regions such as the Peloponnese and Central Greece, EAM was seen not unreasonably as a Communist front, and village leaders often refused to cooperate. In such cases, EAM operatives imposed their authority by force. Some historians refer to a

'Red Terror', but it was certainly the case that EAM was prepared to perpetrate assassinations and other forms of political violence to secure compliance. The EAM attacks launched a new phase of political violence that was to spiral into a much larger conflict.

In the meantime, however, the chief preoccupation of EAM was with the Axis. During the course of 1942, the National People's Liberation Army (ELAS) emerged as the military arm of EAM. There were other groups, but ELAS was by far the largest and most effective resistance force. By the latter part of 1942, the Greek resistance had begun to challenge Axis forces in a variety of ways. Enemy guard positions, barracks and motor convoys were targeted. In May 1943, ELAS operatives seized Grevena, a major town, and captured its Italian garrison. By that stage, 30,000 *andartes* (resistance fighters) were operating in the Pindus Ranges and the Peloponnese.

In September 1943, Mussolini fell from power and the Italian army in Greece surrendered. The Germans quickly reoccupied the Italian zone and commenced an intensive counter-insurgency campaign that involved terrorizing the civilian population, with the intention of denying the resistance its main source of food and recruits. Thousands of villages were destroyed and unspeakable barbarities were commonplace. In late 1943, for example, the entire male population of the Peloponnesian village of Kalavryta was marched out into the fields and executed in retaliation for a guerrilla attack that killed 78 Germans. In the meantime, the Greek Jewry was targeted for elimination. Whilst under Italian supervision, Jews could expect sanctuary, but in German hands their only salvation was a Turkish or Spanish passport. All but a few of Greece's 75,000 Jews, which included 55,000 from Thessaloniki, perished at Auschwitz.

The resistance also had to contend with Greek paramilitary formations created by the puppet government in Athens. The purpose of these 'Security Battalions' was to combat the Communists, and, while most recruits appeared to be destitute and desperate for employment, they undertook their mission with zeal. Dressed in traditional *foustanella* (kilt), the Battalions set out across Greece to attack Communist cells. They also launched a wave of 'White Terror': simply running amok, raping, pillaging and shooting people at random. It was against the backdrop of growing political violence and the looming prospect of German defeat in Europe that EAM and its rivals began contemplating life after the war. EAM had no illusions about ruling Greece without British assent, especially as the Soviet Union refused to support a seizure of power. The best that could be hoped for was a stake in the post-war political order, one dominated by the government in exile and George II. In May 1944, EAM accepted the offer of a few minor ministries from George Papandreou, the left-leaning Venizelist and prime minister in exile. EAM also agreed to place ELAS forces under British authority.

The Germans had evacuated Greece during October 1944, by which time Papandreou had arrived to form the new national government. He had little option, however, but to rely on the Security Battalions and the police, who were also compromised by wartime collaboration. These elements, in turn, were determined to keep EAM out of power. Meanwhile, EAM suspicions of the government grew by the day, especially as only a handful of known Axis collaborators had been brought to justice. Relations broke down completely on 4 December when the police opened fire on EAM protesters and massacred 16 people. The incident unleashed a pandemic of violence across the country called the *Dekembriana* ('December events'), during which time ELAS eliminated rival resistance groups and consolidated its authority in the countryside. However, it suffered defeat in Athens, where British troops and right-wing paramilitaries had the upper hand.

In February 1945, all parties had agreed to lay down their arms and abide by a treaty signed in a seaside suburb of Athens (Varkiza), but once ELAS fighters had laid down their weapons the Ministry of Justice and the police set about arresting thousands of EAM figures and supporters. Former collaborators wreaked vengeance against their wartime enemy, putting resistance fighters on trial for political crimes. Some 2,900 collaborators were jailed after the war, and only 29 were executed, whereas by the end of 1945 the number of EAM/ELAS members that had been jailed was just under 50,000. The families of leftists were not spared harassment. Many lost jobs or were denied employment in government services. Over the course of 1945 and throughout the following year, the police and state security apparatus was radically expanded to monitor and arrest all known and suspected leftists. By the end of 1946, the anti-Communist government was in control everywhere except the rugged mountain regions. Numerous former resistance fighters again went into hiding and regrouped, and the stage was set for civil war.

CIVIL WAR AND ITS AFTERMATH (1946–1952)

In October 1946, ELAS was renamed the Democratic Army, and as a

Image 9 Americanization: as with other Europeans, Greeks became avid consumers of US products, including Hollywood films. The Orpheus Cinema, Athens, 1947 (*Dimitris A. Harissiadis (PLA12_int12) Photographic Archives, Benaki Museum*).

seasoned military outfit it usually had the better of early clashes with government forces. However, while it used guerrilla tactics to good effect, it could do little more. At the beginning of 1947, less than 10,000 guerrillas were at large in the Pindus Mountains, and there were no more than 13,000 overall. Recruitment was much more difficult during these post-war years, given that thousands of EAM supporters had been imprisoned or kept under tight surveillance in the towns and cities, and given that the Democratic Army was restricted to the remote and under-populated mountain ranges. An important disincentive, too, was the fact that a significant proportion of the Democratic Army was composed of Slav Macedonians who were also fighting for a separate homeland. The Communists also resorted to forcibly recruiting soldiers from mountain villages, including thousands of young women that were removed from their homes and put through political indoctrination. The Red Terror tactics used occasionally by EAM/ELAS operatives during the Axis occupation became standard practice in Communist controlled regions.

Denied Soviet support, the Communists could make little headway against their opponents. Whereas the Democratic Army was supplied with arms and other resources by Yugoslavia, Bulgaria and Albania, each of which had recently come under Communist rule, the Greek government and its National Army were backed initially by Britain and then the United States, which assumed the role of regional bulwark against Communism in 1947. Overall, the government received $353,600,000 worth of military aid, along with $1,237,500,000 in reconstruction funds under the Marshall Plan. Moreover, by 1949 the armed services had upwards of 250,000 men, and by that stage the National Army was better trained and had been placed under experienced military officers such as Alexandros Papagos and Thasyvoulos Tsakalotos. By the summer of 1949, the National Army had reclaimed all the mountain regions, and by the beginning of 1950 all fighting had ceased.

The Greek Civil War was not particularly significant in a military sense, for at no point did a Communist seizure of power seem possible. Typically, civilians bore the brunt of the violence. Something like 60,000 people died and as many as 50,000 were forced into exile in Eastern Bloc countries. The worst aspect of the 1940s, however, was the fact that it polarized Greek society for decades, for nearly every individual had been traumatized by political violence. Typical was the experience of one youth from the village of Dekasti near Mt Olympus, who recalled how right-wing gendarmes beat him and left him unconscious because he happened to be wearing a red sweater. Many without strong political sympathies recall being 'politicized' as a result of such experiences. Private feuds were also reconfigured along ideological lines, as personal enemies were recast as *national* enemies. As one Communist fighter confessed during his trial in 1944 for the murder of 12 people:

> I believe that personal hatred probably played a leading role in the decision to kill them, because the village head [*ipefthinos*] D. Trimis disliked the Tsoungos family with whom he was competing in the olive market.[3]

For such reasons, the Civil War cut deeply, and as such it reshaped Greek political culture. Communities were split by a relatively new kind of social division, and those associated with the Left became second-class citizens. Political affiliation became a primary identity that could determine such things as access to employment opportunities and the success of permit applications for operating say a tavern, cafe or *periptero* (a newspaper stall no bigger than a phone booth, normally reserved for handicapped war veterans). Many were compelled to find gainful employment overseas, where Civil War tensions reverberated among the diaspora communities. In Australia, for example, many of these particular migrants saw themselves as political refugees. They formed clubs like 'Atlas' in Sydney and 'Democritos' in Melbourne, and waged a new struggle for community resources against conservative bishops and their lay supporters.

RECONSTRUCTION AND POLITICAL RESTORATION (1950–1961)

The Marshall Plan played a critical role in reviving the Greek national economy. US aid made up half of the state's expenditure on economic rehabilitation between 1947 and 1957, and much of it was used to upgrade the country's infrastructure. By the end of the Civil War, there were more than twice as many roads than before the Axis occupation, and agricultural output markedly improved with the introduction of tractors and fertilizers. Greece's dependency on aid also left it vulnerable to US political interference. That influence was used in shaping early post-war coalitions, in supporting American multinationals and in demanding tougher action against left-wing elements. US aid also came with the proviso that its recipients subscribe to such American ideals as liberal democracy and free elections, and that the police be restrained from using excess violence. The new 'Pax Americana' was not to be sullied by overt authoritarianism and fascist-styled brutalities from client regimes.

In the post-war years, political power slipped back into the hands of the old political class. The conservative Populists were once again pitted against the Liberals, who were now led by Venizelos' son, Sophokles. The Populists also secured the return of the monarchy, but the fact that it was restored with its traditional constitutional powers had major ramifications for the fate of Greek liberal democracy. For in contrast to the other European royal families, the Greek monarchy felt duty-bound to use its political prerogatives, including its control of the armed forces. Even conservative prime ministers were perturbed by its propensity to ignore ministerial advice and determine military appointments and promotions. Quarrels between the prime minister and monarchy led to resignations in 1951, 1963 and 1965.

On the surface, Greece *looked* like a Western liberal democracy. The KKE was banned, but leftist parties such as the United Democratic Left (EDA) were tolerated and allowed to contest elections. The Venizelist Liberals were at large and keen to reclaim power, although since the demise of EAM no single party had been able to generate a mass following. The early post-war governments usually consisted of unstable coalitions, prompting the American ambassador in 1951 to demand that the existing electoral system of proportional representation be replaced by a first-past-the-post alternative that was likely to favour conservatives. The stage was set for a prolonged phase of conservative domination. In the 1952 elections, General Papagos' 'Greek Rally' party won an absolute majority, and in 1955 the leadership passed to Constantine Karamanlis (1955–1963, 1974–1980), an able Minister of Public Works who enjoyed the blessing of King Paul (1947–1964) and the US embassy. Relatively young and handsome, and untainted by any connection with Metaxas or the wartime puppet regime, Karamanlis cut a respectable image on the world stage. While his predecessors had appeared overly preoccupied with internal security, Karamanlis' energies were focussed on policy agendas and such objectives as joining the European Economic Community. He also commanded immense authority within his party, which he renamed the Greek Radical Union, and which won successive elections in 1956, 1958 and 1961.

In the meantime, the Greek economy continued to grow with US financial assistance. By the late 1950s, the annual growth rate averaged 7.3 per cent. Importantly, post-war governments succeeded in keeping inflation below 2 per cent for the most part. As with most recipients of US aid, the Greek government was required to open its doors to international trade and finance, and an important measure in this regard was the devaluation of the drachma by half in 1953, which made Greek exports cheaper during a boom period in international trade. Greece's economic 'miracle' also featured the expansion of industry, manufacturing and particularly construction, all of which facilitated internal migration from the villages to the larger towns and cities, but particularly Athens and Thessaloniki. By 1970, the majority of Greeks were living in urban centres, with close to 30 per cent living in Athens. Overseas migration also recommenced to meet the voracious demand for labour in the United States, Canada, Australia, West Germany and Belgium; the immense volume of remittances that flowed back to Greece played a vital role in containing the national deficit. By 1960 almost 80,000 had migrated abroad, followed by another 230,000 by 1969. Of the 800,000 international *gastarbeiter* (guest workers) in West Germany in 1963, 103,000 were Greeks.

The post-war economic miracle was nevertheless achieved by suppressing labour costs and by keeping government spending on social welfare to an absolute minimum. For the most part, post-war prosperity was not shared equitably, and only by the 1970s did Greek society at large begin to enjoy the kind of consumption-focused lifestyle that was commonplace in Western Europe. Rather, poverty remained an endemic problem, particularly in rural areas where underemployment meant many families were still dependent on remittances from relatives abroad.

In a way, the great wave of overseas migration represented an indictment against the post-war political order. Unlike Germany's *gastarbeiter*, North American and Australian Greek migrants were not compelled to return, and few did. The typical migrant family in Toronto or Melbourne had access to high quality schooling and health care, and to social services that could be accessed without bribes or the need for personal networks (*meson*). In Greece, job and educational opportunities were tied up. In other words, *ta xena* (foreign lands) continued to offer Greeks a much better future.

MONARCHY, THE MILITARY AND THE *PARAKRATOS* (1961–1974)

Many Greeks, particularly those tainted by past association with the Left, whether real or apparent, and who did not share in the prosperity of the mid- and late 1950s, believed real power was in the hands of a *kathestos* (establishment) that included the monarchy, big business, leading conservative politicians, the military and police hierarchy, and the US Embassy. Most of the injustices of contemporary life, such as the suppression of wages and the protection of wartime collaborators, were the product of deals that had been stitched up between these elements. They were also aware that even the slightest attempt to diminish the power of the establishment might invite punitive retaliation from the police and security forces, including the *parakratos* (para-state): clandestine networks within the police and security forces that were prepared to do anything to maintain the status quo.

It was in 1961 when the *parakratos* made its first brazen intervention in Greek public life. That year, George Papandreou's Centre Union was widely expected to win the national elections, but while Papandreou was no socialist he was regarded by the radical right as the thin end of the wedge. When Karamanlis was re-elected, it emerged that his supporters and the *parakratos* had used intimidation tactics with voters. Indeed, so flagrant was electoral fraud that Papandreou mounted an unprecedented public campaign to force another election, and for the first time since the *Dekembriana* popular resentment towards the state was vented openly in the form of political demonstrations and strike activity. Matters came to a head in May 1963, during a protest rally in Thessaloniki. In broad daylight and before thousands of demonstrators, the *parakratos* perpetrated the assassination of the left-wing politician Giorgos Lambrakis. The internationally renowned composer, Mikis Theodorakis, was moved to speak openly to the press about the existence of the *parakratos*, and called for Greeks to rally against it and the establishment.

Karamanlis seemed unmoved by the Papandreou-led protests, but he did resign in June 1963 after a falling out with the monarchy, when King Paul ignored his advice against a royal visit to Britain. In the ensuing elections (3 November), Papandreou's Centre Union won office. As an avowedly reformist government, it lost no time in pushing through a raft of social and educational changes, including free university education and numerous workplace reforms. All the while, right-wing officers were plotting against the government. To forestall the possibility of a coup, Papandreou sought to make changes to the military hierarchy. For that he sought to gain control of the defence ministry, for which he required royal assent. The young King Constantine II (1964–1967) refused, particularly as Papandreou's son, Andreas, was also implicated in a liberal/left military conspiracy.

Papandreou reacted by resigning in July 1965, so as to bring on another election and win a fresh mandate; but Constantine countered by appointing his own prime minister.

For the next two years, the country was in the hands of caretaker governments of the king's choosing, although none enjoyed the confidence of the parliament. As time wore on, rumours abounded of an impending military coup, including separate coups by various generals, colonels and even captains. The establishment was aware that plotting was rife, and Constantine himself conveyed to Karamanlis, then in exile in Paris, that he was toying with the idea of his own coup. Karamanlis said later (10 April) to a colleague back home, 'I hear you have all gone mad'.[4] Constantine was eventually obliged to set elections for May 1967, but since Papandreou was widely expected to win, a particular coterie within the *parakratos* took decisive action. On the morning of 21 April, the Greek public woke up to find itself under military rule.

The plotters struck at 2 a.m. on 21 April. They quickly nabbed and detained all dissidents and significant political and military personnel, including Papandreou and the leading conservative politician, Panayiotis Kanellopoulos. The coup leaders were seasoned operators from within the secret services: Colonel George Papadopoulos, Colonel Nikos Makarezos and Brigadier General Stylianos Pattakos. 'The Colonels', as they became known internationally, notified the king and had a new government appointed. Initially the conspirators tried to maintain the pretence of constitutional governance, but to all and sundry it was clear that Greece was again under dictatorship.

As expected, there was a wholesale purge of the armed forces, the police, the Church and all public institutions. All suspected left-wing activists were subjected to forms of detention and some were tortured. Heavy state censorship was applied to all media and books, and all manifestations of supposed Western 'licentiousness' were attacked, including hippie-length hair, rock music and miniskirts. The junta's interest in 'moral standards' was revealing. Profiles on the ringleaders revealed that they were mostly of modest rural backgrounds, sharing a bucolic contempt for city life, old-moneyed elites and Western permissiveness. They yearned for a Greek world based on wholesome village community values. They also insisted that government, education and all public communication be conducted exclusively in *katharevousa*, reiterating the standard conservative claim that common vernacular (demotic) was an adulterated idiom.

Although the stated justification for the coup was to rescue the country from the Left, what the Colonels actually managed to do was create an irreparable rift within the Right. The establishment was greatly discomforted by the fact that power was in the clutches of a band of yokels and by the image the junta presented to the world. Very few conservative politicians rallied to the junta, and the monarchy played along with gritted teeth, at least initially. In the latter months of 1967, Constantine tried to organize a countercoup with the support of loyal officers, but his plot was betrayed and he was forced to leave the country. Plotting continued, and there were a number of assassination attempts, but little seemed to get past the security apparatus. For its part, the international community condemned the dictatorship, including the United States, which was the only country to apply sanctions. The EEC broke off relations completely in 1970. Critically, the United States reappraised its attitude once problems flared in the Middle East, and particularly when another colonel, Mu'ammar Gaddafi, forced the withdrawal of US bases in Libya (1969). The Nixon Administration then became a stolid supporter of the Colonels.

The junta was never popular, but the potential for social unrest was limited by the ubiquity of the security forces, on the one hand, and the low inflation and high growth rates it inherited, on the other. In 1973, however, the regime had to deal with the global economic crisis. Inflation skyrocketed to 15.5 per cent and to 26.9 per cent the following year. Governments around the world were voted out of office because of the Oil Crisis and unprecedented spike in inflation *and* unemployment, but the Colonels held on by not holding elections. In November 1973, however, students of the Polytechnic in central Athens staged a protest and called for a general uprising. The movement drew huge crowds, but the regime sent in the tanks and several students and onlookers were killed. Worldwide condemnation followed, but the immediate fallout of the affair was limited. Papadopoulos was replaced by another shady military figure: Demetrios Ioannides.

THE CYPRUS TRAGEDY

Clearly in trouble, the junta sought a distraction. Ioannides believed his regime might yet be bathed in glory if it could secure the acquisition of Cyprus. Since the mid-1950s, the island's fate had preoccupied all Greek governments, and Greek Cypriots, who constituted 80 per cent of the population, had been calling for *enosis* (unification) with Greece since the 1930s. The greatest obstacle was Turkey. Since the island is just 65 km from its southern coastline, Cyprus was deemed a vital interest to Turkish security. There was also the matter of protecting the island's ethnic Turks, who formed 18 per cent of the population. Successive Ankara governments had made it clear that any attempt to cede Cyprus to Greece would incur a declaration of war. In reaction to Greek Cypriot moves to force the issue of *enosis* on British authorities during the summer of 1955, the Turkish government did little to stop a pogrom against the Greek community in Istanbul: 4000 shops and 70 churches were destroyed. As the celebrated Turkish novelist Orhan Pamuk recalled, the rioters were as 'merciless as the soldiers that sacked the city after it fell to Mehmet the Conqueror'.[5]

In 1960, the Cypriot population was forced to accept independence, rather than *enosis*, and a constitution that granted a disproportionate share of power to Turkish Cypriot leaders. When the island's first president, Mikhail Mouskos, better known as Archbishop Makarios (1913–1977), attempted in late 1963 a wholesale revision of an otherwise unworkable constitution, intercommunal violence erupted. Complicating the issue was the fact that Greeks and Turks were internally divided on the issue of power sharing, but the greatest source of destabilization were paramilitaries that were keen to foment conflict so as to hasten the implementation of the most radical solutions. Extremists such as Giorgos Grivas and Nikos Sampson continued to test the resolve of Ankara by attacking Turkish Cypriot villages. In 1964, a Turkish invasion was averted by US pressure, after 25,000 Turkish Cypriots were corralled into small enclaves. At the time, Ioannides, then a Greek intelligence officer in Cyprus, recommended to Makarios a plan to mass murder all Turkish Cypriots in one swift operation. Makarios recalled:

> I was astonished and speechless. Then I told him that I could not agree with him; I told him that I couldn't even conceive of killing so many innocents. He kissed my hand again and walked away very angry.[6]

In 1974, Ioannidis was now the Greek president, and Makarios had risen to the top of the junta's hit list. By that stage, Makarios had come to terms with the fact that *enosis* was not feasible, and he had no desire to see Cyprus ruled by the strongmen in Athens. In the meantime, extremists and the junta were perturbed by the fact that Greek–Turkish relations on the ground had improved markedly, thus jeopardizing a plan to see the island divided. In July 1974, when Makarios demanded the withdrawal of the Greek military from Cyprus, Ioannidis retaliated by ordering the removal of Makarios and having the island divided with Turkey. Greek officers led the Cypriot National Guard into thinking they were securing *enosis*, when in fact they were simply overthrowing the government. On 15 July, Nikos Sampson, a man with no government experience and believed to be a mass murderer within Turkish Cypriot circles, was installed as the new president. All the while, the US State Department and Henry Kissinger, the Secretary of State, which had been directly informed about the coup in advance, did nothing to deter its Greek and Turkish clients from coming to blows. On 20 July, Turkish forces invaded Cyprus. Ioannidis ordered a general mobilization against Turkey, but the armed forces were in no condition for a major war and the generals refused to obey orders. Turkey proceeded to occupy 40 per cent of the island, displacing 180,000 Greek Cypriots. The city of Famagusta was reduced to a shell, while Nikosia (Lefkosia) was divided along the middle.

The only positive outcome to arise from the Cyprus tragedy was that it completely discredited the far right in Greek politics. The junta collapsed, and the *parakratos* effectively ceased to exist. The generals who disregarded Ioannidis' mobilization orders invited Karamanlis to return from Paris and set up a provisional government. Karamanlis' plane touched down at Athens airport on 24 July, at 2 a.m., and he was immediately sworn in.

LIBERAL DEMOCRACY SINCE 1974

In Greece, much as in Spain and Portugal, where older dictatorships unravelled at roughly the same time, the subsequent transition to democracy appeared an almost seamless process. Across Europe's south, there was a broad-based consensus for restoring liberal democracy, and Karamanlis, as with his Portuguese and Spanish counterparts de Spinola and Suarez, secured the break with the past without opposition. On 11 August, he demanded of the generals who installed him that they play no part in the political process, and when he legalized the Communist Party in September the security apparatus was effectively made redundant. Karamanlis' first government included members of the Centre Union, but he also called for free elections in November to secure a popular mandate for his newly named *Nea Demokratia* (New Democracy Party). The following month, 70 per cent of the voters rejected the monarchy.

When it came to dealing with the junta, there was a determined effort to see justice being served. An extensive purge of junta supporters in the state and the public services was undertaken, and all significant figures of the regime were tried, including the Colonels and Ioannidis. The former were given life sentences, while Ioannidis was given multiple sentences for his role in the Polytechnic killings. Papadopoulos died in 1999, behind bars and unrepentant.

That Karamanlis led the effort to recast the political order was important. Although a stalwart of the old authoritarian system, he was a reassuring presence for conservatives and political moderates, and he was therefore ideal for driving the necessary changes. The advent of a two-party political system signalled another important departure from the past. *Nea Demokratia* was returned to power during the 1977 elections, while Andreas Papandreou's recently formed Panhellenic Socialist Movement (PASOK) supplanted the factious Centre Union as the main opposition party. Although led by domineering personalities, both *Nea Demokratia* and PASOK were modern political parties that were defined by political principles. Members were expected to join because they subscribed to the party's policy agenda and political philosophy, although the prospect of favours, particularly jobs, was still an important additional motivation.

By 1981, the momentum was with PASOK. Karamanlis had spent much of his post-junta premiership reconstituting Greece's place in the international community, including the aim of full membership of the European Community. As a party dedicated to free-market liberalism, however, *Nea Demokratia* had shown markedly less interest in social policy. A large constituency believed Karamanlis had neglected welfare, public health and workplace conditions, while Andreas Papandreou (1981–1989, 1993–1986) promised sweeping reforms in each of these areas, and caught the public mood with the slogan 'Change' (*Alaghi*). PASOK was swept to power in October 1981, and its early reforms did indeed bring significant changes, such as legislation securing equal rights for women, the legalization of divorce and the disestablishment of Greek Orthodoxy as the official state religion. It also introduced civil marriages and banned dowries. Of major importance was the introduction of comprehensive medical insurance, a vast increase in expenditure on education and early measures designed to improve conditions in the workforce. It also gave proper recognition to the Democratic Army and granted pensions to surviving veterans.

During the course of the 1980s, however, much PASOK rhetoric was shown to lack substance, particularly Papandreou's more radical foreign policy pronouncements. All his noise about removing US bases from Greek soil came to nought, as did his threats to withdraw from NATO and the European Community. Of greater political consequence was PASOK's inability to live up to its promises to redistribute wealth and improve drastically the quality of welfare services. The Greek economy had barely recovered from the 1973/4 crisis, and the global recession in 1980/1 provided an inauspicious environment for carrying out his much vaunted welfare reforms. Throughout the 1980s, real wage levels remained stuck at the bottom of the EU league table, as growth rates did not rise above 1.3 per cent and inflation remained in double digits. By the end of his first term, Papandreou's personal life took the media spotlight – after deserting his wife Margaret and taking up with an airline hostess, and when he was implicated in a massive bank fraud (though for this he was acquitted). There was also sustained criticism from abroad regarding the misappropriation of EU funding. For many Greeks, the most significant indictment against his premiership was the warning delivered by an increasingly impatient European Commission that unless a more stringent fiscal regime was implemented, Greece might be excluded from the European Union. In 1989, Papandreou's government lost to a combined *Nea Demokratia* and Communist-led coalition.

Nea Demokratia secured power in its own right the following year under Costas Mitsotakis (1990/3), who promised to meet EU concerns by implementing a very tight budgetary regime, but his austerity measures appeared to shift the greater share of the burden on lower income earners. Faced by an unprecedented public backlash, including widespread strike activity in August 1992, the Mitsotakis government barely lasted a single term, although the catalyst for its demise was the Macedonian issue. Greeks at home and abroad were incensed by the Former Yugoslav Republic of Macedonia's attempts to attain international recognition as 'Macedonia'. Officially, Greek protests were couched in security arguments: that 'Skopya' (Skopje), as Greeks preferred to describe the new republic, had territorial aspirations over Greek Macedonia. But what concerned the average Greek was Slav Macedonian claims to the ancient Macedonian heritage. The issue galvanized Greeks in the diaspora, particularly in Australia and Canada, where there were also large communities of Slav Macedonians. Greece was criticized for imposing a trade blockade, although Mitsotakis' foreign minister, Antonis Samaras, believing his government was too soft on the issue, formed a break away party that split *Nea Demokratia* and paved the way for the return of PASOK in October 1993.

By that stage, it became clear that the two parties were more or less agreed on the nation's economic path. The avowed aim of Papandreou's new government was to meet the tough criteria for inclusion into the European Monetary Union, and while it risked alienating a significant part of its lower-income support base, unlike *Nea Demokratia* it could secure the cooperation of the unions. PASOK remained in government for more than a decade despite the refusal to relax its commitment to tight budgets, low spending and other austerities. The reason for the limited electoral fallout was that stringencies applied since the Mitsotakis period had begun to bear fruit. From 1993, real wages started to climb, Greek industries had become more competitive, there was significantly greater investment in the domestic economy, and Greek enterprises were flourishing in the newly opened Balkan markets. When Kostas Simitis (1996–2004) replaced Papandreou as Prime Minister in January 1996, he resisted strong pressure from within his own party to return to greater public spending. Rather, the cross-party consensus was for economic *eksynchronismos* (modernization), which meant bringing the Greek economy in line with its EU counterparts.

THE GREEKS TODAY

Greek society experienced its most dramatic transformation during the second half of the twentieth century. The peasants that so fascinated Western anthropologists in the post-war years through to the 1980s have all but vanished. Numerous villages lie abandoned, but most survive as open communities that are firmly linked to the broader world through regular commuting, television and the Internet. Regional accents and idioms continue to disappear in favour of a standard national vernacular, though local traditions and folklore are being recovered, recorded and preserved by dedicated dilettantes. Knowledge of the *exotika* (supernatural) is virtually extinct, although there is much interest in faiths other than Orthodoxy. Maintaining the physical appearance of traditional villages and major historic towns like Chania and Rhodes has required special effort. Heritage preservation orders can be a nuisance for families that might otherwise want to demolish the old family cottage and build a larger and more functional concrete structure, of the kind found everywhere in Athens and Thessaloniki. The new Greece, in fact, is overwhelmingly urban and suburban. In 2008, the Greek population edged over 11.2 million, with roughly a quarter living in the greater Athens area and about a million in Thessaloniki. Here, Greek families grapple with the same kind of challenges facing most European cities, such as illicit drug abuse, traffic congestion, energy needs and environmental degradation. Greeks are just as likely as Westerners to divorce, to form subcultures (e.g. sexual, religious) and to cohabit before marriage.

Inevitably, there are numerous problems that continue to make life difficult for average Greek citizens, such as public service inefficiencies and red tape, although there have been vast improvements since the 1970s. Relations with Turkey over Cyprus and territorial sovereignty in the Aegean appear to be as intractable as ever, as does the relationship with FYROM. The status and welfare of Slavs and Muslims in the northern provinces draws the attention of such human rights NGOs as Helsinki Watch. There are also problems that Greeks share with much richer nations like Britain, such as growing income disparities and discrimination towards immigrants. By far the most difficult challenge facing the Greek state is meeting public expectations in the areas of welfare, education and infrastructure needs. The global financial crisis that started in late 2008 suggests many serious domestic challenges lie ahead, such as the looming problem of intergenerational discrimination, as people between the ages of 15 and 25, including university graduates, object to being denied job opportunities and welfare benefits enjoyed by their elders. In December 2008, mass student protests erupted in many European capitals, but it was the scale of the Greek protests, which were exacerbated by the police shooting of a teenager, that grabbed world headlines. Athens was brought to a standstill, as protesters and unions called for the resignation of Costas Karamanlis (2004–2009), whose government held a mere one-seat majority. The following October he was voted out of office.

Overall, however, the transformation of the Greek polity since 1974, the so-called *metapolitefsi*, has succeeded in forging a durable liberal democracy. At no stage since the junta have the legitimacy of the nation's democratic institutions been seriously questioned. As with Portugal and Spain, which experienced a strikingly similar transition, political stability has been underscored by the general improvement in living standards. According to the United Nation's Human Development Index of 2005, which considers life expectancy, literacy, educational attainment and other aspects of societal well being, Greece ranked 23rd in the world and 16th in Europe. Most national statistics indicate a relatively affluent society. Since the early 1970s, emigration has reduced to a trickle, while net immigration has risen. In 2008, life expectancy and literacy rates are at the top end of the global range, while birth rates, infant mortality and indices relating to poverty are at the far bottom end. As elsewhere in Europe, women are well represented in the workforce and occupy positions of power: in politics, universities and in the upper echelons of the public service.

The outlook in Cyprus has been particularly auspicious in recent years. The Greek part has prospered as a haven for offshore investors, with a per capita GDP that is only just below major European economies such as Germany and Great Britain. As with Greece, Cyprus has become a land of immigration, where Filipinos, South Asians and people from the Middle East come to find work. The Greek diaspora has also changed markedly since the 1960s and 1970s. Initially a working-class phenomenon, most Greek Americans, Canadians and Australians have since abandoned the inner city neighbourhoods for the leafy suburbs. Expatriates are characterized by very high levels of home ownership and high educational qualifications. As in Greece and Cyprus, the diaspora Greeks nowadays enjoy a better quality of life than at any time in the past. In fact, if living standards are the ultimate measure of progress, then the Greek *oikoumene* is in better shape than at any time in its history. That, at least, is an assessment that one can confidently make by taking an historical perspective.

Notes

1 PREHISTORY TO 500 BC: BEGINNINGS

1. Hesiod, 'Works and Days' (98–99), in *Hesiod and Theognis*, tr. Dorothea Wender (Penguin, 1973), p. 68.
2. Theognis (33–38), in *Hesiod and Theognis*, tr. Dorothea Wender (Penguin, 1973), p. 68.
3. Strabo, *Geographica* (10.1.10).
4. Plutarch, *Moralia* (760e–761c).
5. Strabo, *Geographica* (8.6.20).
6. Aristotle, *The Athenian Constitution*, tr. P.J. Rhodes (Penguin, 1984), p. 51.

2 CLASSICAL GREECE (500–359 BC): THE GOLDEN AGE OF THE *POLIS*

1. Herodotus (7.21.1), quoted in *The Landmark Herodotus*, tr. Andrea L. Purvis (New York, 2007), p. 505.
2. Herodotus (7.220.1–2), quoted in *The Landmark Herodotus*, tr. Andrea L. Purvis (New York, 2007), p. 591.
3. Simon Goldhill, *Love, Sex and Tragedy: Why Classics Matter* (London, 2004), p. 1.
4. Herodotus (8.144.2), quoted in Paul Cartledge, *Thermopylae* (New York, 2006), p. 250.
5. Hippocrates, quoted in Paul Cartledge, *The Greeks* (Oxford, 1993), p. 40.
6. Thucydides (1.80.3), quoted in Robert B. Strassler (ed.), *The Landmark Thucydides* (New York, 1996), p. 45.
7. Thucydides (1.141.3), quoted in ibid., p. 81.
8. Thucydides (6.1.1), quoted in Josiah Ober, *Political Dissent in Democratic Athens* (Princeton, 1998), p. 105.
9. Thucydides (2.65.9), quoted in ibid., p. 93.
10. Thucydides (3.81), quoted in *The Peloponnesian War*, tr. Rex Warner (Penguin, 1954), p. 241.

11. W. G. Runciman, 'Doomed to extinction', in O. Murray and S. Price (eds), *The Greek City* (Oxford, 1990), pp. 347–67.
12. Demosthenes (1.4), quoted in J.K. Davies, *Democracy and Classical Greece* (London, 1978), p. 249.

3 THE HELLENISTIC ERA (359–327 BC): FROM PHILIP II TO AUGUSTUS

1. Arrian (7.1–4), quoted in M.M. Austin, *The Hellenistic World from Alexander to the Roman Conquest* (Cambridge, 1981), p. 34.
2. Arrian (2.14), quoted in Nicholas Ostler, *Empires of the Word* (Berkeley, CA, 2005), p. 243.
3. Arrian (3.23), quoted in Arrian, *The Campaigns of Alexander*, tr. Aubrey De Sélincourt (London, 1971), p. 187.
4. Arrian (4.9) quoted in Arrian, *The Campaigns of Alexander*, tr. Aubrey De Sélincourt (London, 1971), p. 217.
5. Strabo *Geographica* (17.1.8), quoted in M.M. Austin, *The Hellenistic World from Alexander to the Roman Conquest* (Cambridge, 1981), p. 390.
6. Inscription reproduced in M.M. Austin, *The Hellenistic World from Alexander to the Roman Conquest* (Cambridge, 1981), p. 196.
7. Polybios (36.17), quoted in *The Rise of the Roman Empire*, tr. Ian Scott-Kilvert (Penguin, 1979), p. 537.
8. Tacitus, *Annals* (1.1–2), quoted in Greg Woolf, 'Provincial Perspectives', in Karl Galinsky (ed.), *The Cambridge Companion to the Age of Augustus* (Cambridge, 2005), p. 107.

4 THE GREEK ROMAN EMPIRE I (27 BC–AD 500): FROM THE PAX ROMANA TO LATE ANTIQUITY

1. Plutarch, *Sulla* (102), from Plutarch, *Fall of the Roman Republic*, tr. Rex Warner (Penguin, 1972), p. 73.
2. Aelius Aristides, *To Rome* (102), quoted in David Cherry, *The Roman World* (Oxford, 2001), p. 172.
3. Horace, *Epistles* (2.1.156).
4. Virgil (*Aeneid* 6.847–53), quoted in Christopher Kelly, *The Roman Empire* (Oxford, 2006), pp. 20–1.
5. Quoted in Fergus Millar, *The Emperor in the Roman World* (London, 1977), p. 417.
6. Pliny (Letters x. 23, 24), *The Letters of the Younger Pliny*, tr. Betty Radice (Penguin, 1963), p. 268.

7. Pliny, (Letters x. 93), *The Letters of the Younger Pliny*, tr. Betty Radice (Penguin, 1963), p. 292.
8. Quoted in Fergus Millar, 'The Greek City in the Roman Period', in F. Millar (ed.), *The Greek World, the Jews, and the East* (Chapel Hill, NC, 2006), pp. 126–7.
9. Dio Chrysostom, *Orations* (40.10), quoted in Maude Gleason, 'Greek Cities under Roman Rule', in D.S. Potter (ed.), *A Companion to the Roman Empire* (Oxford, 2006), p. 231.
10. Dio Chrysostom, *Orations* (34), quoted in Susan Alcock, *Graecia Capta* (Cambridge, 2000), p. 85.
11. Lucian, *The Dream* (9.11), quoted in Tim Whitmarsh, *Greek Literature and the Roman Empire* (Oxford, 2001), p. 123.

5 THE GREEK ROMAN EMPIRE II (*c*.500–1200): THE TRIUMPH OF ORTHODOXY

1. Cassiodorus, *Variae* (Ii), quoted in Julia H. Smith, *Europe after Rome* (Oxford, 2005), p. 275.
2. Peter Brown, *The World of Late Antiquity* (London, 1971), p. 200.
3. Quoted in Patricia Karlin-Hayter, 'Iconoclasm', in Cyril Mango (ed.), *The Oxford History of Byzantium* (Oxford, 2002), p. 155.
4. John of Damascus, *On Holy Images*, quoted in Deno John Geankoplos, *Byzantium* (Chicago, 1984), p. 153.
5. William of Tyre, quoted in Michael Angold, *The Byzantine Empire, 1025–1204* (London, 1984), p. 206.
6. Fulcher of Chartres, *A History of the Expedition to Jerusalem, 1095–1127*, tr. Frances Rita Ryan (New York, 1973), p. 79.
7. Geoffrey de Villehardouin, 'The Conquest of Constantinople', in Jean de Joinville and Geoffrey de Villehardouin, *Chronicles of the Crusades*, tr. M.R.B. Shaw (London, 1963), p. 58–9.

6 THE GREEK *OIKOUMENE* (1200–1700): LIVING UNDER FRANKISH AND OTTOMAN RULE

1. Quoted in J. Harris, *Byzantium and the Crusades* (London, 2003), p. 150.
2. Angeliki Laiou and Cécile Morrisson, *The Byzantine Economy* (Cambridge, 2007), p. 167.
3. Quoted in S.J. Allen and Emilie Amt (eds), *The Crusades* (Peterborough, Ontario, 2003), pp. 234–5.
4. Quoted from S.J. Allen and Emilie Amt (eds), *The Crusades* (Peterborough, Ontario, 2003), pp. 239–40.

5. Quoted in Anthony Kaldellis, *Hellenism in Byzantium* (Cambridge, 2008), p. 375.
6. Quoted in Michael Angold, *Church and Society in Byzantium under the Comneni, 1081–1261* (Cambridge, 2000), p. 563.

7 THE MAKING OF MODERN HELLAS (*c.*1700–1910): ETHNICITY AND STATE BUILDING

1. Theodoros Kolokotrones, *Kolokotrones, the Klepht, and the Warrior* (London, 1892), p. 84.
2. Quoted in John Koliopoulos and Thanos Veremis, *Greece: The Modern Sequel* (London, 2004), p. 159.
3. William Martin Leake, *Researches in Greece* (London, 1814), p. 228.
4. Voltaire, *Oeuvres Complétes* (8.491–92) in David Roessel, *In Byron's Shadow* (Oxford, 2002), p. 14.
5. Stephen George Chaconas, *Adamantios Korais: A Study in Greek Nationalism* (AMS Press, 1968), p. 28.
6. Quoted in Richard Clogg (ed.), *The Movement for Greek Independence, 1770–1821* (London, 1976), p. 157.
7. Quoted in David Roessel, *In Byron's Shadow* (Oxford, 2002), p. 61.
8. Quoted in Michael Llewellyn Smith, *Athens* (London, 2004), p. 128.
9. William Miller, *Greek Life in Town and Country* (London, 1905), p. 112.
10. Quoted in ibid., p. 9.
11. Quoted in Philip Carabott (ed.), *Greek Society in the Making, 1863–1913* (London, 1997), p. 90.
12. Quoted in Mark Mazower, *The Balkans* (London, 2002), p. 94.
13. Quoted in Mark Mazower, 'The Messiah of the Bourgeoisie', *The Historical Journal*, 35 (4) (1992), p. 898.

8 GREECE IN THE TWENTIETH CENTURY: THE AGE OF EXTREMES

1. Mark Mazower, *Salonica, City of Ghosts* (London, 2004), p. 295.
2. B. K. Kirli, 'Forgetting the Smyrna Fire', *History Workshop Journal*, 60 (2005), p. 38 p.222 note 4.
3. Stathis N. Kalyvas, 'Red Terror', in M. Mazower (ed.), *After The War Was Over* (Princeton, 2000), p. 177.
4. C.M. Woodhouse, *The Rise and Fall of the Greek Colonels* (London, 1982), p. 15.
5. Orhan Pamuk, *Istanbul* (London, 2005), p. 158.
6. Quoted in Christopher Hitchens, *Cyprus, Hostage to History* (London, 1997), p. 39.

Chronology

Palaeolithic Era (2.6 million to 11,000/10,000 years ago)

300,000–400,000 years ago: earliest hominids in Aegean region
c.20,000 years ago: Last Glacial Maximum
18,000–12,000 years ago: foraging communities at Franchthi

Neolithic Era (11,000/10,000 years ago to 3300 BC)

7000: earliest farmers in the Aegean region
c.4500: agriculture established throughout Greece

Bronze Age (3300–1200/1100 BC)

2700–2000: Greek first spoken in the Balkan/Aegean region
2700–2300: Cycladic culture
2400–2200: House of Tiles at Lerna
2000–1600: Minoan civilization
1500–1200: Mycenaean domination

Early Iron Age or 'Dark Age' (1200–800 BC)

1000–825: Lefkhandi

Archaic Period (800–500 BC)

800–700: Homeric epics
800–600: the 'orientalizing' period
776: traditional date for the first Olympics
733: founding of Syracuse
c.728: founding of Megara Hybleia
657: Kypselos seizes power in Corinth
625: Periander succeeds Kypselos
594: Solon's reforms
546: Peisistratus seizes power

545: Persian conquest of Asia Minor
510: fall of the Peisistratids
508: Kleisthenes' reforms
507: foundation of the Roman Republic
499–494: Ionian Revolt
490: Battle of Marathon
480–479: Persian Wars

Classical Era (500–359 BC)

477: founding of the Delian League
472: Aeschylus' *The Persians* first performed
467: Battle of Eurymedon
465: revolt on Thasos
462: breakdown in Athenian–Spartan relations
461: radical democracy established in Athens
458: Aeschylus' *Eumenides* first performed
457: Athenians extend power over Boeotia
447: Athenians driven out of Boeotia
447: Parthenon construction begins
446/5: Thirty Years' Peace
438: Parthenon frieze completed
431: outbreak of the Peloponnesian War
421: Peace of Nikias
419: Aristophanes' *The Clouds* first performed
416: massacre at Melos
415: Sicilian Expedition
411: Aristophanes' *Lysistrata* first performed
404: Athens loses Peloponnesian War
394–387: Corinthian War
387: Plato founds the Academy
387: the King's Peace
371: Thebes destroys Spartan power at Leuktra
362: death of Theban general Epaminondas
359: Accession of Philip II of Macedonia
356: the Third Sacred War
352: rebuilding of Priene
338: Battle of Chaeronea
336: Philip is murdered; Alexander III succeeds to the throne
334: Panhellenic invasion of Asia; victory at Granicus
333: Battle of Issus
332: Alexander claims Egypt
331: Battle of Gaugamela
330: sacking of Persepolis

327: Alexander marries Roxane and invades the Indus Valley
323: Alexander dies in Babylon

Hellenistic Era (359–27 BC)

322: Greek coalition defeated by Antipater at Krannon
313: Ptolemy makes Alexandria his capital
307: Alexander's successors claim the title 'king' (*basileus*)
304: Agathokles proclaimed monarch of Sicily
301: Battle of Ipsos
300: founding of Antioch by Seleukids
280: Celts invade Greece
c.276–262: Chremonidean War
275: Pyrrhus driven out of Italy by the Romans
245: Aratos of Sikyon leads the Achaean League
226: Kleomenes III of Sparta defeats Achaean League
222: Kleomenes defeated and flees to Egypt
215: Philip V of Macedonia makes treaty with Hannibal
202: Hannibal defeated at Battle of Zama
200: Rome declares war on Philip V
197: Rome leads Greek coalition to victory at Cynoscephalae
196: Flamininus declares the Greeks are free
195: Nabis of Sparta defeated by Rome
191: Rome defeats Antiochus III at Thermopylae
189: Rome defeats Antiochus III at Magnesia
187: Rome neutralizes the Aetolian League
168: Perseus defeated by Romans at Pydna
167: Macedonia divided into four republics; first Maccabean revolt
146: Macedonia becomes Roman province; Achaean revolt
141: Parthians claim Babylon from Seleukids
113: Mithradates VI of Pontus comes to power
89: Rome at war with Mithradates
31: Battle of Actium

Pax Romana (31 BC–AD 180)

27 BC: Greece proper becomes the Roman province of Achaea
21 BC: Augustus visits Sparta
AD 48–55: Christian communities begin to emerge in Greece and Asia Minor
AD 67: Nero tours Greece
AD 131: Hadrian organizes the Panhellenion
AD 143: Aelius Aristides delivers *Oration to Rome*
AD 167–174: Marcomannic War
AD 212: Roman citizenship extended to all free inhabitants of the empire
AD 267/8: Herulian raid on Greece

Late Antiquity (*c*.80–630)

284:	accession of Diocletian
312:	accession of Constantine
325:	Council of Nicaea
330:	foundation of Constantinople
337:	Constantine baptized
361–363:	the reign of Julian
378:	Battle of Adrianople
390:	massacre of civilians in Thessalonica
395:	final division between eastern and western halves of the Empire
476:	overthrow of Romulus Augustulus, the last emperor in the West
529:	Justinian closes the Academy in Athens
532:	Nika Riots in Constantinople
533:	Balisarius reconquers North Africa
535:	Byzantine reconquest of Italy
541:	outbreak of bubonic pandemic
565:	death of Justinian
577:	major Avar invasion of Balkans
582:	accession of Maurice
602:	Phokas' coup
603:	war begins with Sassanid Persia
626:	Persian–Avar siege of Constantinople
629:	defeated Persia sues for peace

Byzantine Empire (634–1453)

634:	Arabs begin raids into Byzantine Near East
636:	Muslims defeat Byzantium at the Battle of Yarmuk
641:	Muslims conquer Egypt; death of Heraclius
668:	assassination of Constans II
674–678:	Arabs besiege Constantinople
679:	Bulgars migrate to the eastern Balkans
698:	Muslims claim Byzantine Carthage
717:	second Arab siege of Constantinople
730:	Iconoclasm: Leo III orders removal of icons from churches
750:	Abbasid takeover of Caliphate
764:	martyrdom of Stephen the Younger
787:	first restoration of icons
800:	Charlemagne crowned in Rome
811:	Nikephoros I defeated by the Bulgar khan Krum
815:	Iconoclasm: second phase
824:	Arabs begin conquest of Sicily
838:	Arabs sack Amorion
843:	second restoration of icons and the 'Feast of Orthodoxy'

226

863:	defeat of Muslims at Lalakaon
902:	fall of Sicily to the Muslims
923:	new phase of Byzantine imperial expansion in the East
960:	Nikephoros Phokas reclaims Crete
969:	Nikephoros claims northern Syria
975:	John I Tzimiskes invades Palestine
989:	Basil II defeats Bardas Phokas
1022:	Basil annexes most of Armenia
1054:	Church Schism between Rome and Constantinople
1071:	Battle of Manzikert, Seljuks begin occupation of Anatolia
1081:	Alexios I Komnenos claims the throne
1091:	defeat of Pechenegs
1096:	Crusader armies begin arriving at Constantinople
1146:	Second Crusade begins
1180:	death of Manuel I Komnenos
1189:	Third Crusade begins
1204:	Fourth Crusade and the first Fall of Constantinople
1224:	Despotate of Epiros claims Thessaloniki
1261:	restoration of Byzantine Empire
1269:	failure of anti-Greek Crusade
1274:	Council of Lyon
1282:	Sicilian Vespers, death of Michael VIII Palaiologos
1299/1300:	founding of the House of Osman
1303:	Catalan Company hired by Andronikos II
1311:	Catalans seize Duchy of Athens
1331:	fall of Nicaea to Ottomans
1341:	Black Death reaches Constantinople
1349:	Principality of Morea ruled by Palaiologoi
1354:	Gallipoli seized by the Ottomans
1369:	John V Palaiologos converts to Catholicism in Rome
1389:	Battle of Kosovo
1390:	Byzantine Army assists in Ottoman siege of Philadelphia
1402:	Mongols defeat the Ottomans
1430:	Thessaloniki sacked by Ottomans
1439:	Council of Florence; Gemistos Plethon lectures in Florence
1444:	Crusade of Varna
1453:	Second fall of Constantinople; Byzantine Empire extinguished

Early Modern (1454–1800)

1460:	Ottomans claim Morea
1461:	Ottomans claim Empire of Trebizond
1473:	Cyprus becomes Venetian protectorate
1476:	first book printed in Greek

1499:	launch of the first Greek printing press in Venice
1500/4:	Michelangelo's 'David'
1510:	Raphael's 'School of Athens'
1573:	opening of San Giorgio dei Greci in Venice
1669:	fall of Candia
1768–1774:	Russo-Turkish War
1770:	Revolts in Crete and Peloponnese
1774:	Treaty of Kücük Kairnaji

Modern (1800 to present)

1806:	'Hellenic Nomarchy'
1814:	Philiki Etereia formed in Odessa
1820:	Ottoman state moves against Ali Pasha
1821:	Greek revolt begins in the Danubian provinces and the Peloponnese
1825:	Egyptian army begins restoration of order in Greece
1827:	Battle of Navarino
1829:	Treaty of Adrianople
1831:	Capodistrias assasinated
1832:	London Convention
1834:	Athens chosen as national capital
1844:	King Otho forced to introduce constitution
1862:	Otho forced to abdicate; replaced by George I
1875:	Trikoupis' first prime ministership
1896:	first modern Olympic Games at Athens
1897:	Greek–Turkish War
1901:	'Evangelika' and 'Sanidhika' riots in Athens
1909:	military overthrows government (Goudi Coup)
1910:	Venizelos forms his first national government
1912–1913:	Balkan Wars; Greece claims Thessaloniki
1915:	Venizelos resigns and the National Schism begins
1916:	Venizelos sets up separate government in Thessaloniki
1919:	Greek troops occupy Smyrna and its environs
1922:	Asia Minor catastrophe; burning of Smyrna
1923:	Treaty of Lausanne; population exchange between Turkey and Greece
1924:	Greek voters opt for a republic
1928:	Venizelos returns to form government
1935:	Monarchy restored
1936:	Metaxas establishes a dictatorship
1940:	Italian invasion repulsed
1941:	Axis occupation begins; EAM established as chief resistance movement
1944:	Germans withdraw from Greece; George Papandreou leads provisional government
1945:	Civil War inevitable after mass arrest of EAM members

1947: National government receives US backing; Dodecanese ceded to Greece
1949: Democratic Army defeated
1952: Papagos' Greek Rally wins absolute majority; Greece joins NATO
1955: Karamanlis replaces Papagos; pogrom against Greeks in Istanbul
1960: Cyprus granted independence
1961: George Papandreou leads 'relentless struggle' following rigged elections
1963: Karamanlis resigns and Papandreou forms government
1965: Papandreou resigns and Constantine II appoints new government
1967: military junta seizes power in April; Constantine goes into permanent exile
1973: student uprising at Athens Polytechnic
1974: Turkish invasion of Cyprus; Karamanlis restores constitutional rule
1980: Greece rejoins NATO
1981: Andreas Papandreou forms first PASOK government; Greece joins European Union
1989: Mitsotakis' *Nea Demokratia* defeats Papandreou
1991: Mass rallies and government sanctions against establishment of FYROM
1993: PASOK return to power under Papandreou
1996: Costas Simitis replaces Papandreou
2002: the euro replaces the drachma
2004: Nea Demokratia wins elections under Kostas Karamanlis; Greek national team wins UEFA European Football Championship; Athens Olympics
2008: youth riots in December
2009: Greek economy in recession: PASOK returned in early October, led by George (Giorgakis) Papandreou

Glossary

ANCIENT

agon   contest

agora   an open space that served as the civic centre

andreia   courage

andron   men's room

annales   histories

aretê   virtue

aristoi   elites

artes   means

basileus (pl. basileis) in Homer, the term means 'king', but by the Archaic and Classical periods it refers to 'aristocrat'

bouleterion   civic assembly house

chresis   value

communis patria   fatherland community

demes   people units

demokratia   democracy

demos   people, citizens

diadochoi   Alexander's successors

ek theou   from God

eleutheria   liberty

Ellines Hellenes; the name by which the Greeks described themselves; by Late Antiquity the term was restricted to pagans

ethnos (pl. ethneis)   people, ethnic group

gerousia   literally a council of elders

gigantomachia   celestial war

Graeculi   'Greeklings'

gymnastirion   gymnasium

habrosyne   luxury-loving

hegemonia   leadership/domination

Hellas   Greece

to hellenikon   the fact of being Greek

helot   chattel-slave belonging to the Spartan state

hetairoi   companions of the King of Macedonia

Hippodamian   rectilinear urban street plan
hoi polloi   'the many', usually refers to the commoners
hubris   overweening pride
humanitas   civilization
istoria   history
koine dialektos   common dialect
Koine Greek   Common Greek
koinos   community
kosmos   ordered whole, universe
libertas   freedom
Megali Ellas   Greater Greece
megalopolis   great city
melete   declamation
oi mesoi   the middling sort
en meson   to bring before [the public]
metropolis (pl. metropoleis)   mother city
nobiles   nobility
oikos   household
oikoumene   world community
oliganthropia   depopulation
optimates   the best of citizens
orthodoxia   orthodoxy
paidea   education
palaestra   exercise yard
Pax Romana   the Roman peace (31 BC to AD 180)
physis   nature
polis (pl. poleis)   city-state
polygragmosyne   enterprising nature
pothos   passion
princeps   first citizen
proskynesis   prostrating before the king
publicani   Italian/Roman tax farmers
prytaneion, prytaneia   civic meeting hall
Romanoi   Romans
sarissa   long pike
Sophists   teacher/philosophers associated with radical democracy
sophrosyne   balance, comportment
soteros   saviour
spolia   materials
stasis   civil conflict
stoa   public warehouse
strategos (pl. strategoi)   military general
synedrion   council
synoikismos   urban coalescence

theos   god
tholoi   warrior tombs
timi   honour
xenia   guest friendship, a formal relationship between citizens of different states

BYZANTINE AND OTTOMAN ERAS TO THE PRESENT

agrafa   unregistered communities
andartes   resistance fighters
anorthosis   regeneration
antikommatismos   anti-partyism
archonates   provincial units
archontes   regional strongmen
archontika   neoclassical mansions
ayans   Ottoman regional power-broker, warlord
barbaroi   barbarians
belle époque   literally 'beautiful period', normally associated with Europe before
   the First World War
bojars   Serb nobility
chettes   Muslim bandit militias
chresis   term used by Christians regarding the value of Classical texts
dar al-Islam   realm of Islam
dynatoi   the military aristocracy of the eastern Anatolian marches
EAM   National Liberation Front, wartime resistance organization
EDA   United Democratic Left
eksynchronismos   modernization
ELAS   National People's Liberation Army, military arm of EAM
Elleniki Demokratia   Hellenic Republic
emir   Muslim prince
enosis   unification
epanastasi   general insurrection
eparchies   subdepartments
Ethnikos Dichasmos   National Schism
exotika   supernatural
foustanella   kilt
Franks, *franggoi*   Latin Christians
FYROM   Former Yugoslav Republic of Macedonia
gaza   holy war
haiduk   bandit
Helladikoi   people of Greece
Hellenes   pagan in Late Antique parlance
helot   serf
hospodar   regents

Iconoclasm policy and movement to ban icon veneration
iconophile one who venerates icons
kafeneia cafes
kales oikogeneiyes 'good' families
kalos cosmos good society
kapetanios (pl. kapetanioi) bandit leader, also used by sea captains
kastron, (pl. kastra) fortified settlement
katharevousa the 'clean language', an Atticized version of modern Greek
kathestos right-wing establishment
KKE Greek Communist Party
klepht bandit
koçabasis Christian warlords, power magnates
koinotita (pl. koinotites) commune
Makedonomachos Greek nationalists who fought in Ottoman Macedonia
Megali Ellas Greater Greece
Megali Idea the 'Great Idea', the national dream to reclaim Constantinople and other territories believed to be Greek
Nea Demokratia New Democracy Party formed by Constantine Karamanlis in 1974
nomarchies departments
oikoumene world community
pantokrator ruler
parakratos parastate
PASOK Panhellenic Socialist Movement formed by Andreas Panandreou in 1974
patrida homeland
Philiki Etereia Friendly Society
pronoia hereditary land grants
Rhomioi Romans; term used by Ottoman Greeks
Rum Turkish for 'Romans', and used to refer to Greek Orthodox subjects
stato da mar Venice's overseas empire
Stratiotikos Syndesmos Military League
tekke dervish convent
thema, (pl. themata) militarized province
xanthos genos fair-haired peoples
zoi life

Lists of Kings, Emperors, Sultans and Prime Ministers

MACEDONIAN KINGS

(dates given for Hellenistic monarchs are approximate and contested)

Amyntas I	547–498
Alexander I	498–454
Alketas	454–448
Perdikkas II	448–413
Arkhelaus I	413–399
Orestes	399–392
Arkhelaus II	396–393
Amyntas III	393–369
Alexander II	379–368
Perdikkas	368–359
Amyntas IV	359
Philip II	359–336
Alexander III	336–323
Philip III	323–317
Alexander IV	317–310
Antigonos I	306–301
Kassander	304–297
Antigonos II Gonatas	277–239
Demetrius II	239–229
Antigonos III	229–221
Philip V	221–179
Perseus	179–168

PTOLEMIES OF EGYPT

Ptolemy I Soter	323–282
Ptolemy II Philadelphos	282–246
Ptolemy III Eurgetes	246–222

Ptolemy IV Philopator	222–204
Ptolemy V Epiphanes	204–180
Ptolemy VI	180–145
Ptolemy VIII Euergetes	145–116
Kleopatra III	116–107, 107–101
Ptolemy X	101–88
Ptolemy XII Auletes	80–58
Kleopatra VII	51–30

SELEUKIDS

Seleukos I Nikator	312–281
Antiochos I Soter	281–261
Antiochos II Theos	261–246
Seleukos II Kallinikos	246–226/5
Seleukos III Keraunos	226/5–223
Antiochos III	223–187
Seleukos IV Philopator	187–175
Antiochos IV Epiphanes	175–164
Antiochos V Eupator	164–162
Demetrios I Soter	162–150
Alexander Balas	150–145
Demetrios II Nikator	145–140, 129–125
Antiochus VI	145–140
Antiochos VII	138–129
Alexander II Zabinas	129–123
Kleopatra Thea	125–121
Seleukos V	125
Antiochos VIII Grypos	121–96
Antiochos IX Kyzikenos	115–95
Seleukos VI Epiphanes	96–95
Demetrios III	95–87
Philip I Philadelphos	95–83
Antiochos X Eusebes	95–83
Antiochos XII	87–84
Tigranes II	83–69
Antiochos XIII Asiatikos	69–64
Philip II Philoromaeos	65–64

ATTALIDS OF PERGAMON

Philetairos	283–263

Eumenes I	263–241
Attalos I Soter	241–197
Eumenes II Soter	197–159
Attalos II Philadelphos	159–138
Attalos III Philometor	138–133
Eumenes III Aristonikos	133–129

KINGS OF PONTUS

Mithridates I Ktistes	302–266
Ariobarzanes	266–250
Mithradates II	250–220
Mithradates III	220–189
Pharnakes I 1	189–155
Mithradates IV Philopator	154–152
Mithradates V Euergetes	152–120
Mithradates VI Eupator	120–63
Pharnakes II	63–47
Darius of Pontus	39–37
Polemon I	37–8
Pythodorida	8 BC–AD 38
Polemon II	AD 38–64

ROMAN EMPERORS

Augustus	31 BC–AD 14
Tiberius	14–37
Caligula	37–41
Claudius	41–54
Nero	54–68
Galba/Otho/Vitellius	68–69
Vespasian	69–79
Titus	79–81
Domitian	81–96
Nerva	96–98
Trajan	98–117
Hadrian	117–138
Antoninus Pius	138–161
Marcus Aurelius	161–180
Commodus	180–192
Septimius Severus	193–211
Caracalla	211–217

Elagabalus	218–222
Severus Alexander	222–235
Maximinus Thrax	235–238
Gordian III	238–244
Philip the Arab	244–249
Decius	249–251
Valerian	253–260
Gallienus	253–268
Claudius II Gothicus	268–270
Aurelian	270–275
Probus	276–282
Diocletian	284–305
Galerius	305–311
Constantine I	306–337
Constantius II	337–361
Constans I	337–350
Julian	361–363
Jovian	363–364
Valentinian I	364–375
Valens	364–378
Gratian	367–383
Valentinian II	375–392
Theodosius I	379–395

EAST ROMAN AND BYZANTINE EMPERORS

Arcadius	383–408
Theodosius II	408–450
Marcian	450–457
Leo I	457–474
Leo II	474
Zeno	474–491
Anastasius	491–518
Justin I	518–527
Justinian	527–565
Justin II	565–578
Tiberios II	578–582
Maurice	582–602
Phokas	602–610
Heraclius	610–641
Constantine III	641
Heraklonas	641
Constans II	641–668

Constantine IV	668–685
Justinian II	685–695, 705–711
Leontinos	695–698
Tiberios III	698–705
Philippikos	711–713
Anastasios II	713–715
Theodosios III	715–717
Leo III	717–741
Constantine V	741–775
Leo IV	775–780
Constantine VI	780–797
Eirene	797–802
Nikephoros I	802–811
Staurakios	811
Michael I	811–813
Leo V	813–820
Michael II	820–829
Theophilos	829–842
Michael III	842–867
Basil I	867–886
Leo VI	886–912
Alexander	912–913
Constantine VII Porphyrogenitos	913–959
Romanos I Lekapenos	920–944
Romanos II	959–963
Nikephoros II Phokas	963–969
John I Tzimiskes	969–976
Basil II	976–1025
Constantine VIII	1025–1028
Romanos III Argyrous	1028–1034
Michael IV	1034–1041
Michael V	1041–1042
Zoe and Theodora	1042
Constantine IX Monomachos	1042–1055
Theodora	1055–1056
Michael VI	1056–1057
Isaac I Komnenos	1057–1059
Constantine X Doukas	1059–1067
Romanos IV Diogenes	1067–1071
Michael VII Doukas	1071–1078
Nikephoros III	1078–1081
Alexios Komnenos	1081–1118
John II Komnenos	1118–1143
Manuel I Komnenos	1143–1180

Alexios II Komnenos	1180–1183
Andronikos I Komnenos	1183–1185
Isaac II Angelos	1185–1195, 1203–1204
Alexios III Angelos	1195–1203
Alexios IV Angelos	1203–1204
Alexios V Angelos	1204
Theodore I Laskaris	1204–1222
John III Vatatzes	1222–1254
Theodore II Laskaris	1254–1258
John IV Laskaris	1258–1261
Michael VIII Palaiologos	1261–1282
Andronikos II Palaiologos	1282–1328
Andronikos III Palaiologos	1328–1341
John V Palaiologos	1341–1391
John VI Kantakouzenos	1347–1354
Andronikos IV	1376–1379
John VII Palaiologos	1390
Manuel II Palaiologos	1391–1425
John VIII Palaiologos	1425–1448
Constantine XI Palaiologos	1448–1453

OTTOMAN SULTANS

Osman	1300–1324
Orhan	1324–1362
Murad I	1362–1389
Bayezid I	1389–1402
Mehmet I	1413–1421
Murat II	1421–1444, 1445–1451
Mehmet II	1444–1445, 1451–1481
Bayezid II	1481–1512
Selim I	1512–1520
Suleyman I	1520–1566
Selim II	1566–1574
Murat III	1574–1595
Mehmet III	1595–1603
Ahmet I	1603–1617
Mustafa I	1617–1623
Murat IV	1623–1640
Ibrahim	1640–1648
Mehmet IV	1648–1687
Suleyman II	1687–1691
Ahmet II	1691–1695

Mustafa II	1695–1703
Ahmet III	1703–1730
Mahmut I	1730–1754
Osman III	1754–1757
Mustafa III	1757–1774
Abdulhamit I	1774–1789
Selim III	1789–1807
Mahmut II	1808–1839
Adbulmejit I	1839–1861
Abdulaziz	1861–1876
Abdulhamit II	1876–1909
Mehmet V	1909–1918
Mehmet VI	1918–1922

KINGS OF GREECE

Otho	1833–1862
George I	1863–1913
Constantine I	1913–1917, 1920–1922
Alexander	1917–1920
George II	1922–1924, 1935–1947
Paul	1947–1964
Constantine II	1964–1967

PRESIDENTS OF GREECE

Ioannis Capodistrias	1828–1831
Augustinos Capodistrias	1831–1832
Pavlos Koundouriotis	1924–1926, 1926–1929
Theodoros Pangalos	1926
Alexandros Zaimis	1929–1935
Giorgos Zoitakis	1967–1972
George Papadopoulos	1972–1973
Phaidon Gizikis	1973–1974
Mikhail Stasinopoulos	1974–1975
Constantine Tsatsos	1975–1980
Constantine Karamanlis	1980–1985
Ioannis Alevras	1985
Christos Sartzetakis	1985–1990
Constantine Karamanlis	1990–1995
Constantine Stephanopoulos	1995–2005
Karolos Papoulias	2005–

PRIME MINISTERS (FROM TRIKOUPIS)

Charilaos Trikoupis	1880, 1882–1885, 1886–1890, 1892–1893, 1893–1895
Theodoros Deligiannis	1885–1886, 1890–1892, 1895–1897, 1902–1903, 1904–1905
Alexandros Zaimis	1897–1899, 1901–1902, 1915, 1916, 1917, 1928
Giorgios Theotokis	1899–1901, 1903–1904, 1905–1909
Dimitrios Rallis	1897, 1903, 1905, 1909, 1920–1921
Eleftherios Venizelos	1910–1915, 1917–1920, 1924, 1928–1932
Demetrios Gounaris	1915, 1921–1922
Stylianos Gonatas	1922–1924
Themistoklis Sophoulis	1924, 1945–1946, 1947–1949
Theodoros Pangalos	1925–1926
Georgios Kondylis	1926, 1935
Panagis Tsaldaris	1932–1933, 1933–1935
Konstantinos Demertzis	1935–1936
Ioannis Metaxas	1936–1941
Alexandros Koryzis	1941
Emmanouil Tsouderos	1941–1944
Sophoklis Venizelos	1944, 1950, 1951
Giorge Papandreou	1944–1945, 1963, 1964–1965
Nikolaos Plastiras	1945, 1950, 1951–1952
Archbishop Damaskinos	1945
Panagiotis Kanellopoulos	1945, 1967
Themistoklis Sophoulis	1945–1946, 1947–1949
Alexandros Papagos	1952–1955
Constantine Karamanlis	1955–1963, 1974–1980
Ioannis Paraskevopoulos	1963–1964, 1966–1967
George Papadopoulos	1967–1973
Adamantios Androutsopoulos	1973–1974
Giorgios Rallis	1980–1981
Andreas Papandreou	1981–1989, 1993–1996
Konstantinos Mitsotakis	1990–1993
Costas Simitis	1996–2004
Costas Karamanlis	2004–2009
George Papandreou (2)	2009–

Selected Bibliography

PREHISTORY TO 500 BC: BEGINNINGS

For the earliest periods it is often advisable to seek works that take account of the most recent archaeological research. For the Bronze Age, see Cynthia W. Shelmerdine (eds), *The Cambridge Companion to the Aegean Bronze Age* (Cambridge, 2008), and Donald Preziosi and Louise A. Hitchcock, *Aegean Art and Architecture (Oxford History of Art)* (Oxford, 1999). The unity of the eastern Mediterranean is proposed in Marc van der Mieroop, *The Eastern Mediterranean in the Age of Ramesses II* (Oxford, 2007). The Iron and Archaic periods are riddled with stimulating controversies. Especially thought-provoking are Ian Morris, *Archaeology as Cultural History* (Oxford, 2000) and Jonathan M. Hall, *A History of the Archaic Greek World, ca. 1200-479 BCE* (Oxford, 2006), but I have found the arguments of Robin Osborne, *Greece in the Making, 1200-479 BC* (London, 1996) most persuasive. For archaeology and art respectively, see James Whitley, *The Archaeology of Ancient Greece* (Cambridge, 2001) and Robin Osborne, *Archaic and Classical Greek Art* (Oxford, 1998). Vitally important is Jean-Pierre Vernant, *The Origins of Greek Thought* (Ithaca, New York, 1982), as are some of the contributions to H.A. Shapiro (ed), *The Cambridge Companion to Archaic Greece* (Cambridge, 2007). On Greek ethnogenesis, see Jonathan M. Hall, *Hellenicity: Between Ethnicity and Culture* (Chicago, 2002).

CLASSICAL GREECE (500–359 BC): THE GOLDEN AGE OF THE *POLIS*

The literature on the Classical period is exceedingly rich, and what is offered here is a very brief selection. Up-to-date narrative surveys include Simon Hornblower, *The Greek World, 479–323 BC*, 3rd edn (London, 2002) and P. J. Rhodes, *A History of the Classical Greek World* (Oxford, 2006), while more thematically organized material can be found in Robin Osborne (ed.), *Classical Greece (Short Oxford History of Europe)* (Oxford, 2000). Why the West has been so entranced by the Greeks is not made readily apparent in standard histories. Simon Goldhill, *Love, Sex and Tragedy: Why Classics Matter* (London, 2004) tells us why the Classical Greeks are special. For illuminating interpretive frameworks, see J. K. Davies, *Democracy and Classical*

Greece, 2nd edn (London, 1993) and Robin Osborne, *Greek History* (London, 2004). On the ways the Greeks framed their world, see Paul Cartledge, *The Greeks* (Oxford, 1993), J.-P. Vernant (ed.), *The Greeks* (Chicago, 1995) and J.-P. Vernant, *Myth and Society in Ancient Greece* (New York, 1980). For Athenian politics there is Josiah Ober, *The Athenian Revolution* (Princeton, 1996), and for warfare, see Paul Cartledge, *Thermopylae: The Battle that Changed the World* (New York, 2007) and Victor Davis Hanson, *The Western Way of War* (London, 1989). For the *polis*, see Mogens Herman Hansen, *Polis: An Introduction to the Ancient Greek City-state* (Oxford, 2006) and the encyclopaedic *An Inventory of Archaic and Classical Poleis* (Oxford, 2004), edited by M. H. Hansen and Thomas Heine Nielsen.

THE HELLENISTIC ERA (359–327 BC): FROM PHILIP II TO AUGUSTUS

Recent histories on the Hellenistic Era include Graham Shipley, *The Greek World after Alexander, 323-30 BC* (London, 2000) and Malcolm Errington, *A History of the Hellenistic World, 323-30 BC* (Oxford, 2008). Short but valuable introductions are provided by two doyens in the field: Frank W. Walbank, *The Hellenistic World*, 2nd edn (London, 1993) and Peter Green, *Alexander the Great and the Hellenistic Age* (London, 2007). Glen R. Bugh (ed.), *The Cambridge Companion to the Hellenistic World* (Cambridge, 2006) and Andrew Erskine (ed.), *A Companion to the Hellenistic World* (Oxford, 2003) provide readers with comprehensive and up-to-date discussions on various topics. There are many biographies on Alexander, but A. B. Bosworth, *Conquest and Empire: The Reign of Alexander the Great* (Cambridge, 1988) is expert and widely praised, while Paul Cartledge, *Alexander the Great* (London, 2004) is an ideal introduction. On Alexander and Hellenism, see Michael Flower, 'Alexander and Panhellenism', in A. B. Bosworth and E. J. Baynham (eds), *Alexander the Great: Fact and Fiction* (Oxford, 2000) and for Hellenism in later times, see Arnaldo Momigliano, *Alien Wisdom* (Cambridge, 1971) and Stanley Burnstein, 'Greek Identity in the Hellenistic Period', in Katerina Zacharia (ed.), *Hellenisms* (Aldershot, 2008). On Roman imperialism and the Greek world, the standard works are Erich S. Gruen, *The Hellenistic World and the Coming of Rome* (Berkeley, CA, 1984) and W. V. Harris, *War and Imperialism in Republican Rome, 327-70 BC* (Oxford, 1979).

THE GREEK ROMAN EMPIRE I (27 BC–AD 527): FROM THE PAX ROMANA TO LATE ANTIQUITY

Roman attitudes to Greeks and the Greek world are discussed in numerous works, including Erich Gruen, 'Rome and the Greek World', in Harriet I. Flower (ed.), *The Cambridge Companion to the Roman Republic* (Cambridge, 2004); Emma Dench, *Romulus' Asylum* (Oxford, 2005); Wallace-Hadrill, 'To Be Greek, Go Greek', in M. Austin, J. Harries and C. Smith (eds), *Modus Operandi* (London, 1998); and Ronald

Mellor, '*Graecia Capta*', in K. Zacharia (ed.), *Hellenisms* (Aldershot, 2008). For Roman attitudes under the Pax Romana, see Karl Galinsky (ed.), *The Cambridge Companion to the Age of Augustus* (Cambridge, 2006). Especially important is Greg Woolf, 'Becoming Roman, Staying Greek', *Proceedings of the Cambridge Philological Society*, 40 (1994), pp. 116–43. On Greece under Roman rule, the important work is Susan Alcock, *Gaecia Capta* (Cambridge, 1993), but in addition, see B. M. Levick, 'Greece (including Crete and Cyprus) and Asia Minor from 43 BC to AD 69', in Alan Bowman, Edward Champlin and Andrew Lintott (eds), *The Cambridge Ancient History*, vol. x, 2nd edn (Cambridge, 1996); Maude Gleason, 'Greek Cities under Roman Rule', in D. S. Potter (ed.), *A Companion to the Roman Empire* (Oxford, 2006); Fergus Millar, 'The Greek City in the Roman Period', *The Greek World, the Jews, & the East* (Chapel Hill, NC, 2006); and Millar, 'P. Herennius Dexippus', *Journal of Roman Studies*, 59 (1/2) (1969), pp. 122–29. The Second Sophistic is covered in Simon Swain, *Hellenism and Empire* (Oxford, 1996), Tim Whitmarsh, *Greek Literature and the Roman Empire* (Oxford, 2001) and Simon Goldhill (ed.), *Being Greek under Rome* (Cambridge, 2001). Further insights on the Classical past and Greek consciousness are to be found in Christopher Kelly, *The Roman Empire* (Oxford, 2006), ch. 4, and Rowland Smith, 'The Construction of the Past', in David S. Potter (ed.), *A Companion to the Roman Empire* (Oxford, 2006).

On the Greek East, there is Maurice Sartre, *The Middle East under Rome* (Cambridge, MA, 2005) and an important study by Fergus Millar, *A Greek Roman Empire* (Berkeley, CA, 2006). For Late Antiquity, the landmark study is Peter Brown, *The World of Late Antiquity, AD 150–750* (London, 1971), while illuminating recent works that have different strengths are Stephen Mitchell, *A History of the Later Roman Empire, AD 284–641* (Oxford, 2007) and Peter Brown, *The Rise of Western Christendom*, 2nd edn (Oxford, 2003). On Hellenism, there is Claudia Rapp, 'Hellenic Identity, *Romanitas*, and Christianity in Byzantium', in K. Zacharia (ed.), *Hellenisms* (Aldershot, 2008).

THE GREEK ROMAN EMPIRE II (527–1200): THE TRIUMPH OF ORTHODOXY

An essential starting point to the study of Late Antiquity is Peter Brown, *The World of Late Antiquity* (London, 1973), but also see the same author's *The Rise of Western Christendom*, 2nd edn (Oxford, 2003); Stephen Mitchell, *A History of the Later Roman Empire AD 284–641* (Oxford, 2007) and Michael Angold, *Byzantium: The Bridge from Antiquity to the Middle Ages* (London, 2001). More focussed on early Byzantium are Michael Mass (ed.), *The Cambridge Companion to the Age of Justinian* (Cambridge, 2005); Averil Cameron, Bryan Ward-Perkins and Michael Whitby (eds), *The Cambridge Ancient History*, vol. xiv (Cambridge, 2000); and John Haldon, *Byzantium in the Seventh Century* (Cambridge, 1990). For later phases, Mark Whittow, *The Making of Byzantium, 600–1025* (Berkeley, CA, 1996) and Michael Angold, *The Byzantine Empire, 1025–1204*, 2nd edn (London, 1997) are quite valuable. There are many general histories of Byzantium. See John Haldon, *Byzantium: A History* (London, 2005); Cyril Mango (ed.), *The Oxford History of Byzantium* (Oxford, 2002); Timothy E. Gregory, *A History of Byzantium* (Oxford, 2005); and Warren Treadgold's monumental *A History of the Byzantine State and Society* (Stanford, CA, 1997). A lively introduction that explains why the Byzantine Empire merits greater public appreciation is Judith Herrin, *Byzantium: The Surprising Life of a Medieval Empire* (London, 2007), while Jonathan Harris (ed.), *Palgrave Advances in Byzantine History* (London, 2005) is a very useful introduction to sources and recent scholarship.

The following important works deal with key themes: Robin Cormack, *Byzantine Art* (Oxford, 2000); Angeliki E. Laiou and Cécile Morrisson, *The Byzantine Economy* (Cambridge, 2007); and John Haldon, *War, State and Society in the Byzantine World, 565–1204* (London, 1999). On the Balkan world, see Florin Curta, *Southeastern Europe in the Middle Ages 500–1250* (Cambridge, 2006), while Chris Wickham, *Framing the Early Middle Ages* (Oxford, 2007) expertly sets the wider economic and social contexts. For the Macedonian and Komnenian periods, see Catherine Holmes, *Basil II and the Governance of Empire (976–1025)* (Oxford, 2005); Paul Magdalino, *The Empire of Manuel I Komnenos, 1143–1180* (Cambridge, 1993); and A. P. Kazdhan and Ann Wharton Epstein, *Change in Byzantine Culture in the Eleventh and Twelfth Centuries* (Berkeley, CA, 1985). There are countless books on the early Crusades, but of specific relevance is Jonathan Harris, *Byzantium and the Crusades* (London, 2003).

THE GREEK *OIKOUMENE* (1200–1700): LIVING UNDER FRANKISH AND OTTOMAN RULE

The later chapters of Jonathan Shepard (ed.), *The Cambridge History of the Byzantine Empire* (Cambridge, 2009) are essential reading for the periods covered in this chapter. A narrative history is provided in Donald M. Nicol, *The Last Centuries of Byzantium, 1261–1453*, 2nd edn (Cambridge, 1993). For conditions on the eve of 1204, see Michael Angold, *The Byzantine Empire, 1025–1204*, 2nd edn (New York, 1997). More specific to the event is Angold's *The Fourth Crusade* (New York, 2003), while the Latin perspective is covered in Jonathan Philips, *The Fourth Crusade and the Sack of Constantinople* (London, 2005). On Byzantine Hellenism, see Paul Magdalino, 'Hellenism and Nationalism in Byzantium', in *Tradition and Transformation in Medieval Byzantium* (Aldershot, 1991) and Roderick Beaton, 'Antique Nation?', *Byzantine and Modern Greek Studies*, 31 (2007), pp 76–95. On Frankish Greece, there is Peter Lock, *The Franks in the Aegean* (London, 1995), and on the Byzantines and the early Ottomans important studies are contained in Elisabeth A. Zachariadou, *Studies in Pre-Ottoman Turkey and the Ottomans* (London, 2007). Daniel Goffman, *The Ottoman Empire and Early Modern Europe* (Cambridge, 2003) is a wonderful introduction to early and classical Ottoman history, while Karen Barkey, *Empire of Difference* (Cambridge, 2008) provides an insightful analysis of the growth of the Ottoman system. There are numerous books on 1453, with the most recent being Roger Crowley, *Constantinople* (London, 2006). On Venetian Crete, see David Holton (ed.), *Literature and Society in Renaissance Crete* (Cambridge, 1991) and Sally McKee, *Uncommon Dominion* (Philadelphia, 2000), and for the Ottoman changeover, see Molly Greene, *A Shared World* (Princeton, 2000).

THE MAKING OF MODERN GREECE (1700–1911): ETHNICITY AND STATE BUILDING

For the later Ottoman Empire, see Donald Quataert, *The Ottoman Empire, 1700–1922*, 2nd edn (Cambridge, 2004). On the Greeks before independence, useful works include Paschalis Kitromilides, *The Enlightenment as Social Criticism* (Princeton, 1992), Helen Angelomatis-Tsougarakis, *The Eve of the Greek Revival* (London and New York, 1990) and Katherine Fleming, *The Muslim Bonaparte* (Princeton, 1999). For European philhellenism, see Constanze Güthenke, *Placing Modern Greece* (Oxford, 2008), Suzanne L. Marchand, *Down from Olympus* (Princeton, NJ, 1996) and David Roessel, *In Byron's Shadow* (Oxford, 2002). For the Greek War of Independence, see Douglas Dakin, *The Greek Struggle for Independence, 1821–1833* (London, 1973) and David Brewer, *The Greek War of Independence* (New York, 2001). On Greece in the nineteenth century, see Thomas W. Gallant, *Modern Greece* (London, 2001) and Richard Clogg, *A Concise History of Modern Greece*, 2nd edn (Cambridge, 2002). Key themes are covered by the following: John S. Koliopoulos, *Brigands with a Cause* (Oxford, 1987); Robert Shannan Peckham, *National Histories, Natural States* (London, 2001); Michael Herzfeld, *Ours Once More* (Austin, TX, 1986) and Philip Carabott (ed.), *Greek Society in the Making, 1863–1913* (Aldershot, 1997). On Athens, see Eleni Bastéa, *The Creation of Modern Athens* (New York, 2000) and Michael Llewellyn Smith, *Athens: A Cultural and Literary History* (London, 2004).

GREECE IN THE TWENTIETH CENTURY: THE AGE OF EXTREMES

The best work on modern periods is in Greek. The quality of recent Greek historiography can be sampled in Christos Hatziiosif (ed.), *Istoria tis Elladas tou 20ou aiona*, 3 vols (Athens, 1999, 2004, 2008). On the Asia Minor Catastrophe, Michael Llewellyn Smith, *Ionian Vision* (London, 1973) is solid and impartial. For the Great Depression, there is Mark Mazower, *Greece and the Inter-war Economic Crisis* (Oxford, 1991) and for interwar politics, G. Mavrogordatos, *Stillborn Republic* (Berkeley, CA, 1983), while the experience of the Second World War is covered in Mazower's award winning *Inside Hitler's Greece* (New Haven, CT, 1994). The Civil War has attracted the most attention from historians, and a good introduction is David Close, *The Origins of the Greek Civil War* (London, 1995). See also important studies contained in David Close (ed.), *The Greek Civil War* (London and New York, 1993) and Philip Carabott and Thanasis D. Sfikas (eds), *The Greek Civil War* (Aldershot, 2004), and for its legacies, see Mark Mazower (ed.), *After the War Was Over* (Princeton, 2000). On the post-war years, see David Close, *Greece since 1945* (London, 2002) and D. Costas and T. Stavrou (eds), *Greece Prepares for the Twenty-First Century* (Washington, DC, 1995). See also on specific themes: Richard Clogg (ed.), *The Greek Diaspora in the Twentieth Century* (London, 2000); Thanos Veremis, *The Military in Greek Politics* (London, 1997); Richard Clogg (ed.), *Greece under Military Rule* (New York, 1972); and the relevant essays in Katerina Zacharia (ed.), *Hellenisms* (Aldershot, 2008).

Index